GRACE AND GLORY

GRACE
AND GLORY

*Sermons Preached in
the Chapel of
Princeton Theological Seminary*

GEERHARDUS VOS

THE BANNER OF TRUTH TRUST

THE BANNER OF TRUTH TRUST
3 Murrayfield Road, Edinburgh EH12 6EL
P.O. Box 621, Carlisle, Pennsylvania 17013, USA

*

© The Banner of Truth Trust 1994
Grace and Glory First Published 1922
First Banner of Truth Edition
with Additional Material 1994
ISBN 0 85151 663 7

*

Typeset in 11/13pt Monotype Bembo
Printed and bound in Great Britain at
The Bath Press, Avon

Contents

Contents

Introduction

The name of Geerhardus Vos is perhaps as well-known today as it has ever been. Yet he remains a lesser figure in many minds by comparison with some of his fellow-professors at Princeton Theological Seminary, such as B. B. Warfield, and later J. Gresham Machen and Cornelius Van Til (the latter two becoming founding faculty members of Westminster Theological Seminary).

In fact, however, Vos was a theological thinker of immense erudition and insight; probably of all the Princeton men, even more so than his friend and noon-time walking companion, Warfield, he was a theologian's theologian.

Born in Heerenveen, Friesland in The Netherlands in 1862, Vos came to the United States in 1881 when his father accepted a call to serve a congregation of the Christian Reformed Church in Grand Rapids, Michigan. Following intensive theological training from which he emerged with great distinction he was invited to fill a new post as Professor of Old Testament Theology in the Free University of Amsterdam. Despite the encouragement of both Abraham Kuyper and Herman Bavinck, he declined, and instead served the theological school of his denomination until 1893 when he accepted the new Chair of Biblical Theology at Princeton Seminary. Here he remained until his retirement in 1932. His wife Catherine (well-known as the author of the widely-appreciated *Child's Story Bible* which the

Trust also publishes) predeceased him in 1937. Vos himself died in 1949 at the age of 87.

Vos was a scholar *par excellence* and devoted his best energies to this calling. He seems to have been relatively little involved in the major issues and controversies of ecclesiastical or social life; researching, teaching, writing, preaching and the leisure activity of composing poetry, were the staple diet of his days.

Richard B. Gaffin is surely right in his assessment that Vos would not have gained a large 'following' among the Princeton students, and in analysing why that was the case: 'By many, perhaps the majority, he was probably more respected than understood. No doubt his lectures were like his writings, intrinsically difficult because of the wealth of insight packed into virtually every sentence.'[1]

But there were some who particularly appreciated him and were profoundly influenced by his teaching. The young J. Gresham Machen wrote home enthusiastically to his mother following Vos's sermon 'Rabboni'[2]:

We had this morning one of the finest expository sermons I have ever heard. It was preached by Dr Vos . . . and rather surprised me. He is usually rather too severely theological for Sunday morning. Today he was nothing less than inspiring . . . Dr Vos differs from some theological professors in having a better-developed bump of reverence.[3]

[1] R. B. Gaffin Jr., ed., *Redemptive History and Biblical Interpretation: The Shorter Writings of Geerhardus Vos*, Philipsburg, New Jersey, 1980, p. xiii.

[2] See below, pp. 67–81.

[3] N. B. Stonehouse, *J. Gresham Machen: A Biographical Memoir* (Grand Rapids 1954), reprinted Banner of Truth Trust, Edinburgh, 1987, p.72.

Another student in whose life Vos's influence would be multiplied to many others, John Murray, described him in these terms:

Dr Vos is, in my judgment, the most penetrating exegete it has been my privilege to know, and I believe, the most incisive exegete that has appeared in the English-speaking world in this century.[4]

A number of Vos's works have been reprinted in recent decades and continue to be carefully studied. These include *The Self Disclosure of Jesus* (1926), *The Pauline Eschatology* (1930) and his *Biblical Theology* (1948) which was edited by his son. Now to these highly-valued treatises is added the long out-of-print *Grace and Glory*.

In possessing a copy of *Grace and Glory* the reader has in his or her hands a book of sermons which are almost as rare as they are remarkable. Not only so, but in addition to the six sermons which originally constituted the volume *Grace and Glory* the present edition includes a further nine sermons which Vos preached in the Chapel of Princeton Theological Seminary between 1896 and 1913, as well as an undated exposition of Ephesians 2:4-5 translated from Dutch. This additional material has been provided to the publishers by James T. Dennison, the Librarian of Westminster Theological Seminary in California and the editor of the journal *Kerux*, in which the bulk of it has already been printed. Mr Dennison originally uncovered Vos's personal sermon book in 1971 in the Heritage Hall Archive of Calvin Theological Seminary and transcribed the material. As heirs of his

---

[4] These words were written by Murray in 1974 in commendation of the reprinting of Vos's *Biblical Theology* by the publishers.

labours the publishers are also indebted to the Heritage Hall Archive of Calvin Seminary for the privilege of reproducing the material in this more permanent form.

But the uniqueness of these sermons extends far beyond the difficulty of obtaining the original edition of *Grace and Glory* or the providences which led to the rediscovery of the manuscript material now in book form for the first time. It is the nature of the sermons themselves which will have a stunning effect on the reader. For they combine such constantly penetrating depths of biblical and theological understanding with such soaring heights of eloquence that it is difficult to imagine their like being heard in any pulpit in the world today. They are at one and the same time intensely demanding on the reader and glorious in their exposition of Scripture. These pages contain a thesaurus of theological riches, a gold mine whose every vein is packed with gleaming insight.

Such is the character of these sermons that, to a world which is obsessed with 'sound-bites' and in a church which has become unused to concentrated thought, their content and style may seem almost overwhelming.

No doubt some small element in this lies in the fact that Dutch and not English was the native tongue of Vos's formative years through teenage. But far outweighing that is the fact that what Vos hears Scripture teaching cannot be reduced to a few easily-grasped thoughts, an alliterated outline, a ten-minute homily. He wishes to speak to his hearers about God. He wants to instill in them precisely the sense that God is gracious *and* God is glorious. Nothing short of an eloquence which is both gracious and glorious will suffice him. Every sensitive and thoughtful reader will be struck by the mountain peaks which Vos's mind and vocabulary seemed to be capable of scaling.

In these pages the reader is invited, almost commanded and certainly demanded, to become a spiritual mountaineer. There are times when many will be left gasping for the higher oxygen levels of the lower slopes. But Vos was aiming for the summit, and those who follow him there will find panoramic views of the wonders of God and his ways which will make the ascent immensely rewarding. Having been taken to such mountain peaks, the vision of God we have beheld in Scripture will produce in us a new and more holy and heavenly perspective on the whole of life.

So remarkable are these sermons that we may even be tempted to ask, 'What group of people—even of theological students—could have taken in the substance of any of these sermons at one hearing?' Perhaps the answer is 'very few, either then or now'. Certainly the judgement of the brilliant young Machen quoted above would seem to confirm that. But it would be a mistake to lay them aside on that account for two reasons. Firstly, because with the publication of these pages we now have the privilege to 'read, mark, learn and inwardly digest' them at our own pace. But secondly, because their sheer all-demanding weight teaches us a principle which our present generation has both rejected and forgotten: all of Scripture, all of its rich teaching, is for all of the people of God; its deepest and highest theology is not the exclusive preserve of the sophisticated intellectual, but has been given for the maturing of the whole congregation of the faithful.

There is no doubt that if Vos assumed that all of his hearers would be able to follow him he was mistaken;

even the supposition that most of his listeners would be able to do so was perhaps too complimentary to theological students. But for those errors of judgement grateful readers of these pages will forgive him. And many will believe that the benefit of having them now in print is adequate compensation.

Here, then, is material calculated to enrich the mind, heart, will and emotions; grace and glory indeed.

Sinclair B. Ferguson
Westminster Theological Seminary
Philadelphia, Pennsylvania
January 31, 1994

I: The Wonderful Tree

Hosea 14:8: *'I am like a green fir-tree; from me
is thy fruit found.'*

This prophetic utterance represents one of the two inseparable sides in the make-up of religion. If we say that religion consists of what God is for man, and of what man is for God, then our text in the divine statement, 'From me is thy fruit found', stands for the former. To balance it with the other side some such word as that of Isaiah might be taken, 'The vineyard of Jehovah of Hosts is the house of Israel.' Nor would it be an arbitrary combination of disconnected passages thus pointedly to place the one over against the other. In each case a careful study of the prophet would reveal that not some incidental turn of thought, but an habitual point of view, imparting tone and colour to the entire religious experience, had found expression in a characteristic form of statement. The two points of view are supplementary, and, taken together, exhaustive of what the normal relation between God and man involves. Until we learn to unite the Isaiah type of piety with that of Hosea, we shall not attain a full and harmonious development of our religious life.

Let us look at the half-circle of truth expressed by the older prophet. The text stands in the most beautiful surroundings, not merely within Hosea's own prophecy, but in the entire Old Testament. There is a charm about this chapter more easily felt than described. It is like the clear shining after rain, when the sun rises, a morning without clouds. In what precedes there is much that is hard to understand. Hosea's style is abrupt, full of strange leaps from vision to vision. But here we suddenly pass out of the labyrinth of involved oracles into the clear open. It is a prophecy suffused with deep feeling. All the native tenderness of the prophet, the acute sensitiveness and responsiveness of his emotional nature, rendering him, as it were, a musical instrument expectant of the Spirit's touch, are here in striking evidence; the dissonances of the many prophecies of woe resolve themselves in the sweet harmony of a closing prophecy of promise. And besides, the incomparable light of the future shines upon this chapter. It is bathed in the glory of the latter days, those glories which no prophet could describe without giving forth the finest notes of which his organ was capable. In the repertoire of the prophets the choicest always belongs to the farthest. When their eye rests on the world to come, a miracle is wrought in their speech, so that, in accord with the things described, it borrows from the melodies of the other world.

Still the spell thrown upon our minds by this piece is by no means wholly, or even chiefly, due to its form. It is the peculiar content that captivates the heart as the music captivates the ear. It is not to be expected of any prophet that he shall put into his prophecies relating to the end indiscriminately of his treasure, but chiefly what is to him its most precious part, that which the Spirit of revelation had led him, and him above others, to apprehend and appreciate. From utterances of this kind, therefore, we get our best perception of what lay nearest to the prophet's heart. So, certainly, it is here with Hosea.

In its last analysis, the charm of this chapter is none other than the innate charm of the prophet's most cherished acquaintance with Jehovah. And, applied to the future, this may be summed up in the idea that the possession of Jehovah himself by his people will be of all the delights of the world to come the chief and most satisfying, the paradise within the paradise of God. The whole description leads up to this and revolves around it. As preparing for it, the return to Jehovah is mentioned first. The end of the great change is that the people may once more live in the presence of God. The prayer the prophet puts upon their lips is, 'Take away all iniquity', with the emphasis upon the all, so as to indicate that not otherwise than by the absolute removal of all sin can the cloudless atmosphere be created for the supreme enjoyment of God. And the people pledge that their eyes and hearts henceforth shall be closed to the lure of idols. As a helpless orphan Israel casts herself upon Jehovah's grace: 'We will not say any more to the work of our hands, Ye are our gods: for in thee the fatherless findeth mercy.' But Jehovah also addresses the people on that day, to the effect that he himself is eager to pour out the riches of his affection upon the heart of Israel and meet her desire for him to the utmost measure of its capacity: 'I will be as the dew to Israel: he shall blossom as the lily, and cast forth his roots as Lebanon. His branches shall spread, and his beauty shall be as the olive-tree, and his smell as Lebanon . . . They shall revive as the grain, and blossom as the vine . . . I have answered and will regard him. I am like a green fir-tree . . . from me is thy fruit found.'

It will be seen from this that our text is really the climax of this speech of Jehovah. Through the addition of image to image the divine purpose of giving himself gathers intensity, till at last God appears as a green tree, bearing fruit for his people. This is truly a marvellous representation, well adapted to startle us, when we think ourselves into it. It seems to imply something in God that, in the desire for self-communication exceeds even the strongest affection of a human parent for his children.

And yet, when reflecting upon it for a moment, can we fail to observe that the marvel in it is nothing else than the heart-miracle of all true religion, the great paradox underlying all God's concern with us? That he, the all-sufficient One, forever rich and blessed in himself, should, as it were, take himself in his own hands, making of himself an object to be bestowed upon a creature, so as to change before the eyes of the prophet into a tree, showering its fruit upon Israel, lavish as nothing in all nature but a tree can be, this surely is something to be wondered at, and something which, though it recurs a thousand times, no experience or enjoyment ought to be able to rob of its wonder. There is in it more than we convey by the term 'communion with God'. That admits of relativity, there are degrees in it, but this figure depicts the thing in its highest and deepest possibility, as flowing from the divine desire so to take us into the immediate, intimate circle of his own life and blessedness, as to make all its resources serve our delight, a river of pleasures from his right hand. It might almost seem as if there were here a reversal of the process of religion itself, inasmuch as God appears putting himself at the service of man, and that with the absolute generosity born of supreme love. This relation into which it pleases God to receive Israel with himself has in it a sublime abandon; it knows neither restraint nor reserve.

Using human language one might say that God enters into this heart and soul and mind and strength. Since God thus gives himself to his people for fruition, and his resources are infinite, there is no possibility of their ever craving more or seeking more of him than it is good for them to receive. To deprive religion of this, by putting it upon the barren basis of pure disinterestedness, is not merely a pretence to be wiser than God; it is also an act of robbing God of his own joy through refusing the joy into which he has, as it were, resolved himself for us. So far from being a matter of gloom and depression, religion in its true concept is an exultant state, the supreme feast and sabbath of the soul.

Of course, in saying this, we do not forget that such religion in its absoluteness can be for a fallen race but a memory and a hope. The painful and distressing elements that enter into our Christian experience are by no means the product of a perverted and bigoted imagination.

Religion need not be in error or insincere when it makes man put ashes on his head, instead of every day anointing his countenance with the oil of gladness. In order to be of any use whatever to us in a state of sin it must assume the form of redemption, and from redemption the elements of penitence and pain are inseparable. Here lies the one source of all the discomfort and self-repression entering into the occupation of man with God, of the sad litany which revealed religion, and to some extent even natural religion, has chanted through the ages. Let no one in a spirit of superficial light-heartedness ridicule it, for, though it may have its excrescences and hypocrisies, in itself it is as inevitable as the joy of religion itself. There is as much reason to pity the man to whom religion has brought no sorrow as the one to whom it has brought no joy. The bitter herbs may not be omitted from the Paschal feast of deliverance.

Perhaps the saddest thing to be said of sin is that it has thus been able to invade religion at its very core of joy, injecting into it the opposite of its nature. And yet it is equally true that there is no religious joy like the joy engendered by redemption. Nor is this simply due to the law of contrast which makes the relief of deliverance proportionate to the pain which it succeeds. A more particular cause is at work here. In redemption God opens up himself to us and surrenders his inner life to our possession in a wholly unprecedented manner of which the religion of nature can have neither dream nor anticipation. It is more clearly in saving us than in creating us that God shows himself God. To taste and feel the riches of his Godhead, as freely given unto us, one must have passed not only through the abjectness and poverty and despair of sin but through the overwhelming experience of salvation. He who is saved explores and receives more of God than unfallen man or even the unfallen angel can. The song of Moses and of the Lamb has in it a deeper exultation than that which the sons of God and the morning stars sang together for joy in the Creator.

This redemptive self-communication of God is what the prophet has particularly in mind in recording the promise of our text. As already stated, it is a gift of the

future, and, of course, the entire future stands to him, as
to every prophet, in the sign of redemption. Not as if
the future meant only redemption. There is no more
characteristic trait in prophecy than that it never makes
the crisis of judgement a road to mere restoration of
what existed before, but the occasion for the bringing
in of something wholly new and unexperienced in the
past, so that Jehovah comes out of the conflict, not as
one who has barely snatched his work from destruction,
but as the great Victor who has made the forces of
sin and evil his servants for the accomplishment of
a higher and wider purpose. There is an exact correspondence in this respect between the large movement
of redemption, taken as a whole, and the enactment of
its principles on a smaller scale within the history of
Israel. As the second Adam is greater than the first, and
the paradise of the future fairer than that of the past, so
the new-born Israel to the prophet's vision is a nobler
figure and exists under far more favourable conditions
than the empirical Israel of before. Once its Peniel-
night is over, it will live in the light and feed upon the
goodness of God, and be beautified through its religious
embrace of him.

This thought is not unclearly suggested by the very
figure of our text. Whatever may be the precise tree
species designated by the word *berosh*, here rendered as
fir-tree, at any rate an evergreen is meant, a tree retain-
ing its verdure in all seasons of the year, never failing in
its power to shade and to refresh. The reason is none
other than that for which in verse six Israel in its beauty
is compared to the olive-tree, a tree likewise perennially
clothed with foliage. But there is still something else
and far more wonderful about this tree. While by nature

not a fruit-bearing tree in the ordinary sense, it changes itself into one before the eyes of the prophet. If nothing more than the idea of fruitfulness were intended, the figure of the olive-tree would have lain closer at hand. But the labour of the olive is a process of nature and bound to the seasons, and evidently what Hosea wishes to express is the concurrence in the same tree of miraculous fruitage, perennial yield and never-failing shade, for the context emphasizes all three.

It is evident that we are here in another tree-world than that of Palestine; it is the neighbourhood of the tree of life of which we read elsewhere that it yields its fruit every month. Plainly Jehovah is thus represented on account of his specific redemptive productiveness, and that in its heightened future form, when new, unheard of influences shall proceed from him for the nourishing and enjoyment of his people. Surely here is something that nature, even God's goodness in nature, could never yield.

Perhaps we are not assuming too much by finding still another element in the comparison. In emphasizing the verdant, living character of Jehovah with reference to Israel, the prophet may have had in mind, by way of contrast, the pagan deity from which these qualities of life and fruitfulness and miraculous provision are utterly absent. There used to stand beside the altar of idolatry a pole rudely fashioned in the image of Asherah, the spouse of Baal and goddess of fruitfulness. Nothing could have more strikingly symbolized the barrenness and hopelessness of nature worship than this dead stump in which no bud could sprout, and on which no bird would alight, and of which no fruit was to be found forever. How desperate is the plight of those Canaanites, modern no less than ancient, who must look for the satisfaction of their hunger to the dead wood of the Asherah of nature, because they have no faith in the perpetual miracle of the fruit-bearing fir-tree of redemption.

But let us endeavour to ascertain what concrete meaning the prophet attaches to the image of the text. What is the fruit that is promised to Israel? To answer this we shall have to go beyond the confines of the text and look around us in the preceding prophecy. The study of this will teach that there are four outstanding features to Jehovah's gift to Israel of the fruition of himself. We find that it is eminently personal, exclusive, individual and transforming in its influence.

In the first place, then, Israel's fruition of Jehovah is eminently personal. One might truthfully say that the idea of the possession of one's God in this pointedly personal sense is an idea grown on the soil of revelation, nurtured by the age-long self-communication of God to his own. To be sure, the thought that the fortunes of life must be related to the deity is a common one in Semitic religion. Edom and Moab and Ammon also have joy before their gods. But this is still something far different from having joy in one's God. The latter is Israel's distinction. To have a god and to have God are two things. The difference can be measured by the presence and the absence of the covenant idea in the two different circles. When Jehovah, entering into covenant with Israel says, 'I will be unto you a God, and ye shall be unto me a people,' this means infinitely more than the trite idea: henceforth you shall worship me and I will cultivate you. It is the mutual surrender of person to person. Jehovah throws in his lot with Israel, no less truly than

Israel's lot is bound up with Jehovah. To express it in terms of the text one would have to force the figure and say that not merely the fruit, nor merely the tree for its fruit, but the tree itself, as a glorious living being, is the cherished treasure of the owner.

The sense of this is so vivid that it has given rise to the phrase 'Portion of Israel' as a personal name of God. To the mind of Hosea the most forcible, indeed final and absolute, expression of this precious truth had been reached in the form of the marriage-union between God and Israel. That is simply a closer specification of the covenant idea, and it brings out precisely that side of it on which we are dwelling, the personal aspect of the union involved. While this is from the nature of the case conceived of as mutual, yet the emphasis rests perceptibly on the divine side of it. To be sure, Israel also personally surrendered herself to Jehovah, for we read that she made answer in the days of her youth, and through Jeremiah God declares: 'I remember thee, the kindness of thy youth, the love of thine espousals, when thou wentest after me in the wilderness, in a land that was not sown.'

But that was in the beginning; in the sequel Israel soon proved indifferent and faithless. The burden of the message lies in the ascription of this to Jehovah as a permanent, unchangeable disposition. He had not for one moment ceased to be the personal and intimate life companion of Israel. The covenant might be suspended, but so long as it lasted, it could have no other meaning than this, for this lay at its heart. In a number of delicate little touches the prophet reveals his consciousness of it. After the dire calamities of the judgement have overwhelmed the people and seemingly left nothing further to be swept away, then, as a climax, by the side of which all else shrinks into insignificance, Jehovah announces that he will now personally withdraw from Israel. And corresponding to this, after they have sat many days in the desolation of exile, all but divorced from God, the first and supremely important step in their conversion is that they come trembling unto Jehovah and unto his goodness in the latter days.

Even in the Messianic outlook this strongly personal view-point appears. With a peculiarly affectionate turn to the thought, the prophet represents the people as in the end seeking David their king, through remembrance of the sure covenant mercies attaching to the name of one who was the man after God's heart, and thus in himself a pledge of the divine love towards the people. In the sphere of external, terrestrial gifts the same principle applies.

Here, of course, revealed religion comes nearest to the circle of ideas of paganism. Baal, no less than Jehovah, is supposed to give to his servants the produce of the soil. But what a principal difference between the attitude in which paganism entertains this idea and the spirit in which the prophet expects Israel to cherish it! The pagan cult cleaves to the sod, and buries itself in the heaps of grain and the rivers of oil, and remembers not, except in the most external way, the god who gave. The worship sits loosely upon the life; it is a habit rather than an organic function, and subject to change, if the turn of fortune requires. Paganized Israel herself is introduced as speaking in the distress of harvest failure, 'I will go after my lovers, that give me my bread and my water, my wool and my flax, mine oil and my drink.' 'But,' says Jehovah, 'she knew not that I gave her the grain and the wine and the oil and multiplied unto her silver and gold.'

To Hosea the main principle is that the gifts shall come to the people with the dew of Jehovah's love upon them, deriving their value not so much from what they are intrinsically but from the fact of their being tokens of affection, to each one of which clings something of the personality of the giver. And Jehovah knows such a special art of putting himself into these favours; he is not imprisoned in them as are the Baals, but freely lives in and loves through them, so as to make them touch the heart of Israel. When the time of her new betrothal comes, and she sees the gifts for her adornment, she exclaims, 'Ishi, my husband!' and no longer, 'Baali, my lord!'

Notice the role that nature plays in effecting this; the externals are by no means despised; they have simply ceased to be externals, and been turned into one great sacramental vehicle of spiritual favour. Jehovah sets in motion the whole circuit of nature for the service of his people: 'It shall come to pass in that day, I will answer the heavens and they shall answer the earth, and the earth shall answer the grain and the new wine and the oil, and they shall answer Jezreel.' The things do not mutely grow, they speak, they answer, they sing, and the voice that travels through them is the voice of Jehovah. Nature becomes the instrument of grace.

That in the spiritual sphere everything proceeds along the same line need hardly be pointed out. God speaks comfortably unto Israel to call her back to repentance. He loves her freely, and it is through making her realize this fact that he effects her return. His bridal gifts to Israel are righteousness and mercy and faithfulness and lovingkindness. The mercy that he shows them in their distress is at bottom something far deeper, finer and more spiritualized than the generic sense of pity. It is *chesed*, lovingkindness, that is, mercy intensified a thousand times by the tenderness of an antecedent love. It is not compassion that saves Israel, for compassion, though truly spiritual in itself, lies but on the circumference of that mysterious saving movement that springs in the divine heart from love and grace as its centre.

In the second place the possession and enjoyment for which Jehovah offers himself to Israel are an exclusive relationship. Here the figure of marriage comes into play. Hosea has greatly idealized this figure, at least as compared with the customs of his time. No matter which side we choose in the exegetical dispute as to whether the first three chapters are allegory or recite facts, in either case, be it by a unique experience or through a unique vision, the prophet has produced a marriage ideal fit to be the parable of the covenant. In this idealized form it renders most faithfully the latter's essential features. For emphasizing the pure spirituality of the relation nothing could be more suitable. In this respect it excels even the figure of fatherhood and sonship. For these originate in nature without free choice. The bond of marriage, as conceived by Hosea, was established through a spiritual process. God, after having created Israel, sought and cultivated her affection. He did this in the beginning and will do it again in the future. So intent is the prophet upon guarding the ideal, ethereal perfection of the union that he studiously avoids representing the coming state of blessedness as a restoration of the previous bond, lest the sin-clouds of the past should project their shadows into it. Therefore the consistency of the figure is disregarded; no reparation, no remarriage is mentioned; the past is blotted out; the sin loses both stain and sting; the future arises as a fresh creation out of the waters of oblivion beneath which Israel's guilt has been buried. It is the new, otherwise unrepeatable, love of the first bloom of youth shedding its fragrance over all: 'I will betroth thee unto me in faithfulness, and I will say, Thou art my people, and they shall say, Thou art our God.' Now this same idealization also appears in regard to the mutual exclusiveness of the covenant attachment. For we must remember that the prophet affirms this with equal absoluteness with reference to the covenant husband as to the wife, and in this respect custom in his day fell far short of the ideal. When God gives himself to Israel it is with the clear understanding and promise that he does not do so to any other people. And the exclusiveness on the part of God demands an equally exclusive return of love and service such as shall leave no room for strange devotion. Still at this point the reality somehow again transcends the figure. Not that God is husband, but the kind of husband he is, comes under consideration. It is not merely his general honour that is at stake, as would be the case in ordinary human marriage; apart from all else the specifically divine character of his Person and love renders exclusiveness imperative. Even in giving himself God remains God and requires from Israel the acknowledgement of this. The gift is divine and desires for itself a temple where no other presence shall be tolerated. If we feel God to be ours, then we also feel that no one but God can ever be ours in the same exclusive ineffable sense and that every similar absorption by any

purely human relationship would partake of the idola-
trous. The only thing that can give a faint suggestion of
the engrossing character of the divine hold upon his
people is the first awakening of what we call romantic
love in the youthful heart with its concentration of all
the intensified impulses and forces and desires upon one
object and its utter obliviousness to all other interests.
This actually in some measure resembles the single-
minded, world-forgetful affection we owe to God, and
for that very reason is called worship. But it is a state of
momentary, supernormal exaltation, which cannot last,
because in the creature there is not that which will
justify and sustain it. Eternalize this and put it into the
divine instead of the human, and you will have a dim
image of what the mutual exclusiveness of devotion
between God and man in the covenant bond implies.
Here lies the infallible test of what is truly religious in
our so-called religion. Everything that lacks the unique
reference to God, as its supreme owner and end, is
automatically ruled out from that sphere. Anything that
is cherished and cultivated apart from God (in such a
sense that we cannot carry it with us in the Godward
movement of our life) becomes necessarily a hindrance,
a profanation, and at last a source of idolatry.

Man's nature is so built that he must be religious
either in a good or in a bad sense. Ill-religious he may
be, but simply non-religious he cannot be. What he fails
to bring into the temple of God, he is sure to set up on
the outside, and not seldom at the very gate, as a rival
object of worship. And often the more ostensibly spiritual and refined these things are, the more potent and
treacherous their lure. The modern man who seeks to
save and perfect himself has a whole pantheon of ideals,

each of them a veritable god sapping the vitals of his religion. No, the prophet goes even farther than this: Jehovah himself can be made an object of idolatry. If one fails to form a true conception of his character and weaves into the mental image formed of him the false features gathered from other quasi-divine beings, then, whatever the name employed, be it God or Jehovah or even 'the Father', the reality of the divine life is not in it. In such a case it is the perverted image that evokes the worship, instead of the true God. Hence the prophet does not hesitate to place the calf of Bethel, in which all Israel meant to serve Jehovah, on a line with the idols of the Canaanites, and to call it outright by the name of Baal.

This may remind us that the rival interest which interferes with the exclusiveness of our devotion to God is not seldom taken from the sphere of religion itself. Where that happens, the most insidious form of adultery ensues, because it permits the delusion to remain that with an undivided heart we are cleaving to the Lord. Our outgoing activities, our good works of service, our concern with the externals of religion, all this, unless kept in the closest, most vital contact with God himself, will inevitably tend to acquire a degree of detachment and independence in which it may easily withdraw from God the consecration that ought to go to and the satisfaction that ought to come from him alone.

There is even such a thing as worshipping one's religion instead of one's God. How easily the mind falls into the habit of merely enlisting God as an ally in the fight for creature-betterment, almost oblivious to the fact that he is the King of glory for whose sake the whole world exists and the entire battle is waged! Sometimes it is difficult not to feel that God is reckoned with, chiefly because his name and prestige and resources are indispensable for success in a cause that really transcends him, and that the time may yet come when as a supernumerary he will be set aside. Is it not precisely this that often makes the atmosphere of Christian work so chill and uninspiring? Though we compel the feet to move to the accelerated pace of our modern religious machinery, the heart is atrophied and the lukewarm blood flows sluggishly through our veins. Let each one examine himself whether to any extent he is caught in the whirl of this centrifugal movement. The question, though searching, is an extremely simple one: Do we love God for his own sake, and find in this love the inspiration of service, or do we patronize him as an influential partner under whose auspices we can better conduct our manifold activities in the service of the world? It was not said with a manward reference alone, that if one should bestow all his goods to feed the poor, and give his body to be burned, and not have love, it would profit him nothing. That which is necessary to hallow an act towards our neighbour must be certainly indispensable in any service for rendering it sacrifice well-pleasing unto God.

In the third place the fruition of himself granted by God to us is individual. There can be no division to it; each must of necessity receive the whole, if he is to receive it at all. This follows from the nature of the gift itself. If the gift consisted of impersonal values, either material or spiritual, the supply might be quantitatively distributed over many persons. But being, as it is, the personal favour of God, it must be poured as a whole into the receptacle of the human heart. The parable of marriage not only teaches that the covenant relation is a monogamic one, but implies besides that it is a bond binding unitary soul to soul. There is an inner sanctuary of communion, where all else disappears from sight, and the believer shut in with God gazes upon his loveliness, and appropriates him, as though outside of him nothing mattered or existed. These may be fugitive moments, and they may be rare in our experience, but we surely must know them, if God's fruitbearing for us is to be a reality in our lives.

The prophet evidently had a feeling for this, although the dispensation of the covenant under which he lived made it far more difficult to attain than in our time. The collective method of procedure pursued at that stage related everything in the first instance to the nation of Israel. To it belong the election, the love, the union with God, the future. It is quite in accordance with this that Israel as a body appears as the bride and wife of Jehovah, or in the terms of a different figure as the son he has called out of Egypt. None the less it yields a pure abstraction, when this is carried to the extreme of a denial of every individual bond between the single Israelite and Jehovah. On the basis of the collective relationship, in which the many unite as one, there must of necessity have sprung up an individual attachment, in which the single believer and Jehovah directly touched each other. As there was private sacrifice alongside of the public ritual service, so there must have flourished personal worship and affection for God in the hearts of the pious.

The devotional fragrance wafted to us from so many a page in the Old Testament bears abundant witness to this. But, while no true Israelite could be entirely without this, there existed doubtless many degrees in the individualizing of what was so largely a common possession. The nature of the prophetic office brought with it a certain detachment from the mass and a peculiar intimacy with Jehovah. And yet the note of individualism is not equally strong in all the prophets. It is interesting to observe where and when and how it emerges. Its two great exponents are Hosea and Jeremiah. These two speak not only from and for Jehovah but also to Jehovah. They are pre-eminently the prophets of prayer. In the case of each there appears to be some connection between the temperament of the prophet and the cultivation of this element. Both exceptionally endowed in their emotional nature, they instinctively sought, and under the influence of the Spirit were enabled to find, what could satisfy this deep instinct.

Religion as centred in the heart cannot but incline towards individualism, for the heart with its hidden feelings is the most incapable of duplication of all the factors that enter into it. Belief and intent of will may be standardized; the emotional reaction is like the wind of heaven: we hear the sound thereof, yet know not whence it cometh nor whither it goeth; so it is with the world of religious feeling; it has a colouring and tone of its own in each individual child of God.

Hosea being of a most tender and impressionable temperament was on that account chosen to secure for the covenant-bond in his own life, and through his influence in the life of others, that sweet privacy and inwardness which forms the most precious possession of every pious soul. Here lies the cause of that vivid, life-like personification to which the prophet subjects the people of Israel, putting words upon their lips expressing a mode of feeling such as, strictly speaking, only an individual can experience. It is his own heart that the prophet has put into the body of Israel. The construction is in the plural, but the spirit is in the singular, and it needs only to be translated back into the singular to render it a most appropriate speech for every believer in addressing Jehovah: 'Come and let us return unto Jehovah; for he hath torn, and he will heal us; he hath smitten and he will bind us up. After two days will he revive us; on the third day he will raise us up, and we shall live before him. And let us know, let us follow on to know Jehovah: his going forth is sure as the morning; and he will come unto us as the rain, as the latter rain that watereth the earth.' And thus the prophet, and through him doubtless others, had the wonderful experience that the God of Israel could give himself to a single person with the same individual interest and undivided devotion, as if that person were the only one to whom his favour extended. This is necessary to complete the fruition of God.

Every child of God, no matter how broad his vision and enlarged his sympathies, is conscious of carrying within himself a private sanctuary, an inner guest-chamber of the heart, where he desires to be at times alone with God and have his Saviour to himself. So instinctive and irrepressible is the craving for this, that it may easily give rise to a sort of spiritual jealousy, making it difficult to believe that the God who has given himself to millions of others should receive us alone into absolute intimacy and show us the secret of his covenant. Does it seem improper to pray, 'Come, Lord, to me alone, and close the door, that I may have thee to myself for a day and an hour'? Should this feeling come to us and perplex us, the best way to meet it is to consider the existence of the same mystery in the relation of earthly parents to their children. It does not matter whether there be one or ten, each child has the full affection of the father's and mother's heart. If we that are creatures can experience the working of this miracle in our finite lives, how much more can the infinite God be present to a countless number of souls and give to each one of them the same ineffable gift? He is God and not man, the Holy One, both in our midst and in our hearts.

Finally, the possession and enjoyment of Jehovah by Israel has according to the prophet a transforming effect. Here we touch upon the greatest wonder in our fruition of God. This tree, unlike the probation-tree of paradise, has the veritable power of making man like God. Those who dwell together in the holy companionship of the covenant grow like each other. There is an assimilative influence in all the spiritual intimacies of life. But here the mystery is deepest, because it plays between God and man. It works in both directions: as it has caused God's gift of himself to us to assume even the form of the incarnation, in which he became flesh of our flesh and bone of our bones, so in the opposite direction it makes us partakers of the divine nature, putting upon our souls God's image and superscription. This is not, of course, the fusing of two entities; such a thought lay far from Hosea's mind. It is the interpenetration of the two conscious lives of God and man, each holding the other in the close embrace of a perfect sympathy.

The prophet has developed this thought also in connection with the marriage idea. As the wife becomes
like the husband, and the husband unto the wife,
through the daily association of years, so Israel, the wife
of Jehovah, is bound to undergo an inner change
through which the features of God are slowly but surely
wrought out in her character. The beauty of the Lord
God is put upon her. This law works with absolute
necessity. The prophet traces it even in the shameful
pagan cult, which in other respects is the caricature of
the true religion of Israel. Those who come to Baal-
Peor and consecrate themselves to the shameful thing
become abominable like that which they love. The
principle laid down applies to all idolatry, open or dis-
guised; whatever man substitutes for the living God as
an object of his supreme devotion not only turns into
his master, but ends with becoming a superimposed
character fashioning him irresistibly into likeness with
itself. There is no worshipper but bears the image of his
god. The self-sovereignty and independence affected by
sin are not allowed to exist. With a sure nemesis religion
reclaims its own and in each one of its pseudo-forms
thrusts man back into the attitude of worship. Likeness
to God, however, is not merely the effect of his giving
himself to us, it is also the condition on which the
reality of such divine self-communication is suspended.
To have God and to be owned by God in the profound
covenant sense would be impossible and result in doing
violence to the nature of God and man alike, if the
character of man could not be made to fit into the
nature and will of God. The basis of all religion is that
man must exist in the image of God. Only on this basis
can the further assimilation proceed. But the prophet

has given this thought the warm baptism of affection. A power of conscious love is at work in the process. To bring out his own image in Israel is the delight of Israel's lover and husband. This is the reason why the likeness is represented as beginning with the day of betrothal, and the chief qualities entering into it appear as a bridal gift from God to Israel, God giving her, as it were, of his own attributes: 'I will betroth thee unto me in righteousness and in justice, in lovingkindness and in mercies, and thou shalt know Jehovah.' That the gift is a gift of likeness appears also in this, that it is equivalent to the knowledge of Jehovah. Hence the emphasis thrown on the need of knowledge in Hosea's prophecy. God is declared to have known Israel in the wilderness, in the land of great drought. And of Israel it is required, 'Thou shalt know no God but me.' In both cases the meaning of the word goes far beyond the intellectual sphere; to know is not a mere act or process of becoming informed, but an act of sympathetic absorption in the other's character. It describes Jehovah's original choice of Israel as a most affectionate determination of what Israel was to be, and the attitude of the people as a passionate searching after the perfections of the divine nature. It is that self-projection of the lover into the beloved which is more than knowledge through the understanding. Hence also the trait of eagerness which the prophet ascribes to it. It is not a state of contentment, but partakes of the extreme restlessness of love in motion: 'O let us know, let us follow on to know Jehovah!' This is to such an extent the heart and soul of the marriage, that the one great adultery consists in this: that Israel does not know, and does not care to know Jehovah. For that is to fail of the end for which the covenant exists; it makes the marriage idle and fruitless. And finally, my hearers, from this falls some light upon the mystery that a finite creature can receive and possess the infinite God. To speak of giving and possession and enjoyment is after all but speaking in figures. When we try to resolve the figure into the thing itself, the reality grows so great and deep that it transcends our minds, and we must resign ourselves to an experience without understanding. But here is something that we can at least make relatively clear to ourselves: the fruition of God consists in the reception by us of his likeness into ourselves, so that his beauty of character becomes literally our own. So close and so precious an identification no other love can dream of and no other union attain. In it the fruit and the tree become one; we feel and taste that the Lord is for our delight. And when that picture, which Hosea saw as in a glass darkly through the tracings of the imagery of lily and olive-tree and grain and wine, when that picture shall have resolved itself for us into the spiritual realities of the life to come, then also the covenant climax will have been reached, every sacrament shall fall away, and our fruition shall be of God within God; we shall at last be like him, because we know him as he is.

II: Hungering and Thirsting After Righteousness

Matthew 5:6: *'Blessed are they that hunger and thirst after righteousness, for they shall be filled.'*

The Sermon on the Mount is rightly accorded a chief place in the teaching of our Lord. It carries a weight of authority, sets an ethical standard, and reveals heights and depths of the religious life, nowhere surpassed in the Gospels. The Evangelists in recording it seem to have been aware of this. Matthew does not, as on other occasions, introduce the discourse with the conventional phrase, 'Jesus said', but with the quite solemn statement, 'And he opened his mouth', thus giving us to understand that the utterance of these words was to Jesus' own mind an act to which he deliberately proceeded. And Luke conveys somewhat of the same impression by the introductory statement, 'And he lifted up his eyes on the disciples and said'. Jesus never spoke without a clear sense of the consequence with which his words were fraught. And blessed is the preacher of whom it can be truly said that ministering the Word of God is to him an holy task. But, while the sense of this was always present with our Lord, it was heightened on this occasion. This was the first time that he set himself to teach his disciples. Here he assumes that peculiar ministry of breaking the bread of life for his own, which he has ever since unceasingly performed through the ages, and even now performs for us, as in these moments we gather round his feet to receive his teaching. In fact it is here for the first time that the term 'disciples' occurs in Matthew's Gospel. Hence also the statement that our Lord 'sat down', and, having made the disciples draw near, so taught them. The sitting posture, with the hearers standing around, was characteristic of the relation between teacher and pupils, in distinction from the standing position, marking the prophet or gospel-herald.

To note these details of description is not of merely historical interest, but also of practical religious importance, because it may warn us at the outset against a view all too commonly prevailing concerning the purpose of this 'Sermon on the Mount'. The sermon is often represented as a succinct summary of Jesus' message. It passes for an epitome of Christianity, the test-stone of what is essential to our religion. All that is not here, we are told, can without detriment be neglected. Every later type of Christian life and teaching is to be judged, not by the standard of Scripture as a whole, nor even by the authority of the words of Christ as a whole, but by the content of this one discourse.

This deplorable error is due to more than one cause. The beauty and glory of truth concentrated here may easily beget a feeling that all else in the New Testament is in comparison of minor value.

A second motive coming into play is that many people in the matter of religious belief wholly abandon themselves to their ungoverned tastes and feelings. They scorn every hard and fast rule of faith and practice. Even submission to the indiscriminate teaching of Jesus they find distasteful. At the same time, unwilling to appear entirely emancipated from all historical bonds of faith, they fall back upon some choice portion of the gospel, preferably the Sermon on the Mount, and cling to it as to the last remaining shreds of the garment of creed, barely sufficient to cover the nakedness of their subjectivity. It is thus that the Sermon on the Mount has become the creed of the creed-less.

But by far the most influential force driving people to such a view comes from the flattery it supplies to the natural man. It flatters him by taking for granted that he needs no more than the presentation of this high ideal, and that Jesus does him the honour of thinking him capable of realizing it by his own natural goodness. And, last of all, it is not so much what people find in the Sermon on the Mount, it is what they congratulate themselves upon not finding there, that renders them thus enamoured of its excellence. It is because they dislike the story of the helplessness of sin, of man's utter condemnation in the sight of God, and the insistence upon the necessity of the cross; it is because of all this that they evince such eagerness to adopt as their exclusive creed a portion of the gospel from which in their opinion these offensive things are absent.

Now all such forget that both Jesus and the Evangelist expressly relate the Sermon on the Mount to the disciples, and consequently place behind what is described in it the process of becoming a disciple, the whole rich relationship of saving approach and responsive faith, of calling and repentance and pardon and acceptance and the following of Jesus, all that makes the men and women of the Gospel such disciples and Jesus such a Lord and Saviour as this and other records of his teaching imply. It is therefore folly to insist that no specific doctrine of salvation is here. It is present as a living doctrine incarnate in the Person of Jesus.

We are apt to forget that in the days of our Lord's flesh there was no need for that explicit teaching about the Christ found in the epistles of the New Testament. At that time he, the real Christ, walked among men and exhibited in his intercourse with sinners more impressively than any abstract doctrine could have done the principles and the process of salvation. If we have but eyes to see, we shall find our Saviour in the out-door scenes of the Gospels no less than within the walls of the school of the Epistle to the Romans. And we shall find him too in the Sermon on the Mount. For this discourse throughout presupposes that the disciples here instructed became associated with Jesus as sinners needing salvation, and that their whole life in continuance is lived on the basis of grace.

At the beginning stand the beatitudes, engraven in golden script upon its portal, reminding us that we are not received by Jesus into a school of ethics but into a kingdom of redemption. It is blessedness that is promised here, and the word does not so much signify a state of mind, as that great realm of consummation and satisfaction, which renders man's existence, once he has entered into it, serene and secure for evermore. And again, foremost among the beatitudes stand those that emphasize the emptiness, the absolute dependence of man upon divine grace. As at the dawn of the gospel Mary sang: 'He has put down princes from their thrones, and has exalted them of low degree; the hungry he has filled with good things and the rich he has sent empty away,' so here those pronounced blessed are the poor in spirit, the mourners, the meek, and they that hunger and thirst after righteousness. It is in no wise to the self-satisfied mind that the Lord addresses himself; his call is not a call to exertion, not even to exertion in holiness; it would be too little to say that it is an invitation to receive; it goes farther than that; it amounts to the declaration that the consciousness of having nothing, absolutely nothing, is the certain pledge of untold enrichment. So much is salvation a matter of giving on God's part that its best subjects are those in whom his grace of giving can have its perfect work. The poor in spirit, those that mourn, the meek and the hungry, these are made to pass before our eyes as so many typical forms of its embodiment. And because this is so, they are here also introduced as having the promise of the infinite. To be a child of God and a disciple of Jesus means to hold in one's hand the treasures of eternity.

Look for a moment at the second clauses of these beatitudes. Some of the things spoken of may, in a relative sense, be obtained in the present life. Comfort and mercy and the vision of God and sonship are bestowed during our pilgrimage on earth. As a matter of fact, however, these things are here held in prospect not in relative but in absolute measure. In the consummate life only can it become true that the meek inherit the earth, that the eyes of the pure behold the beatific vision of God, that the hungry and thirsty are satisfied with righteousness. This absolute character of the promise writes the principle of redemption large on the face of the Sermon on the Mount. To join together after this manner creature-emptiness and the riches of divine benediction is the prerogative of God the Saviour. So long as this voice of the beatitudes is distinctly heard, it will not be possible to find any other religion here than the religion of salvation through the grace of God in Christ.

But is it not true, you are perhaps inclined to ask, that at least from the words of our text the opposite view receives a measure of support? 'Righteousness'—in this word certainly the stress seems to be laid on ethical conduct without any particular admixture of the redemptive element. Men are willing to admit that, so far as the specifically religious qualities are concerned, our attitude must be a receptive one, leaving all the energizing to God. When, however, the sphere of the moral life is reached, the principle seems no longer to apply, this being the field of co-operation between the divine and the human.

That people are rash to draw such a conclusion is partly due to the modish social colouring which the term 'righteousness' receives at the present day. But we may not determine its meaning for our text in the light of this modern association. The important question to answer is what meaning the word carried to the mind of Jesus. As soon as this is done, we shall soon discover that no greater mistake could be made from Jesus' point of view than to assume that in the matter of righteousness the divine is less and the human more than in other relations. It would be crude to be sure, straightway to inject into our text the doctrine of Paul according to which righteousness is something wrought out in Christ and transferred to us by imputation. And yet, it would be a far more serious mistake to suppose that our Lord's idea of righteousness and that of Paul differed in principle and did not grow from the same root. There need be no difficulty in showing that Jesus, and in fact all preceding revelation, carefully laid the basis for this crowning structure of apostolic revelation. In order to do this let us note in the first place that righteousness is in Scripture an idea saturated with the thought of God. Throughout the Old Testament this is so. It is a commonplace of its teaching, especially in the prophets, that there can be no true obedience of heart and life without the constant presence to the mind of man of the thought of Jehovah. Not only is ethics without religion a fragmentary thing; even more important is the principle that in such a case it lacks the true quality of right, the inner essence of what renders it conformable to its very idea. Righteousness is the opposite of sin, and as the reference to God is inseparable from the conception of sin, so the reference to God is in precisely the same manner inherent in the idea of righteousness.

To put it very plainly: if there were no God to see and judge and punish, one might perhaps still continue to speak of good and evil, meaning thereby what is beneficial or injurious, subject to the approval or disapproval of men, but it would be meaningless to speak of sin on such a supposition. And so, by equal reasoning, while what is commonly called good might without the existence of God be conceivable in the world, yet it could not properly bear the name of righteousness, for the simple reason that, in order to deserve this name, according to the biblical way of thinking, it needs first to be placed in the light of the divine nature, the divine will, the divine judgement. At the very birth of the people of God this principle was embedded deep in their life, when God said to Abraham: 'I am El-Shaddai,

walk thou before me, then shalt thou be blameless.'
To walk before God means so to walk as to have the
thought of God's presence and supervision constantly in
mind, and to shape one's conduct accordingly.

Our Lord's whole teaching on the subject of righteousness is but one emphatic reaffirmation and further
development of the same principle. Although the religious atmosphere in his day was surcharged with the
notions of law-keeping and merit and retribution, there
was lacking the vivid consciousness of God as a perpetual witness and interested participant in every moral
transaction. The automaton of the law had taken the
place of the living God. Well might our Lord quote the
words of the prophet Isaiah: 'This people honoureth me
with their lips, but their heart is far from me.'

Alas, this fault with which Jesus had to contend is not
so exclusively peculiar to the spirit of that age as we
might perhaps be inclined to assume. A Jew lives in you
and me and in every human heart by nature. If we ever
were tempted to think ourselves able to fulfil the law of
God, was it not perhaps for this reason—that the sense
of God's absolute claim upon us and knowledge of us
had become dim to our conscience?

Since, then, this fault reappears in every sinner, the
Preacher of the Mount repeats his sermon in the ears of
each generation. He stands to plead the right of God,
no matter what substitutes for him we may have put up
in our lives, nay not even though it were, as in the case
of Judaism, a counterfeit of God's own law. And, great
physician that he is, he directs his probe straight to the
root of the disease. Christ drives us back into the inner
chambers of our consciousness, where God and we
are alone, and good and evil assume a proportion and

significance never dreamt of before.

The law in the hands of Jesus becomes alive with God's own personality. Majestic and authoritative, he is present in every commandment, so absolute in his demands, so observant of our conduct, so intent upon the outcome, that the thought of giving to him less than heart and soul and mind and strength in the product of our moral life ceases to be tolerable to ourselves. Much has been preached and written about the internal character of the law-observance which the Sermon on the Mount requires. Truly, it does teach with powerful emphasis that the righteousness is in the intent and disposition, not first in the outward act, just as the sin is not committed first when the hand reaches out to strike, but when anger surges up in the heart. But we do not, I am afraid, realize with sufficient clearness what is the ultimate reason for this internalizing emphasis.

Why are evil and good with such insistency pushed back into the region of the heart? The reason is none other than that in the heart man confronts God. In the recesses of the inner man, where deep calls unto deep, where the Lawgiver and the creature are face to face, there and there alone the issue of righteousness and of sin can be decided. Nor does this merely mean that the conscience is brought under the direct gaze and control of the will of God. It is the divine nature lying behind the divine will in the light of which the creature is led to place itself. The inner man enters, if we may so speak, into the inner forum of the Most High. There God, besides requiring obedience to his will, is heard to ask conformity to his moral nature. The law is perceived to coincide with what he is. The majesty, the inevitableness, the self-evidencing and self-enforcing power of the eternal are put into it. To fulfil the law becomes but another form of the imperative, to be like God. It is God's inalienable right as God to impress his character upon us, to make and keep us reflectors of his infinite glory.

But in a state of sin this can only intensify a thousand times the consciousness of man's utter inability even to begin to realize what nevertheless is the very core of his end in life, the sole ultimate reason for his existence. Thus apprehended the range and scope of the moral circle drawn around our being become enormous, so much so indeed that they would almost seem to exceed the possibilities of frail human nature. So long as man's moral life is not illumined by this central glory of the nature of God, it may remain possible for the illusion to spring up that the sinner can at least aspire towards ful-filment of the law. He then imagines that the command is relaxed and lowered to the limitations of his abnormal state. The limitless perspective, all that makes for the eternal seriousness and solemnity of the values of righteousness and sin, are forgotten. 'To be righteous' acquires the restricted meaning of being law-like, instead of God-like. Sin also loses its absolute character of disharmony with the divine nature. It appears a mere shortness in one's account, easily rectifiable by future extra-payments. To all this delusion Jesus puts an end by the simple word: 'Ye shall be perfect as your Father in heaven is perfect,' and: 'Thus shall ye pray: Thy will be done, as in heaven so on earth.'

And, still further, the purpose of this demand of God-likeness is not to be primarily sought in the desir-ability for man of patterning himself after the highest example; it has its deeper ground in the right of God to possess and use us as instruments for the revelation of his supreme glory. If God desires to mirror himself in us, can it behove man to offer him less than a perfect reflection? Shall we say, that he must overlook the little blemishes, the minor sins, the mixed aspirations, the half-hearted efforts, must take the will for the deed, and an imperfect will at that? Or shall we confess with the speaker in Job that the heavens are not clean in his sight?

Once this point of view is adopted, our whole estimate of sin and righteousness undergoes a radical change. We then begin to measure and appraise them in their bearing on God and their value for him. Obedience becomes sacrifice; the light that is in us no longer shines for our own delectation, but in order that through the perception of our good works by men glory may come to our Father in heaven. Here lies also the reason why, notwithstanding all the emphasis placed on the secretness and inwardness of righteousness, our Lord none the less insists upon the necessity of works as essential to the issue of the moral process. Because it does not exist for itself, therefore the right must leap to the light of day. Jesus, no more than Paul, would have assented to the view that in sanctification the good will or intention is the sole thing required. The tree of righteousness is planted in us by God for his own sake, and consequently he delights in its blossoms and desires to eat of its fruit.

We have now explored a little of the length and breadth and height and depth of what the Sermon on the Mount proclaims as the whole duty of man. The task of fulfilling this is so stupendous that a sinless being might almost contemplate it with misgiving. Where, then, shall the ungodly and sinner appear? Can our

Lord have meant that it is even remotely possible for the disciple by his own strength to attain unto this? Our text implies the very opposite. No, not the possession of such a righteousness is characteristic of the members of the kingdom, but that they hunger and thirst after it.

Notice sharply the implications of the striking figure employed. It implies, of course, in the first place that the disciple has not in himself, and is conscious of not having the thing described. That, however, is only the negative side; to the absence there corresponds the desire for its presence. And a very specific kind of desire is referred to. Its strength is emphasized, and that not merely in general, but in the very particular sense of its being an elemental desire, a life-craving, in which the deepest instincts of the disciple assert themselves. To hunger and thirst after a thing means the recognition that without that thing there can be no life. It involves that in this one desire and its satisfaction the whole meaning of life is centred, that the whole energy of life is directed towards it, that the goal of life is identified with it. To the sense of this fundamental spiritual craving all other things are obliterated. As to the hungry and thirsty gold and silver become worthless, so to the disciple in whom this desire has awakened, the wealth of the universe, were he offered it, would have no attraction.

And let us remember that this intensified desire has for its object the righteousness of God as previously described. What renders this thing desirable is the vision of it as associated with God. In its ultimate analysis it is the passion for God himself. Here is the cry of the psalmist: 'Whom have I in heaven but thee, and there is none upon earth that I desire besides thee,' translated into terms of ethics. Still further, the form of hunger and thirst which the desire assumes presupposes the clearest conceivable perception of the nature of its object. As there is no more vivid picture of the nourishing and refreshing power of food and drink than that which stands before the imagination of a hungry and thirsty person, so there is no truer, no more adequate reproduction of God's own idea of righteousness than that which exists in the mind that hungers and thirsts after the manner here portrayed. Herein lies one of the chief glories of the work of redemption, that it produces in the heart and mind of the sinner such a profound, ineffaceable impression of the realities in God. Nothing will lay so bare the foundations of our relationship to him as the experience of salvation.

The thing spoken of in the text appears nowhere else in such an intense form as it does through its connection with sin. The beginning of hungering and thirsting after righteousness lies in the birth of conviction of sin. In fact the presence of this element in it is what distinguishes true, deep repentance from every kind of superficial regret for the secondary consequences of sin. True repentance strips sin of all that is accidental. It resembles an inner chamber where no one and nothing else is admitted except God and the sinner and his sin. Into that chamber all the great penitents like David and Paul and Augustine and Luther have entered, and each one in the bitter anguish of his soul has borrowed the words of the psalmist: 'Against thee, thee only have I sinned, and done this evil in thy sight, that thou mightest be justified when thou speakest, and be clear when thou judgest.' A repentant sinner acquits God and condemns himself. And for the very reason that his consciousness of sin is God-centred, he is also alive

[37]

to his inward seriousness. He learns to trace it in the recesses and abysses of his inmost life, where even the eye of self-scrutiny would otherwise scarcely penetrate, but in which the eyes of God are at home, where all our iniquities stand naked before him and our secret sins in the light of his countenance. If it is characteristic of sin to excuse itself, it is no less characteristic of repentance to scorn all subterfuge and to judge of itself, as it were, with the very veracity of God.

Herein indeed is shown the first grace of God to an awakened sinner that he lets in upon the soul this cleansing flood of moral truth. It is a painful experience, but even through the pain the penitent feels that his relation towards God has been in principle rectified, that the sorrow of repentance is a sorrow after God himself. Without that much of faith there is no repentance, by that much of faith gracious repentance differs from the remorse of the hopelessly lost. And from such saving penitence there is but one more step to the recognition that the claims of the divine righteousness in their widest extent must be satisfied.

To a mind thus disposed the thought of atonement is no longer an offence or foolishness, but something commending itself by its inherent justice. The doctrine of satisfaction ages before it was elaborated by religious thinkers had vindicated itself, as it still continues to do, to thousands of hearts in the bitter theology of repentance. The fact of sin, while as such irrevocably accomplished, yet so far as the guilt is concerned must be undone, if God is to remain the God of sinners. Here the truth taught by Jesus leads directly to Paul's doctrine of atonement and justification. To the heart that has had the Sermon on the Mount interpreted to itself by the Holy Spirit there is no other solution and refuge than the cross underneath which Paul found shelter. To such as hunger and thirst after righteousness the flesh of the Son of man is meat and his blood is drink, indeed.

But the principle expressed in our text reaches still farther out. The hungering and thirsting also include a desire to exhibit the righteousness of discipleship in a sanctified life. And this Christian pursuit of holiness likewise is centred in God. It is not as if in justification the divine grace, and in sanctification human endeavour, were the sole factor to be reckoned with. Much rather in sanctification itself the old alternative again presents itself, whether in all its parts, in the acting upon by God and in the being moved to responsive action of the believer, the divine glory or human merit shall be the principal concern. There is a striving after moral excellence in which the selfish sinful nature most vigorously reasserts itself, involving merely a transition from the gross and carnal to the more refined and elusive type of sin. The true disciple does not seek to be made better for his own glory but in the interest and for the glory of God. He feels with Paul that he must apprehend, because he was apprehended for that very purpose.

The image of God restored in the soul cannot help turning back towards its original. The new man is created after God in righteousness and holiness of truth. The believer, therefore, sanctifies himself, that God's purpose may not be frustrated in him, but find glorious fruition. Only he does so in constant reliance on divine grace. It would be a mistake to confine the province of faith to justification. All progress in holiness depends on it. It is the element, the atmosphere in which the

Christian lives, that which imparts to his works their sacrificial character and makes them pleasing to God. And, because, thanks to God, it is deeper in him than his deepest sin, even when he fails and falls, he does not despair, nor is utterly forsaken. God's witness remains in him; he can say with Peter: 'Lord, thou knowest all things, thou knowest that I love thee!'

Finally, the Lord here assures the hungry and thirsty ones that they shall be satisfied. Every instinctive desire, when normal, carries in itself the knowledge that there is that which can satisfy it. The great gifts of God and the great desires of life have been created for each other, and call for each other. If this be true in the natural world, it is equally true in the spiritual world, in the sphere of redemption. The craving described in our text is a prophecy; it tells of a law in the kingdom of God, a sure creative appointment, out of which, twin children of the divine grace, the hunger after righteousness and the righteousness itself are born. It is God, and God alone, who can produce in the deepest heart of man a thing so instinctive as what is here spoken of. No sinner can give this to himself. If we feel it at all, to however slight a degree, it is from no other cause than that the love of God has found us, and the breath of the Spirit Creator has blown upon us, quickening us into newness of life. If this were a desire artificially awakened or stimulated by man, there could be no assurance of either the existence or the satisfying character of its object.

Even in the case of our noblest and most elevating desires after the creature, we too often make sad experience of the failure of our ideals to meet the expectation. The reason is that in our dreams we ourselves are the creators of the excellence we crave, and because we cannot also create the satisfaction, we hunger in vain. But it is different here. He that gave the thirst likewise provides the water, and the one exactly meets the other. It is not the will of our heavenly Father that any longing in our hearts, prompted by himself, and therefore sincerely seeking him, shall perish unsatisfied. A satisfying righteousness therefore must be provided for the people of God. And it must be provided outside of us. To eat means to be nourished from without. Since the sinner is devoid of all righteousness, it is self-evident that the source of his supply must be sought beyond the confines of his own evil and empty nature. For it to be otherwise would mean that hunger could be stilled with hunger. Our Lord's meaning obviously is that the coming order of things, the new kingdom of God, brings with itself, chief of all blessings, a perfect righteousness, as truly and absolutely the gift of God to man as is the entire kingdom. What is true of the kingdom, that no human merit can deserve, no human effort call it into being, applies with equal force to the righteousness that forms its centre. It is God's creation, not man's. The prophet recognized it as such when, despairing of sinful Israel, he promised that in the future, in the new covenant, God would remember the sin no more, and would write his law upon the tablets of the heart. Our Lord here simply declares that what prophets and psalmists saw from afar is on the point of becoming real. The acceptable year of Jehovah is about to begin. His beatitudes are the evangel, giving answer across the ages to the prophecies of old. It means that with comfort and riches and mercy and sonship and the vision of God, righteousness will be given in abundance to a destitute people. True, Jesus does not enter here upon any description of the method by which this is to be accomplished. As little as he specifies what will bring comfort in the place of mourning, does he tell how righteousness will banish sin. But does not the very fact of his foregoing to tell this afford a presumption that he is conscious of carrying the source and substance of all these things in his own Person? The same Jesus who immediately afterwards in interpreting the law puts side by side with the commandment of God his sovereign 'I say unto you', the same Jesus here takes into his hands all the riches of prophecy, as only the God of prophecy can take them, and disposes of them as his own sovereign gift: 'Theirs is the kingdom,' and 'They shall be filled.' What gives him the right to speak thus, not merely in the sphere of power, but also in the sphere of righteousness? As God he could change sickness into health, and mourning into joy, but even as God he cannot change sin and guilt into righteousness by a mere fiat of his will. When, nevertheless, he here declares that this will be done, the reason is that in his own life, his life of a servant, this greatest of all tasks is being accomplished. In one sense the Sermon on the Mount was a sermon preached out of his own personal experience. The righteousness he described was not a distant ideal, it was an incarnate reality in himself. He alone of all mankind fulfilled the law in its deepest purport and widest extent. His keeping of it proceeded from that sanctuary of his inner life where he and the Father always beheld each other's face. He made it his meat and drink to do the will of God. His human nature was an altar from which the incense of perfect consecration rose ceaselessly day and night. He submitted to the cross and endured the shame, not merely on our behalf, but first of all in order that not one jot or one tittle of the divine justice should fall to the ground. He not only hungered and thirsted but was satisfied with the travail of his soul. And now you and I can come and take of the bread and water of life freely. Through justification we are even in this life filled with the fullness of his merit, and appear to God as spotless and blameless as though sin had never touched us. Through sanctification his holy character is impressed upon our souls, so that, notwithstanding our imperfections, God takes a true delight in us, seeing that the inner man is changed from day to day after the likeness of Christ. And the full meaning of our Lord's promise we shall know in the last day, when he shall satisfy himself in us by presenting us to God perfect in body, soul and spirit. Then shall come to pass the word that is written: 'They shall hunger no more, neither thirst any more.' For we shall behold God's face in righteousness and be satisfied, when we awake, with his image.

III: Seeking and Saving the Lost

Luke 19:10: *'For the Son of man came to seek and to save that which was lost.'*

The words of our text are Jesus' own commentary on the event described in the preceding verses. His meeting with Zacchaeus and, as a result of this, the publican's salvation, were in the last analysis due to the fact that the Son of man came to seek and to save that which was lost. And in the light of this interpretation the event itself in turn becomes a commentary upon the Saviour's ministry in the largest sense, both upon that which he served while on earth and upon that which he now fulfils, walking through the lands and the ages, as he once walked through the fields and cities of Palestine. Neither this nor any other occurrence in the Gospel history was a casual thing.

It is true, these days of our Lord's flesh which he lived among his countrymen, acting and acted upon, were a real concrete piece of life interwoven with the life of Israel. They belong to that age and generation as truly as any section of human history can be said to belong to the times in which it happened. But it is also true that this is not common history, but sacred, redemptive history, which means that there runs through it, from beginning to end, a special design, ordering its course, shaping its frame, and fixing its issues, so as to make of it a proper stage for the enactment of the great mystery of redemption, whose spectators and participants were not merely the Jews of that age but the inhabitants of all subsequent ages.

Nothing is casual here; every moment, every circumstance, every person that our Lord touched became fraught by that touch with a profound actuality and an eternal significance. How marvellously adapted was the setting of these scenes to serve their unique purpose! What sharp contrasts of human state and condition were here brought together! What pronounced types of sin, exhibiting in their development the root-principles of all evil, appear side by side! The Pharisee and the publican come together to the temple of God! Truly, in this world of the Jewish land a microcosmic picture was presented of the realms of sin and suffering and sorrow and death. And because this is so, you and I can come to the story of two thousand years ago and find a present salvation there, an ever open door to the house of peace and hope. These are not strange, outlandish scenes and surroundings we are invited to; it is the familiar ground of sin and salvation; those who people it are flesh of our flesh and bone of our bone, and the Saviour, who comes to meet them, in their persons meets us and transacts his business with us individually about matters of eternal importance.

For a few moments with the statement of our text in mind let us look at what passed between Zacchaeus and the Saviour. The time is that of Jesus' last journey to Jerusalem shortly before the great Passover in which all things were to be fulfilled. These were the last hours of the day during which it is possible to work; closer and closer drew near for him that night of suffering and death in which it is not given to any man to work. Could one have wondered, if in this critical hour our Lord's thoughts had been wholly turned forward and inward, if, oblivious to his surroundings, he had been intent upon the tremendous experience of his passion with which he was now almost face to face? We do find him faithful and busy in the outward duty until the last moment. As he loved his own until the end, so it may be said that he sought his own until the darkness of death closed in upon him. But a moment ago he had helped the blind beggar at the entrance to Jericho and, scarcely within the city, a publican becomes the object of his quest.

Notice how vividly the sense of a specific duty, here and now to be performed, is present to the Saviour's mind, for he announces to Zacchaeus: 'Today I must abide at thy house.' His times and ways and works were not his own but the Father's who had sent him. But let us further notice the precise expression that principle receives in the statement: 'The Son of man came to seek and to save that which was lost.' There is no need to ask for the moment, whence he came; the fact of his coming in itself sufficiently claims our attention. For this 'coming' means his coming into the world; it covers his entire earthly life; he was born for this purpose, and this purpose only, to seek and save the lost. Never in all human history was there such an absolute concentration of life upon a single specific task as that which our Lord here affirms of himself. Every man comes into the world to work out a design of God in his existence. But in the case of each one of us this design embraces a number of various ends, all of which we legitimately pursue, and in all of which we serve the will of God. Our Lord's life was a human life which derived its meaning from beginning to end from his vocation as a Saviour; in seeking and saving its significance exhausted itself. To that even the most sacred and private concerns of his soul with God, his prayer, his trust, all his intercourse with the Father were wholly subservient. The personal was swallowed up in the one great devotion to the work of God. Into this the full stream of his strength flowed, from this its hidden sources were nourished: he made it his meat and his drink to do the will of his Father in heaven. He lived for this will and he lived on it. Thus only can we explain to ourselves the sensitiveness of our Lord, where his right to prosecute this task was called into question, for then he felt himself assailed in the centre and sanctuary of his being. Hence on this very occasion, when after his entrance of the house of Zacchaeus the people murmured, saying, 'He is gone in to lodge with a man that is a sinner,' our Lord did not content himself with pointing out the propriety and beneficence of the act, but vindicated his conduct by an appeal to the supreme law of life under which he stood and from which he could not free himself without ceasing to be what he was. With what sublime simplicity he takes for granted that his entering into a house could be for no other purpose than to introduce salvation there! Of course, there is in this something unique, incapable of reproduction in precisely that sense by even the most consecrated servant of God. He was made incarnate for the work of salvation, and we are dedicated to our ministry on the basis of a natural life we already possess. Paul perhaps in this respect approached nearest to the example of the Lord, having been separated from his mother's womb for the apostleship. In his words, 'Woe is me, if I preach not the gospel,' we imagine to hear an echo of our text and other similar declarations of our Lord. But surely, though with an almost equal distance between, we likewise ought to possess some reproduction of this mind of Christ within us. Pitiable indeed is the plight of the steward of Christ, who cannot say from a conviction as profound as the roots of his spiritual life itself, that he came into the kingdom for the very purpose of seeking and of saving that which was lost.

The Lord's statement, however, obtains a still richer and more forceful meaning by our enquiring whence and out of what state he came to enter upon this life-task. It may be in a certain sense true that in the Synoptic Gospels there is not that emphatic expression of his eternal pre-existence in the world of heaven, not that sublime consciousness of transcending the sphere of time, as are met with in the discourses recorded by John. But, surely, if we will only come to them with believing minds, we shall not fail to find even in these simpler narratives indications of the great mystery of godliness sufficiently clear to satisfy us, when in the helplessness of our sins we cry out for a divine, an eternal Saviour. Such a message our text brings us, when it declares that 'the Son of man came to seek and to save that which was lost'.

The word 'came' is in itself suggestive of a previous sphere and state which he exchanged for our world, a sphere and state wherein no seeking nor saving was required, because there all live secure and blessed in God. But much more suggestive is this word when coupled with the name 'Son of man'. It is not accidental that our Lord makes use of this self-designation in a connection like this. Elsewhere also we read that 'The Son of man came not to be ministered unto, but to minister, and to give his life a ransom'. And in a number of other passages the title is associated with his abode in the world of heaven, whence he descended to these lower regions of ours. In the prophecy of Daniel, where first the phrase 'Son of man' is used to describe the Messiah, twice a 'coming' is affirmed of the Person so designated: 'There came with the clouds of heaven One like unto the Son of man, and he came even to the Ancient of days.'

Now, while our Lord often identifies the 'coming' thus described with his return to judgement, yet he likewise once and again retrospectively associates it with his first advent, when he came out of the glory he had with the Father before the world was. Being told, therefore, that it was the 'Son of man', who came to seek and to save, our first thought surely should be of that unspeakable grace of our Lord, who, being rich as God alone can be rich, yet for our sake became poor as sinful man only can be poor, that by his poverty we might be made rich. The depth to which this seeking and saving brings him down should be measured by the distance there is between the highest in God and the lowest in man. To lodge with publicans and sinners might be condescension for a high-placed personage— what language will express its meaning in the case of the infinite God?

The 'Son of man', who unites in himself all that Deity and humanity together can lend of glory to the Messianic state, he it is who came to seek and to save the lost. It was such a glorious life that was wholly given up to its very last thought, poured out to the very last residue of its strength, and that for the task of helping us, the lowest of us, who would have turned away from one another, because the sinful felt it a degradation to stoop to such as were a degree more sinful than they acknowledged themselves to be. When we combine this consciousness of ineffable glory sacrificed with the consciousness of absolute surrender to the service of the most despised, then, and only then, do we begin to understand somewhat of the indignation with which Jesus repudiated the charge, brought by sinful men, that it was unworthy of him to associate with publicans and sinners. With superhuman dignity the one 'Son of man' silences that voice of murmuring in the streets of Jericho, and every echo, we may add, of that same voice from any quarter, or any age, when it presumes to criticize the gospel of Christ on the ground that it speaks in accents of the sovereign grace of God.

But the fact that he came as the 'Son of man' is important for our Lord's seeking and saving of the lost in still another respect. By reason of it he retains even on earth the exercise of that divine knowledge and power which such a task calls into requisition. Love is far-sighted and wields great influence, but love alone, even divine love alone, would not be sufficient to find and save the sinner. Seeking and saving are acts in which God puts forth his omniscience and omnipotence, as the searcher of hearts and the Lord of spirits. To these divine prerogatives the 'Son of man' lays claim in the pursuit of his task. He brings to it all the qualifications which its character as a strictly divine work requires. When making to Nathanael the marvellous disclosure of his supernatural knowledge, he declares, 'Ye shall see the heaven opened and the angels of God ascending and descending upon the Son of man.'

It is in the 'Son of man' that the mystic ladder, which Jacob saw at Bethel, has been truly set up, so that God visits man, and man is made aware of the saving presence of God. In healing the sick of the palsy he demonstrated the authority of the 'Son of man' to forgive sins on earth by bidding him arise, take up his bed and go to his house. Here the very point in question was, whether during his sojourn on earth such power belonged to the 'Son of man'. That he possessed it in his heavenly state even the scribes would scarcely have doubted; what they disputed was that any person on earth should pretend to share this right with God. But Jesus claims, and by the miracle proves his claim, that he is on earth invested with the power of saying to a guilty soul, 'Thy sins are forgiven thee,' and to say it so that the conscience, which obeys no other voice than the voice of God himself, will acknowledge him as its Sovereign and be silent at his behest. But what need to look for illustrations elsewhere, when the connection of our text itself gives the most striking example of how our Lord places these divine attributes in the service of his seeking and saving love? When Jesus came to the spot where Zacchaeus had stationed himself for observation, it was surely not by accident that his eye discovered the publican amidst the branches of the tree. His looking up precisely at that point may convince us that he acted deliberately; it was a step in that process of seeking for which he had come. He calls the publican by name, though to all appearance the two had never met before. Before that spot on the roadside was reached, he had not only discovered his person, but had read with omniscience the innermost thoughts of his heart. He who could say, 'Before Philip called thee, when thou wast under the fig-tree, I saw thee!' had likewise seen Zacchaeus in advance of the latter's seeing him.

Here is a look from which no man can hide himself, the same that saw our first parents behind the branches of the fateful trees, and has since that hour, wherever sinners seek to conceal themselves, penetrated into the recesses of their guilt and shame, called them up from their depths of despair and brought them down from their heights of pride, a look from the eyes of the Lord which are in all places and see the small no less than the great. More than this, we need not hesitate to affirm that the publican, though unaware of the fact, was there at his station by the appointment of Jesus.

In all probability Zacchaeus in his desire to see Jesus, who he was, was not so exclusively actuated by curiosity as is usually assumed. But suppose it to have been curiosity and nothing more, even that was in no wise exempt from the Lord's control. Open to him are a thousand ways to bring you and me to the very place and point where he desires to meet us. How many of us would have been saved, if the Lord had waited till we sought him out?

Thanks be to God, he is a Saviour who seeks the lost, who with eyes supernaturally far-sighted discerns us a long way off, and draws our interest to himself by the sweet constraint of his grace, till we are face to face with him and our soul is saved. As once, in the incarnation, he came down from heaven to seek mankind, so he still comes down silently from heaven in the case of each sinner, and pursues his search for that individual soul, following it through all the mazes of its waywardness and the devious paths of its folly, sometimes unto the very brink of destruction, till at last his grace overtakes it and says, 'I must lodge at thy house.' For, besides the divine omniscience here manifested, we are made witnesses of the Lord's sovereign and almighty power. Having found Zacchaeus he addresses to him that call, which makes the lame to leap, the blind to see, the deaf to hear, the dead to arise. It is a call like the voice of God at the first creation, 'Let there be light,' and there was light: 'Zacchaeus, make haste and come down, for today I must abide at thy house.'

Note the instantaneous effect. Zacchaeus, who perhaps had never before encountered the Saviour, who would have hardly ventured to approach Jesus, at a single word is transformed into a disciple of the Lord. He knows the voice of the Shepherd immediately, makes haste to come down and receives him with joy. This is that wonderful effectual calling by name, which takes place wherever a sinner is saved, and which, while it may not always take place with such suddenness and under such striking circumstances as happened here, yet is in substance everywhere equally supernatural and immediate. The use of the divine word not only does not detract from its immediacy, but serves the very purpose of expressing the fact that nothing but the omnipotent volition of God is at work in it. For it is characteristic of God, and of God alone, thus to produce effects by a mere word. He gives life to the dead and calls the things that are not, as though they were. Thus Lazarus was summoned from the grave, and thus Zacchaeus was brought into the Shepherd's fold. Of course, there is no cause for denying that as the result of, and simultaneously with, this call, many thoughts and convictions may be released and spring into action

that were previously latent. Images may have floated
before Zacchaeus' mind picturing Jesus in his ways and
works. The gospel summons may have come to him
through rumour or report of the Saviour's life, for even
in regard to these outward instrumentalities for conveying the knowledge of Christ it is sometimes true which
is written elsewhere concerning the inward birth itself,
'The wind bloweth where it listeth, and thou hearest
the sound thereof, but knowest not whence it cometh,
and whither it goeth.' The Spirit of God who makes all
things new, can so baptize an ancient fragment of truth,
a dimly remembered shadow of knowledge, as to give it
in our perception all the radiant newness of a flash of
light fresh from the womb of revelation. But, while all
these old elements of consciousness may work, as out of
the past, they are in no case the actual producers of the
new creature. On the contrary it is only through the
immediate impartation of the higher life that they can
be roused from their dormant state to the active vitality
of a heartfelt experience. Whatever antecedently dwells
in our souls of religious knowledge, of reasonable persuasion of the truth, of recognition of God's claim upon
us, of stirrings of conscience—it all needs to be regenerated and quickened by the touch of Christ, before it can
blossom into saving faith. We speak of our saving men,
but this, while conveying a legitimate idea, is a metaphor. At bottom it signifies no more than that through
the means of grace we arrange and prepare the situation
in which it pleases God to perform the unique saving
act. It is ours to let in the light and lay ready the
garments which afterwards Lazarus will need, but we
cannot wake the sleeper under the stone. Let us rejoice
that this is so. Precisely that at the centre there lies

something that we cannot do constitutes the glory of our message. If the gospel-dispensation were a matter of mere intellectual enlightenment and moral suasion, such as fall within the limits of human power to produce, then indeed it might be urged, that what is reserved for the divine action is subtracted from the scope of human opportunity, the intrusion of God, as it were, diminishing our glory. But on such a view of the gospel ministry its distinction is reduced to a level, where it matters little, whether the minister accomplishes more or less of it. If, on the other hand, the gospel service is incorporated in a creative movement of supernatural character, involving at its core what lies absolutely beyond human power, then to feel this inevitable limitation as a drawback would evince a strange blindness to the most glorious aspect of the preacher's office.

To move on the outermost fringe of a process of that kind, to have even the slightest connection with it, confers an unspeakable distinction, because it associates one with what is specifically divine. How much greater still is the grace, if we are permitted not a minimum but the highest conceivable degree of proximity to the wonder-world of God! Is not the underlying cause of the failure to perceive this, that we too much individualize and isolate ourselves, instead of feeling strongly our organic appurtenance to the mighty, supernaturalizing movement introduced by God into this world? If we could only more adequately realize the irresistible omnipotence of its momentum and the robe of splendour it casts around the smallest of its servants, we would exult with Paul and give thanks to God 'who always leadeth us in triumph in Christ'.

But let us return to Zacchaeus and note how our

Lord further illustrates the nature of the saving act for which as 'Son of man' he claims to possess the full qualifications. It is an act of seeking and saving the 'lost'. What it implies can be ascertained from the state affirmed of its objects. There is a sure correlation between these two, and, if at any time we are apt to lose the proper perspective in regard to either of them, we should immediately rectify our view by reflecting upon the inherent significance of the other term. The 'lost' are such as require a 'Seeker' and 'Saviour'; when tempted to dilute or tone down the meaning of this word, it should suffice to remember, that in the same proportion as this is done we also detract from the Saviour-title of our Lord a substantial part of its significance. And conversely, if we allow ourselves to lose sight of even the smallest part of what the words 'to save' and 'Saviour' connote, it necessarily modifies the sound which the word 'lost' carries to our ear. There is no escape from this; it is the inherent logic of the structure of the gospel. To refuse to be bound by it puts one beyond the pale of consistent Christianity. It will therefore well repay us to scan most closely the exact correspondence of these two ideas in our text.

There is perhaps no passage that enables us to do so to the same degree of definiteness and clearness as this saying of our Lord's. The reason is that here he has, in response to the peculiar situation of Zacchaeus, taken pains to resolve the Saviour-function in its two component parts, so as to give us a double light for the purpose. The 'Son of man' came not merely to seek, but 'to seek and to save'. Nor is this in the nature of a mere addition of a second thing to a first: these two likewise mutually illumine each other; the seeking determines the saving, and the saving in turn the seeking, and both as thus joined together receive their interwoven significance from the 'being lost'. Now it is not difficult to ascertain what the word 'lost' expresses in the vocabulary of Jesus. 'To be lost' in its simple, primary sense, which it scarcely needs knowledge of the original to understand, is 'to be missing', to have passed out of the active possession and use of one's owner. The word, of course, in order to be intelligible, requires the supplementary thought of a definite possessor. It is not the vague general notion of forsakenness and misery Jesus has in mind when using it, but very particularly the fact of the sinner's being missing to God, that is, missing to the normal relations man sustains to God. Because these relations to God constitute in our Lord's opinion the fundamental thing in human life, the state of 'being lost' acquires that sad connotation of total derangement and dissolution of all the factors and forces of spiritual existence; the word has about it the solemn, ominous sound of darkness and chaos. The light and health of life, which are religion, have departed with the departure from him who is the one source of both. The lost sinner is swung out of the orbit appointed for him by the central position of God, deprived of all the attractions of fellowship, trust, obedience and blessedness that were his birthright ever since God, in infinite grace, constructed the circle of religion around himself.

Furthermore, being out of harmony with God, man, as a sinner, has lost the rhythm of his own spiritual life; he is full of discords and inner conflicts, law clashing with law and in consequence the deepest self falling a prey to these disruptive forces which attack it at its core. The very moment the prodigal leaves the Father's house he carries this fatal disorder within him, he is beside himself in principle, so that, when in bitter repentance he begins to realize his desperate condition, this is described as a 'coming to himself'.

This then, in the first place is 'being lost', and to this in the first place addresses itself the task of the Son of man. Hence its first part must of necessity be a 'seeking' of the sinner. And the 'seeking' must be such an act as will be able to undo the 'being lost'. We should, therefore, take a far too superficial view of it, were we to confine it to the bare effort at approach, or perhaps even to the search for locating the sinner, as the figure, taken by itself, might tempt us to do. No, the finding is not the mere discovery, it is the actual bringing back to God, something by which the sinner is restored to the blessed reality of what God is to him and he is to God: 'And when he came to himself he said, I will arise and go to my Father.'

Are we not made to feel by this, that not first in the saving but already in the finding begins the uniqueness of the Saviour's work, that which differentiates it from any finding that we can do, however glorious the latter may be in itself? For, after all, our finding of a man can be only preparatory to his becoming partaker of salvation. In the case of Christ it is identical with the saving act itself. Yes, already the seeking is a part of the finding, because with unfailing certainty and directness the feet and the arms of the Saviour move to the point where the saving embrace is accomplished.

In the last analysis the difference between this and our part appears due to the difference between Christ as God and ourselves as mere human instrumentalities. To be found by Jesus is to be saved for the simple reason that in his Person God himself restores the lost contact, gathers up the cords of life into his own bosom, and throws about us the circle of his divine beatitude, so that our soul, like a star in its native course, once more moves around him, and knows no other law or centre. So far as Christ was a preacher he preached with the voice of God, and in his message salvation was not merely potential but incarnate. He silently takes this for granted in his whole treatment of sinners, when he deals with them sovereignly in the supreme issues of life and death. In a word he saves as God saves.

On this ground, and on this ground only, can we understand why so seldom in the matter of salvation he points beyond himself to God, but constantly places his own Person in the centre of the sinner's field of vision, so as to focus belief and trust and hope and surrender and attachment in himself. Consequently it is true not only in the abstractly logical, but in the most realistic, one might almost say in the local, sense that where Jesus is, there is salvation, and away from him there is none. As he rebuked the disciples in the storm, because they forgot this fact, and feared that with him on board they still might perish, even so he requires of us that in every tempest of life we shall be tranquil, because our ship carries him. Was it not so in this very case of Zacchaeus? Because he had entered, salvation in him and through him had entered into the publican's house.

Salvation, however, according to our Lord's teaching is not exhausted by restoring the sinner to a sense of the realities of his belonging to God. There is another equally indispensable side to it. What this is we may learn by considering the second element that enters into the state of 'being lost'. 'To be lost' is more than to be missing to God. It has also the passive, even more terrible sense of 'being ruined', 'given up to destruction'. The former sense remains within the sphere of the negative; it describes what is absent from the sinner's state; this other sense is positive, denoting the presence of something dreadful there. If our Lord's discourse dwells chiefly, and with a noticeable predilection, on the first aspect of the matter, this is perhaps due to the vividness with which by very reason of the concrete, detailed picture of what is wanting, the glorious realities of religion are brought out. The rule that we do not clearly visualize a thing until through its departure and its consequent failure to function it recalls its image to our mind, is here put to practical use. Strange to say, the face of religion appears in our Lord's teaching most clearly in the form of a description of its opposite: 'In my father's house there is bread enough and to spare, while I perish with hunger'. What glowing words could have more powerfully expressed the blessedness of spiritual satisfaction near the heart of God than this pitiful cry of want!

There is a lesson for us in this. We shall never succeed in impressing men, untouched by grace, with the riches and glory of religion, until we learn from Jesus to hold up to them the mirror of their sin and destitution. To say that there is no experience of redemption without the knowledge of sin sounds like a truism; perhaps it will appear less so, if we go one step farther and add, that there is, as things are, no proper, no deep knowledge either of religion or of redemption than through the sorrowful journey into the far country of famine and husks. But, while for this obvious reason the greater part of Jesus' teaching on the lost is concerned with the first aspect of their state, it would be wrong to infer that the other side only slightly or perfunctorily figured in his mind. The contrary is true. The subject possessed for him such a fearful reality, that, except on the most solemn and imperative occasions, he hesitated to contemplate or draw it into the glare of open speech. It is none the less there with the ominous darkness of untold, no, unspeakable things spread over it like a semi-opaque curtain. To be sure, it is something future, but this only deepens the gloom that covers it. It is born of the womb of the judgement. 'Broad is the way that leads to perdition' and the lost are those walking on it. Only this should not be taken to mean that the loss contemplated is purely future. It overhangs and envelops the sinner even in this life. As the narrow path to the city of God, notwithstanding its straightness, is already bordered with some of the flowers and fruits of paradise, so the highway to the land of destruction, in spite of its seeming delights, has long stretches of shadow from the storm-cloud that is seen to thicken at the end.

Even in this ultimate, more perilous, sense it is not sufficient to say that the sinner will suffer loss in the last day; according to the conception of Jesus he in principle is already lost. We feel something of the awful import conveyed, when in his high-priestly prayer the Saviour declares: 'Holy Father . . . I kept them in thy name which thou hast given me; and I guarded them, and none of them is lost except the son of perdition.' For, although Judas' sin in degree was altogether beyond comparison, it was not in substance different from each sin of every one of us. Except for the intervention of God no one has ever turned back on the broad way to perdition. Herein verily is seen the uttermost divine grace, that Christ seeks and saves from the plight of that despair. If our eyes delight to see him as the friendly Shepherd on the trail of the lost sheep, let us not turn our looks away from him in this more solemn occupation of rescuing the lost from the judgement. Let us see him in the darkness of the cross. For this part of the saving also takes place in no other way than the more gentle one we have already considered. Here too he not merely announces or promises the salvation, but carries it in his own Person. He is the impersonation of the God who pronounces the judgement and of the God who sovereignly takes it away, the one who bears our curse, and, while bearing it, speaks peace to our souls. For this reason he came to the cross, so that he might be able to act for God in this solemn, anticipated judgement through which every sinner passes. When he speaks of sin and pardon and escape, the voice is the voice of God and the arms stretched underneath us are the everlasting arms of the Almighty himself.

There is one other point on which we must briefly touch before closing. The text represents the object of the saving in the impersonal form as 'that which was lost'. The impersonal form of expression carries with it a generalizing effect. It amounts practically to 'whatsoever is lost'. The motive in our Lord's mind for this is not difficult to discover. A murmuring populace had excluded the class of publicans from the sphere that was worthy of his attention. To this Jesus replies with the emphatic declaration that all that is lost falls under the legitimate scope of his task, that, since the very fact of salvation is evoked by there being lost ones, no exception can be allowed from its grace on the mere ground that the object appears lost.

Within the realm of sin distinctions between class and class or degree and degree of sinners become obliterated. In comparison with the one tremendous fact of sin as such they dwindle into insignificance, or if there is any differentiation observable it assumes rather the opposite, paradoxical form of those taking the precedence, in whom, by reason of excessive sinfulness and most poignant sense of guilt, salvation's opportunity for magnifying itself is increased. The harlots and publicans enter first into the kingdom of God. But we should surely misinterpret this, if we took it to mean that Jesus, after precisely the same fashion, seeks and saves each single one that is lost. Grace knows no jealousy except for the honour of God. With wide generosity, such as only a renewal of heart can give, it yearns and prays for the ingathering of many. None the less, when as saved sinners we place ourselves individually before God, who would not feel it as a denial of salvation itself to forget that pointedly and with a special mysterious determination the search, which in its issue placed him among the saved, was instituted and pursued for him on the part of God and Christ? Let us not from hyper-altruistic squeamishness allow ourselves to gloss this over, for, besides withholding from God the glory which is his due in it, we should lose for ourselves the most precious portion of God's saving grace.

It is not as if Christ at random wandered through this world on the chance of finding someone upon whom to exercise his power of salvation. With reference to each one of the children of God there was with him from the beginning a unique compassion, a personalized love, and in result of this a singleness and determination of purpose, that imparted to his seeking

of the least one of us the glory of a private inclusion in
the intimate circle of God's saved ones. Of such seeking
Jesus was conscious, and with all the wideness of his
compassionate heart, which no world of sinners could
overcrowd, he was not ashamed to acknowledge the
gracious privileges and distinctions that pertained to the
Lord's people or to any individual child of God. On this
very occasion he gave expression to them in the words:
'Inasmuch as he also is a son of Abraham,' words which
trace back the blessed issue of Zacchaeus' encounter
with Jesus to the covenantal promise made ages before
to the patriarch, and ultimately to the sovereign election
of which this promise was the outcome. It is with this as
it is with the Pauline statement: no more than one can
say, 'Who loved me and gave himself for me,' is it possible to say, 'Who sought me and saved me,' except by a
profound faith in the elective purpose as the ultimate
cause of the personal inheritance of salvation.

Now what in conclusion are the lessons that we,
seekers of the salvation of others, ought to draw from
this episode in our Lord's life? They are chiefly two, and
I shall indicate them with the briefest of words. The first
relates to the specialized character we as servants of
Christ ought to make our work to bear. If his procedure
is normative for us—and who would deny this?—then
all our seeking and saving, that is, all our religious
endeavour, ought to carry the image and superscription
of Christ's. And here the salient point is undoubtedly
this, that the purpose, the goal of seeking and saving
were for our Lord pronouncedly religious. Seeking and
saving meant for him, before anything else, seeking
and saving for God. It had no humanitarian or world-
improving purpose apart from this. It began with the

thought of God and ended there. For that he came. And at that we should aim. This conception will not narrow our work any more than it did his, it will only centralize it. Beginning there we shall find that everything else will follow that ought to follow. Was it not so in the case of Zacchaeus? Once Jesus had entered his house with salvation, he could not help taking his stand as one morally and socially reconstructed before the crowd of detractors: 'Behold, Lord, the half of my goods I give to the poor; and if I have wrongfully exacted anything of any man, I restore fourfold.' Provided the precious nard of religion be poured into it, no vessel is unworthy. But, on the other hand, the finest flagon of the world, when bearing a false trademark, and under the guise of religion offering some inferior substitute, has no proper place in the service of Christ. It belongs to the hidden things of shame which Paul had discarded. No servant of Christ should touch it. And even though other things are not positively deceitful or harmful in themselves, our duty of bringing salvation is so transcendently important and exacting that the Christian minister cannot afford to lose time or energy over them.

The second lesson relates to what our specifically religious task of saving should centrally consist in. It may all be summed up in the simple formula, to bring Christ to men and men to Christ. It sounds simple, but is in reality a most difficult and most delicate task. No painter portraying face upon canvas ever used more exquisite art than is his who in preaching the gospel succeeds in so delineating the face of Christ as to make him look out with his immortal Saviour-eyes straight and deep into the hearts of sinners. Let your one concern be to bring the two together in the house

where salvation is needed, and having led the Saviour
in, go thou out and shut the door silently behind thee. I
tell you they shall not come out thence until salvation
has done its perfect work.

IV: 'Rabboni!'

John 20:16: *'Jesus saith unto her, Mary.*
She turneth herself and saith unto him, Rabboni;
which is to say, Master.'

O ur text takes us to the tomb of the risen Lord, on the first Sabbath-morning of the New Covenant. It is impossible for us to imagine a spot more radiant with light and joy than was this place immediately after the resurrection. Even when thinking ourselves back into the preceding moments, while as yet to the external eye there was nothing but the darkness of death, our anticipation of what we know to be about to happen floods the scene with a twilight of super-natural splendour. The sepulchre itself has become to us prophetic of victory; we seem to hear in the expectant air the wingbeat of the descending angels, come to roll away the stone and announce to us: 'The Lord is risen indeed!' Besides this, we have learned to read the story of our Lord's life and death so as to consider the resur-rection its only possible outcome, and this has to some extent dulled our sense for the startling character of what took place. We interpret the resurrection in terms of the atoning cross, and easily forget how little the disciples were as yet prepared for doing the same. And so it requires an effort on our part to understand sympa-thetically the state of mind they brought to the morning of this day. Nevertheless we must try to enter into their thoughts and feelings, if for no other reason, for this, that something of the same fresh marvel and gladness that subsequently came to them may fill our hearts also. Whether we may be able to explain it or not, the gospel tells us that, notwithstanding the emphatic prediction by the Saviour of his death and resurrection, they had but little remembrance of these words, and drew from them no practical support or comfort in the sorrow that overwhelmed them. In part this may have been due to the fact of our Lord's having only predicted and not fully explained these tremendous events.

At any rate the circumstance shows that there is need of a deeper faith than that of mere acquaintance with and consent to external statements of truth, when the dread realities of life and death assail us. Dare we say that we ourselves should have proved stronger in such a trial, if over against all that mocked our hope we had been able to see no more than a dimly remembered promise? Let us thank God that, when we ourselves enter into the valley of the shadow of death, we have infinitely more than a promise to stay our hearts upon, that ours is the fulfilment of the promise, the fact of the resurrection, the risen Lord himself present with rod and staff beside us.

Supplementing the account of John with the statements of the other Evangelists, we gain the following conception of the course of events previous to what the text relates. A small company of women went out at early dawn towards the garden, carrying the spices prepared as a last offering to honour Jesus. From among these Mary Magdalene in the eagerness of her desire to reach the place, ran forward, and discovered before the others that the stone had been rolled away. Without awaiting the arrival of her companions she hastens back to tell Peter and John what she supposed to be true: 'They have taken away the Lord out of the tomb.' Roused from the lethargy of their grief by this startling announcement the apostles immediately went to the place, and by their own observation verified Mary's report. John came first, but merely looked into the tomb. Peter, who followed, entered in, and saw the linen cloths lying and the napkin that was upon the Saviour's head rolled up and put by itself. Then John also entered, saw and believed. As yet they did not know the Scripture that he must rise again from the dead. Their eyes were so holden that the true explanation never occurred to them. Perplexed, but not moved from a despairing state of mind, they returned to their abode.

Mary must have followed the apostles at a distance when these came in haste to see for themselves. We find her standing outside the tomb weeping. Is it not remarkable that, while both John and Peter departed, Mary remained? Although the same hopeless conclusion had forced itself upon her, yet it could not induce her to leave. In her mind it only intensified a thousand times the purpose with which she had come. How striking an illustration of the Saviour's word that much forgiveness creates abounding love!

But may we not believe that still something else reveals itself in this? Mary's attitude towards Jesus, more perhaps than any other disciple's, seems to have been characterized by that simple dependence which is the consciousness of an ever present need. It was a matter of faith, as much as of love, that made her differ at this time from the others. Unmixed with further motives, the recognition of Jesus as the only refuge from sin and death filled her heart. In a measure, of course, he had been this to the others also. But whilst to them he stood for many other things in addition, the circumstances under which she had become attached to him made Mary's soul the mirror of saving faith pure and simple. And because she was animated by this fundamental spiritual impulse, drawing her to the Saviour more irresistibly than affection or sorrow could have done, therefore she could not but continue seeking him, even though unable for the moment to do anything else than weep near his empty tomb.

In vain does Calvary proclaim that the Lord is dead, in vain does the tomb declare that he has been buried, in vain does the absent stone suggest that they have taken him away—this threefold witness will not convince Mary that he has gone out of her life forever. And why? Because in the depth of her being there was an even more emphatic witness which would not be silenced but continued to protest that she must receive him back, since he is her Saviour. Contact, communion with Christ had become to her the vital breath of her spiritual life; to admit that the conditions rendering this possible had ceased to exist would have meant for her to deny salvation itself. There is, it is true, a pathetic incongruousness between the absoluteness of this desire and the futile form in which for the moment she thought it could be satisfied. In the last analysis what was she doing but seeking a lifeless body, in order that by caring for it and feeling near it she might still the longing of a living faith? Suppose she had received what she sought, would not in the next moment the other deeper desire have reasserted itself for that in him which it was absolutely beyond the power of a dead Jesus to give her? Still, however incongruous the form of expression, it was an instinct to which an outward reality could not fail to correspond. It arose out of a primary need, for which provision must exist somewhere, if redemption exists at all. Though unaware of the resurrection as a fact, she had laid hold upon the supreme principle from which its necessity flows. Once given the intimate bond of faith between a sinner and his Saviour, there can be no death to such a relationship.

Mary, in her simple dependence on Jesus, had risen to the point where she sought in him life and sought it ever more abundantly. To her faith he was Conqueror over death long before he issued from the grave. She was in rapport with that spiritual aspect, that quickening quality of his Person, of which the resurrection is the sure consequence. Here lies the decisive issue for everyone as regards the attitude to be assumed towards this great fact. Ultimately, stripped of all accidentals, the question resolves itself into this: What does Christ mean for us? For what do we need him? If we have learned to know ourselves guilty sinners, destitute of all hope and life in ourselves, and if we have experienced that from him came to us pardon, peace and strength, will it not sound like mockery in our ears if somebody tells us that it does not matter whether Jesus rose from the dead on the third day? It is of the very essence of saving faith that it clamours for facts, facts to show that the heavens have opened, that the tide of sinful nature has been reversed, the guilt of sin expiated, the reign of death destroyed and life and immortality brought to light. And because this is the insuppressible cry of faith, what else should faith do, when it sees doubt and unbelief emptying the gospel of the living Christ, what else should it do but stand outside weeping and repeating the cry:

'They have taken away my Lord and I know not where they have laid him'?

But, although these things were in principle present in Mary's heart, she did not at that moment perceive the pledge of hope contained in them. Her grief was too profound to leave room for introspection. It even hid from her vision the objective evidence of the resurrection that lay around her. Worse than this, she turned what was intended to help her into an additional reason for unbelief. But who of us shall blame her? Have not we ourselves under as favourable circumstances made the mistake of nourishing our unbelief on what was meant to be food for our faith? Do we not all remember occasions when we stood outside the grave of our hopes weeping, and did not perceive the hand stretched out to prepare us by the very thing we interpreted as sorrow for a higher joy?

From Mary's experience let us learn to do better. What the Lord expects from us at such seasons is not to abandon ourselves to unreasoning sorrow, but trustingly to look sorrow in the face, to scan its features, to search for the help and hope, which, as surely as God is our Father, must be there. In such trials there can be no comfort for us so long as we stand outside weeping. If only we will take the courage to fix our gaze deliberately upon the stern countenance of grief, and enter unafraid into the darkest recesses of our trouble, we shall find the terror gone, because the Lord has been there before us, and, coming out again, has left the place transfigured, making out of it by the grace of his resurrection a house of life, the very gate of heaven.

This was just what happened to Mary. She could not stand forever weeping, forgetful of what went on around her. 'As she wept she looked into the tomb, and she beholdeth two angels in white sitting one at the head and one at the feet, where the body of Jesus had lain.' It was a step in the right direction that she roused herself from her inaction. Still, what strikes us as most characteristic in this statement is its implying that even the vision of angels did not sufficiently impress her to raise the question, to what the appearance of these celestial messengers might be due. Probably this was the first time she had come in direct contact with the super-natural in that particular form. The place was doubtless charged with the atmosphere of mystery and wonder angels bring with themselves when entering into our world of sense. And yet no tremor seems to have run through her, no feeling of awe to have made her draw back. A greater blindness to fact is here than that which made her miss the sign of the empty grave. What more convincing evidence of the truth of the resurrection could have been offered than the presence of these two angels, silently, reverently, majestically sitting where the body of Jesus had lain? Placed like the cherubim on the mercy-seat, they covered between themselves the spot where the Lord had reposed, and flooded it with celes-tial glory. It needed no voice of theirs to proclaim that here death had been swallowed up in victory. Ever since the angels descended into this tomb the symbolism of burial has been radically changed. From this moment onward every last resting-place where the bodies of believers are laid is a furrow in that great harvest field of Christ whence heaven draws upward into light each seed sunk into it, whence Christ himself was raised, the first fruits of them that sleep.

Let us not overlook, however, that Mary's disregard

of the angels revealed in a most striking form something good also: her intense preoccupation with the one thought of finding the Lord. For him she had been looking into the tomb. He not being there, it was empty to her view, though filled with angelic glory. She would have turned aside without speaking had not the angels of their own accord spoken to her: 'Woman, why weepest thou?' These words were meant as an expression of sympathy quite natural in beings wont to rejoice over repenting sinners. But in this question there is at the same time a note of wonder at the fact that she should be weeping at all. To the mind of the angels the resurrection was so real, so self-evident, that they could scarcely understand how to her it could be otherwise. They felt the discord between the songs of joy with which their own world was jubilant and this sound of weeping coming out of a world of darkness and despair. 'Woman, why weepest thou?' Tears would be called for indeed, hadst thou found him in the tomb, but not at a time like this, when heaven and earth unite in announcing: he is risen in glory, the King of life!

Mary's answer to the angels shows that neither their sympathy nor their wonder had succeeded in piercing her sorrow. 'She saith unto them, Because they have taken away my Lord, and I know not where they have laid him.' These are almost the identical words in which she had informed Peter and John of her discovery of the empty tomb. Still a slight change appears. To the Apostles she had said 'the Lord' and 'we know not.' To the angels it is: 'my Lord' and 'I know not.' In this is revealed once more her intense sense of proprietorship in Jesus. In that sense the angels could not have appropriated him for themselves. They might hail him as their matchless King, but to Mary he was even more than this, her Lord, her Saviour, the One who had sought, saved and owned her in her sins.

Having given this answer to the angels she turned herself backward and beheld Jesus standing, and knew not that it was Jesus. No explanation is added of the cause of this movement. It matters little. Our interest at this stage of the narrative belongs not to what Mary but to what Jesus did. On his part the encounter was surely not accidental but intended. He had witnessed her coming once and again, her weeping, her bending over the tomb, her answer to the angels, and had witnessed not only these outward acts, but also the inward conflict by which her soul was torn. And he appears precisely at the point where his presence is required, because all other voices for conveying to her the gladsome tidings have failed. He had been holding himself in readiness to become in his own Person the preacher of the gospel of life and hope to Mary.

There is great comfort for us in this thought that, however dim our conscious faith and the sense of our salvation, on the Lord's side the fountain of grace is never closed, its connection with our souls never inter-rupted; provided there be the irrepressible demand for his presence, he cannot, he will not deny himself to us. The first person to whom he showed himself alive after the resurrection was a weeping woman, who had no greater claim upon him than any simple penitent sinner has. No eye except that of the angels had as yet rested upon his form. The time was as solemn and majestic as that of the first creation when light burst out of chaos and darkness. Heaven and earth were concerned in this event; it was the turning-point of the ages. Nor was this merely objectively so: Jesus felt himself the central figure in this new-born universe, he tasted the exquisite joy of one who had just entered upon an endless life in the possession of new powers and faculties such as human nature had never known before. Would it have been unnatural, had he sought some quiet place to spend the opening hour of this new unexplored state in communion with the Father? Can there be any room in his mind for the humble ministry of consolation required by Mary? He answers these questions himself. Among all the voices that hailed his triumph no voice appealed to him like this voice of weeping in the garden.

The first appearance of the risen Lord was given to Mary for no other reason than that she needed him first and needed him most. And what more appropriate beginning could have been set for his ministry of glory than this very act? Nothing could better convince us, that in his exalted state he retains for us the same tender sympathy, the same individual affection as he showed during the days of his flesh. It is well for us to know this, because otherwise the dread impression of his majesty might tend to hinder our approach to him. Who of us has not at some time of communion with the Saviour felt the overwhelming awe that seized the seer on Patmos, so that we could not utter our prayer, until he laid his hand upon us and said: 'Fear not'?

We should be thankful, then, for the grace of Christ which has so arranged it, that between his rising from the dead and his departure for heaven a season of forty days was interposed, a transition period, helping, as it were, the feebleness of our faith in the act of apprehending his glory. Perhaps the Lord for the same reason also intentionally placed his meeting with Mary at the

threshold of his resurrection life. Like other acts
recorded in the fourth Gospel this act rises above the
momentary situation and acquires a symbolic significance, enlarging before our eyes until it reveals him
in his priestly ministration conducted from the throne
of glory.

However not the fact only of his showing himself to
Mary, but likewise the manner of it claims our attention. When first beholding him she did not know the
Lord, and even after his speech she still supposed him to
be the gardener. The chief cause for this may have lain
in the change which had taken place in him when the
mortal put on immortality. Now behold with what
exquisite tact the Lord helps her to restore the broken
bond between the image her memory retained of him
and that new image in which henceforth he would walk
through her life and hold converse with her spirit. Even
these first words: 'Woman, why weepest thou? Whom
seekest thou?', though scarcely differing in form from
the question of the angels, go far beyond the latter in
their power to reach Mary's heart. In the word 'woman'
with which he addresses her speaks all the majesty of
one who felt himself the Son of God in power by resurrection from the dead. It is a prelude to the still more
majestic, 'Touch me not' spoken soon afterwards. And
yet in the words, 'Why weepest thou? Whom seekest
thou?' he extends to her that heart-searching sympathy,
which at a single glance can read and understand the
whole secret of her sorrow. He knew that such weeping
results only there where one who is more than father or
mother has been taken away. And how instantaneous the
effect these words produced! Though she still supposes
him the gardener, she takes for granted that he at least

could not have taken the body with evil intent, that he will not refuse to restore it: 'Sir, if thou hast borne him hence, tell me where thou hast laid him, and I will take him away.' A certain response to his sympathy is also shown in this, that three times she refers to Jesus as 'him', deeming it unnecessary to mention his name. Thus in the way she met the gardener there was already the beginning resumption of the bond of confidence between her and the Lord. And thus Jesus found the way prepared for making himself known to her in a most intimate manner. 'Jesus saith unto her, "Mary." She turneth and saith unto him, "Rabboni."' It happened all in a moment, and by a simple word, and yet in this one moment Mary's world was changed for her. She had in that instant made the transition from hopelessness because Jesus was absent, to fullness of joy because Christ was there. We may well despair of conveying by any process of exposition the meaning of these two words. This is speech the force of which can only be felt. And it will be felt by us in proportion as we clearly remember some occasion when the Lord spake a similar word to us and drew from us a similar cry of recognition. Doubtless much of the astounding effect of Jesus' word was due to the tone in which he spoke it. It was a tone calling to her remembrance the former days of closest fellowship. This was the voice that he alone could use, the same voice that had once commanded the demons to depart from her, and to which ever since she had been wont to listen for guidance and comfort. By using it he meant to assure her, that, whatever transformation had taken place, there could be and would be no change in the intimate, personal character of their relationship. And Mary was quick to apprehend this.

The Evangelist takes pains to preserve for us the word she uttered in its original Aramaic form, because he would have us understand that it meant more at this moment than could be conveyed by the ordinary rendering of 'Teacher' or 'Master'. 'Rabboni' has a special untranslatable significance. It was the personal response to the personal 'Mary', to all intents a proper name no less than the other. By speaking it Mary consciously re-entered upon the possession of all that as 'Rabboni' he had meant to her. Only one thing she had yet to learn, for teaching her which the Lord did not deem even this unique moment too joyful or sacred. In the sudden revulsion from her grief Mary would have given some external expression to the tumult within by grasping and holding him. But he restrained her, saying: 'Touch me not, for I am not yet ascended unto my Father; but go unto my brethren and say to them, I ascend unto my Father and your Father, and my God and your God.' At first sight these words may seem a contrast to those immediately preceding. And yet no mistake could be greater than to suppose that the Lord's sole or chief purpose was to remind her of the restrictions which henceforth were to govern the intercourse between himself and her. His intention was much rather to show that the desire for a real communion of life would soon be met in a new and far higher way than was possible under the conditions of local earthly nearness. 'Touch me not' does not mean: touch is too close a contact to be henceforth permissible; it means: the provision for the highest, the ideal kind of touch has not been completed yet: 'I am not yet ascended to my Father.' His words are a denial of the privilege she craved only as to the form and moment in which she craved it; in their larger sense they are a pledge, a giving, not a withholding of himself from her. The great event of which the resurrection is the first step has not yet fulfilled itself; it requires for its completion the ascent to the Father. But when this is accomplished then all restrictions will fall away, and the desire to touch that made Mary stretch forth her hand shall be fully gratified. The thought is not different from that expressed in the earlier saying to the disciples: 'Ye shall see me, because I go to the Father.' There is a seeing, a hearing, a touching, first made possible by Jesus' entrance into heaven and by the gift of the Spirit dependent on that entrance. And what he said to Mary he commissioned her to repeat to his brethren, that they also might view the event in its proper perspective.

May we not suitably close our study by reminding ourselves that we too are included among the brethren to whom he desired these tidings be brought? Before this he had never called the disciples by this name, as he had never until now so suggestively identified himself with them by speaking of 'your Father and my Father' and 'your God and my God'. We are once more assured that the new life of glory, instead of taking him from us, has made us in a profounder sense his brethren and his Father our Father. Though, unlike Mary and the disciples, we have not been privileged to behold him in the body, yet together with the believers of all ages we have an equal share in what is far sweeter and more precious, the touch through faith of his heavenly Person for which the appearances after the resurrection were but a preparation. Let us then not linger at the tomb, but turn our faces and stretch our hands upwards into heaven, where our life is hid with him in God, and whence he shall also come again to show himself to us as he did to Mary, to make us speak the last great 'Rabboni', which will spring to the lips of all the redeemed, when they meet their Saviour in the early dawn of that eternal Sabbath that awaits the people of God.

V: The More Excellent Ministry

2 Corinthians 3:18: *'But we all, with unveiled face, beholding as in a mirror the glory of the Lord, are transformed into the same image from glory to glory, even as from the Lord, the Spirit.'*

This second letter of Paul to the church at Corinth is marked by a pronounced polemic strain. In this respect it somewhat resembles the Epistle to the Galatians. In each instance a serious crisis in the life of the church had evoked it. It is further common to both writings that in certain passages the polemic assumes a sharply personal character. In neither case is this due to any temperamental difficulty on Paul's part to control his outraged feelings, although even if this had been so, much could have been said in excuse of the apostle. His opponents had certainly not been sparing in personalities. He had been represented as a deceiver, as one who preached himself and praised himself. It had been charged that in his quasi-apostolic authority he lorded it over the church, employed his usurped power for casting down instead of for building up, and that, in spite of all this bluff and bluster of prestige, he lacked the ability to make good his pretensions, being indeed weighty and strong in his letters, but weak in his bodily presence, and in his speech, of no account. The insinuation had been made that Paul himself was aware of the hollowness of his claims, because he would not take from the church the support to which, if a true apostle, he ought to have felt himself entitled. He had been held up as a man who by his fickleness betrayed the duplicity of his position.

The Apostle had not even been spared that meanest of all aspersions—that he was spending money collected for the poor saints in Judea on his own person. His sincerity as a minister of the truth had been called into question. It was charged that, while aware of his subordination to the original apostles, he was disloyal to them, and substituted for their gospel an entirely different one spun out of his own mind. Thus the truth of the very substance of his preaching was challenged. In this respect again a certain resemblance to the tactics of his Galatian opponents may be observed. The charge in both instances was that he preached 'a different gospel'. Nevertheless the point of attack had been somewhat shifted. In Galatia the main question had been that of salvation with or without the law. Here in Corinth, on the other hand, the controversy raged around Paul's teaching concerning the Christ. It was with another Jesus that his opponents had approached the Corinthians. No effort had been spared to prove this the true Jesus, by the side of whom the Christ of Paul's preaching was a pure figment of the imagination. Suspicion had been cast on the source of his knowledge of the Saviour on the ground that the visions through which it was obtained belonged to the class of wild, fantastic experiences, and that these marked Paul as one beside himself, not merely in this one point, but in the entire tone and temper of his religious life. The exalted, spiritual, heavenly nature, in which his gospel clothed

the glorified Christ, was construed as convincing proof
of the darkness and incomprehensibleness of the apostle's message. He preached a gospel that was veiled. And
over against these elusive and intangible things had been
placed the palpable institutions of the Mosaic covenant,
carrying with them the demand for a Messiah corre-
spondingly substantial and realistic in his make-up. This
is an early illustration of the principle which from that
time onward has shaped all forms of teaching in the
church. For in each instance the view about the method
of salvation is reflected in the conception of the Saviour.
A certain gospel requires a certain kind of Christ, and a
certain type of Christ a certain gospel.

It might have seemed as if the attack upon the
apostle had therewith reached its logical conclusion and
could not possibly go farther. Still this was not the case.
With a curious retroversive movement the issue had
been carried back from this point to the question of the
personality of Paul, with this difference only, it
was now his dignity in office that had been assailed.
Paul's office as such was made out to be mean and
contemptible. Such a Christ and such a cause could
engage one who laboured for them only in the weakest
and most ignoble kind of service. Paul was not permitted to escape the immemorial stigma reflected upon the
minister from the apparent foolishness and weakness of
the cross. And the apostle was sensitive, if anywhere, on
this point of the nobility and glory of his office. Moral
aspersions against his character he might, had it not
been for fear of danger to the churches, have passed
by as unworthy of notice. But the pride of office was
stronger in him than the sense of personal honour.
And thus it happens that we are indebted to these

disturbers of the Corinthian church, whose names have long been forgotten, for an encomium upon the gospel service, which for power and splendour has no equal in the records of Christian apology. It deserves to be placed beside the song of triumph in the eighth chapter of the Epistle to the Romans. As there the apostle is carried on the crest-wave of assurance of salvation, so here he moves with the full tide of enthusiasm over the excellence of his calling. The very words are, as it were, baptized in the glory of which they speak.

Let us briefly examine the several elements that enter into this high consciousness. The form of argument which Paul adopts is evidently determined by the method of his detractors. At the climax of their calumny they had concentrated their attack on the meanness and weakness of his message. Consequently he chooses to defend himself on the same basis by arguing from the glory of the message to the distinction of the bearer. While thus adjusted to the manner of attack, this method was also in keeping with Paul's innate modesty, still further refined by grace.

But there was another tactical motive besides. Paul recognized that by thus approaching the subject a more substantial title to official prestige could be made out than in any other way, such, perhaps, as calling attention to outward results. After all it is not so much by what the minister contributes of himself to the cause of Christ, but rather by what he is enabled to draw out and utilize from the divine resources, that his office and work will be tested. It is not chiefly the question whether we are strong in the cause, but whether the cause is strong in and through us. And herein lies the practical value of the argument in its application to the servants of Christ under all conditions. If Paul had staked the issue on the personal factor, then there could be in his testimony but little comfort and encouragement for others, for there are not many Pauls. Now that the subject is dealt with in the other way the apostle's words contain something heartening for you and me and the simplest, obscurest bearer of the gospel.

We are too often told at the present day that the official, professional distinction of the minister is a matter of the past, that it has become purely a question of what is called personal magnetism whether he shall earn success or failure. Paul certainly was far from this opinion. To be sure, to such things as ecclesiastical position or rank he would hardly have attributed much importance. Even the difference between the apostolate and other forms of service in the church seems scarcely to enter into the reckoning here. But within the realm of the invisible and spiritual there remains such a thing as an intrinsic prestige. Paul is conscious of belonging to a veritable élite of the Spirit. I beg you to notice on how large a scale this thought is projected. It gives rise to the conception of a ministry of God's covenant, that is, a ministry identified with an all-comprehensive dispensation of divine grace. Thus Moses was a minister of the Old and Paul is a minister of the New Covenant.

To have such a covenant-ministry means to be identified with God in the most intimate manner, for the covenant expresses the very heart of God's purpose. It means to be initiated into the holiest mysteries of redemption, for in the covenant these are transacted. It means to be enrolled on the list of the great historic servants of God, for in the organism of the covenant these are united and salute each other across the ages. It means to become a channel through which supernatural currents flow. In the covenant the servant is, as it were, made part of the wonder-world of salvation itself. The apostle has embodied this grandiose thought in a most striking figure. 'Thanks be to God,' he exclaims, 'who always leadeth us in triumph in Christ.' The onward march of the gospel is a triumphal procession, God the victorious Conqueror, Paul a follower in God's train, burning the incense to his glory, making manifest the savour of his knowledge in every place!

What has been said so far applies to the ministry of the covenant of grace under both dispensations. It describes a glory common to Moses and Paul. The apostle ungrudgingly recognizes that the Old Testament had its peculiar distinction. To be a prophet or priest of the God of Israel conferred greater honour than any secular prominence in the pagan history of the race. Even the ministration written and engraven on stones came with glory. This excellence of the Old Covenant found a symbolic expression in the light upon the face of Moses after his tarrying with God upon the mount, a light so intense that the children of Israel could not steadfastly look upon its radiance. Paul's purpose, however, is not to emphasize what the two dispensations have in common, but that in which the New surpasses the Old.

Since the opponents had clothed their attack upon him in the invidious form of a comparison with the Mosaic administration, it was natural for him to take up the challenge and fight out the battle along the same line. None the less the comparison, as followed up by Paul, is startling in its exceeding boldness. A more impressive disclosure of his exalted sense of office is

GRACE AND GLORY

scarcely conceivable. In order to feel the full force of
this we ought to make clear to ourselves that not
two single persons but two pairs of persons are set over
against each other. On the one side stand God and
Moses, the reflector of his glory, on the other Christ
and Paul, the reflector of his glory.

It would be interesting, but beside our present purpose, to consider what it implies as to the nature and
rank of Christ, that the apostle feels free simply to
put him on a line with God as a fount and dispenser of
glory in the New Covenant after no different fashion
than God was under the Old Covenant. Without pursuing this further, we now wish to make the point, that
the comparison lies not between Moses and Christ, but
between Moses and Paul. Than Moses no greater name
was known in the annals of Old Testament redemption.
Prophet, priest, lawgiver in one, he towers high above
all the others. And to Paul, the son of Israel, all this
wealth of sacred story gathered round the head of
Moses must have been a thousand times more impressive than it can be to us. What an overwhelming sense
then of the greatness of his own ministry must Paul have
possessed, when he dared conceive the thought of being
greater than Moses! 'Verily that which has been made
glorious has been made not-glorious in this respect, by
reason of the glory that surpasseth.'

The apostle, however, does not give expression to
this lofty consciousness in an outburst of unreasoning
enthusiasm. He carefully specifies wherein the surpass-
ing excellence of his ministry above that of Moses
consists. The first point relates to the contrast between
transitoriness and eternity. Putting it in terms of the
figure, Paul affirms that the glory of the Old Covenant

had to pass away, whereas that of the New Covenant must remain. When Moses descended from the mount his face shone with a refulgence of the divine glory near which he had been permitted to dwell for a season.

But his face could not retain this brightness for any length of time. It soon disappeared. Thus what Moses stood for was glorious but lacked permanence. The day was bound to come when its splendour would vanish. On the other hand the New Covenant is final and abiding. The times cannot outgrow, the developments of history cannot age it, it carries within itself the pledge of eternity. But not only did such a difference actually exist—both Moses and Paul were aware of the state of things in each case. Moses was aware of it, for we are told that he put the veil on his face for the purpose of hiding the disappearance of the glory. And Paul was, since in pointed contrast to this procedure, he professes to minister with open face: 'Not as Moses, who put a veil over his face.' It was further inevitable that in Paul's estimation the speedy abrogation of Moses' work detracted from his glory as a servant of the covenant, and that, on the other hand, the enduring character of his own work added greatly to the honour wherewith Paul felt it clothed him and the satisfaction he derived from it. Time, especially time with the wasting power it acquires through sin, is the arch-enemy of all human achievement. It kills the root of joy which otherwise belongs to working and building. All things which the succeeding generations of mankind have wrought in the course of the ages succumb to its attacks. The tragic sense of this accompanies the race at every step in its march through history. It is like a pall cast over the face of the peoples. In revealed religion through the grace of redemption it is in principle removed, yet not so that under the Old Covenant the dark shadow entirely disappears. The complaint of it is in Moses' own psalm: 'Thou turnest man to destruction—Thou carriest them away as with a flood.' And something of this bitter taste of transitoriness enters even into the Old Testament consciousness of salvation.

Now put over against this the triumphant song of life and assurance of immortality that fills the glorious, spacious days of the New Covenant, especially where first it issues from the womb of the morning bathed in the dew of imperishable youth. The note of futility and depression has disappeared, and in place of this the rapture of victory over death and decay, the exultant feeling of immersion in the atmosphere of eternity prevail. And this particularly communicated itself to the spirit in which the covenant-ministration was performed. The joy of working in the dawn of the world to come quickens the pulse of all New Testament servants of Christ. Paul felt that the product of his labours, the output of his life, would shine with unfading splendour in the palace of God. Thus also the honour of being a fellow labourer of God first obtains its full rich meaning. It is the prerogative of God, the Eternal One, to work for eternity. As the King of the ages he discounts and surmounts all the intervening forces and barriers of time. He who is made to share in this receives the highest form which the divine image can assume in its reproduction in man. Neither things present nor things to come can conquer him, he reigns in life with God through Jesus Christ, his Lord.

In the second place, there is a difference operating to the advantage of Paul between the two ministries in

regard to the measure of openness and clearness with
which they are conducted. Moses ministered with covered, Paul ministers with open, that is uncovered, face.
As regards Moses this was that the children of Israel
should not perceive the passing away of the glory
underneath the veil. Not that Moses acted as a deceiver
of his people. Paul means to say, that in receiving the
glory, and losing it, and hiding its loss, he served
the symbolic function of illustrating, in the first place,
the glory of the Old Covenant, in the second place
its transitoriness, and in the third place the ignorance
of Israel in regard to what was taking place. The chief
point of ignorance of the people related to the eclipse
and abrogation their institutions would suffer. But the
symbolism permits generalization, so as to include all
the limitations of self-knowledge and self-understanding
under which the Old Covenant laboured. As a matter
of fact Paul immediately afterwards extends it to
Israel's entire reading of the law, that is, to Israel's self-
interpretation and Scripture-interpretation on a large
scale. Ignorance as to the end would easily produce
ignorance or imperfect understanding with reference
to the whole order of things under which the people
were living.

Everything temporal and provisional, especially if it
does not know itself as such, is apt to wear a veil. It
often lacks the faculty of discriminating between what is
higher and lower in its composition. Things that are
ends and things that are mere means to an end are not
always clearly separated. Every preparatory stage in the
history of redemption can fully understand itself only
in the light of that which fulfils it. The veil of the
Old Covenant is lifted only in Christ. The Christian

standpoint alone furnishes the necessary perspective for apprehending its place and function in the organism of the whole. So it came about that the Mosaic covenant moved through the ages a mystery to itself and to its servants. According to Paul this tragical process reached its climax when Israel came face to face with him who alone could interpret Israel to itself. It is not for us to unravel the web of self-misinterpretation and unbelief wrought by the Jews on the ancient loom previously to the appearance of Christ. Paul implies that both causes contributed to the sad result. There was an element of original guilt as well as of subsequent hardening involved. Their minds were blinded. The veil was on the reading of Moses, but the veil was also on their hearts. And the apostle's word still holds true: the veil remains until the present day. It can be taken away only when Israel shall turn to the Lord. Then, and not until then, that ghost of the Old Covenant which now accompanies Israel on its wandering through the ages, will vanish from its side. As a double gift of grace it will then receive the treasures of Moses and those of Paul from the hand of Christ.

It is in sharp contrast to all this that Paul describes his own mode of ministering under the New Covenant. He serves with unveiled face, and in this one figure all the openness, the self-intelligence, the transparency of his ministry find expression. The proclamation of the Word of the gospel has left behind all the old reserve and restrictions and limitations under which Moses and his successors laboured. Its ministers can now speak fully and freely and plainly the whole counsel of God. Paul glories in being able to do this. He uses great boldness of speech. There is nothing to withhold, nothing to conceal: the entire plan of redemption has been unfolded, the mystery hidden through the ages has been revealed, and there is committed to every ambassador of Christ an absolute message, no longer subject to change. Not the delicate procedure of the diplomat, who hides his aim, but the stately stepping forward of the herald who renders an authoritative pronouncement characterizes his task to Paul's own mind. He discards all human artifice and invention, all insincere and undignified devices evidently employed by some at that time, as they are still not infrequently at the present time, to render the gospel palatable to his hearers. He scorns, where principles are concerned, all compromise and concession: 'Therefore, seeing we have this ministry, even as we obtained mercy, we faint not, but we have renounced the hidden things of shame, not walking in craftiness, nor handling the word of God deceitfully, but by the manifestation of the truth commending ourselves to every man's conscience in the sight of God.'

There is a straightforwardness, a simplicity in preaching, which is proportionate to the preacher's own faith in the absoluteness, and inherent truthfulness of his message. No shallow optimism about the adjustableness of Christianity to ever-changing conditions, about its self-rejuvenating power after apparent decline, can possibly make up for a lack of this fundamental conviction. Unless we are convinced with Paul that Christianity has a definable and well-defined message to bring, and are able to tell wherein it consists, all our talk about its vitality or adaptability will neither comfort ourselves nor deceive others. A thing is not immortal because it is long-lived and dies hard. Only when through all changes of time it preserves unaltered its essence and source of power, can it be considered worthwhile as a medicine for the sickness of the world. Something that needs the constant use of cosmetics to keep up the appearance of youth is a caricature of the Christianity of the New Testament. Its case is worse than it imagines: it has not merely passed its youth, but is in danger of losing its very life.

In the next place, the greater distinction of the ministry of the New Covenant springs from this, that it is in the closest conceivable manner bound up with the Person and work of the Saviour. It is a Christ-dispensation in the fullest sense of the word. What is possessed by the New Covenant is not the glory of God as such, but the glory of God in the face of Jesus Christ. Moses had a great vision on the mountain, but Paul had a greater one, even as Moses himself had a greater, when he stood with Elias on the New Testament mount of transfiguration. Paul beholds the glory of Christ as in a mirror, or, according to another rendering, reflects it as a mirror. His entire task, both on its communicative and on its receptive side, can be summed up in his reflecting back the Christ-glory, caught by himself unto others. To behold Christ and to make others behold him is the substance of his ministry.

All the distinctive elements of Paul's preaching relate to Christ, and bear upon their face his image and superscription. God is the Father of our Lord Jesus Christ. The Spirit is the Spirit of Christ. In the procuring of righteousness Christ is the one efficient cause. In Christ believers were chosen, called, justified, and will be glorified. To be converted is to die with Christ and to rise with him. The entire Christian life, root and stem and branch and blossom, is one continuous fellowship with Christ. But to say that the gospel is full of Christ is still too general a statement. What the apostle affirms is that it is particularly the gospel of the glory of Christ, and that, therefore, its ministry also has specifically to do with this.

Now this is not a mere metaphorical way of speaking, as if it meant no more than that in every possible manner the gospel-preaching brings out and promotes the honour of the Saviour. Paul intends it in a far more literal sense. The glory of Christ transmitted by his gospel is an objective reality. It is that which effects the Saviour's exalted state since the resurrection. While including the radiance of his external appearance, it is by no means confined to this. Paul reckons among this glory the whole equipment of grace and power and beauty, all the supernatural potencies and forces stored up in the risen Lord. It consists of energy no less than of splendour. Taken in this comprehensive, realistic sense, it is equivalent to the content of the gospel, and determines the nature of its ministry. The rendering, 'beholding as in a mirror', admirably fits into this representation. As a mirror is not an end in itself but exists for the sake of what is seen through it, so the gospel serves no other purpose than to bring men face to face with the glory of Christ. It is nothing else but a tale of Christ, a Christ in words, the exact counterpart of Christ's Person and work in their glorious state.

Because of the consciousness of this Paul felt himself greater than Moses, for the partial light that shone on the latter's face has now become omnipresent and fills the New Covenant. Under the old dispensation the servants of God saw only from afar the brightness of the Messiah's rising. Now he is visible from nearby, the One filling all in all, occupying the entire field of vision. The humblest of preachers surpasses in this respect the greatest of Old Testament evangelists. He carries a gospel all-fragrant and all-radiant with Christ.

In the fourth place the excellence of the ministry of the New Covenant is seen in this that it is a ministry of abundant forgiveness and righteousness. This aspect of it also is intimately connected with the glory of the Lord, although it requires a somewhat closer inspection to perceive this. It should be remembered that the glory possessed by Christ in heaven is, to Paul, the emphatic, never-silent declaration of his absolute righteousness acquired during the state of humiliation. It sprang from his obedience and suffering and self-sacrifice in our stead. It is righteousness translated into the language of effect, the crown set upon his work of satisfaction. Consequently the servant of the New Covenant can attach his ministry of pardon and peace to the glory of Christ. Hence Paul in working out the comparison between Moses and himself with special reference to the question of righteousness reduces the difference to terms of glory: 'For if the ministry of condemnation is glory, much rather does the ministry of righteousness exceed in glory.'

In a broad sense the Old Testament was the economy of conviction of sin. The law revealed the moral helplessness of man, placed him under a curse, worked death. There was, of course, gospel under and in the Old Covenant, but it was for its expression largely dependent on the silent symbolic language of altar and sacrifice and lustration. Under it the glory which speaks of righteousness was in hiding. In the New Covenant all this has been changed. The veil has been rent, and through it an unobstructed view is obtained of the glory of God on the face of Jesus Christ. And with this vision comes the assurance of atonement, satisfaction, access to God, peace of conscience, liberty, eternal life. For Paul the commission to proclaim these things constitutes no small part of the excellence of his task. As Jesus delighted in announcing release to the captives, in setting at liberty those who were bruised, in proclaiming the acceptable year of Jehovah, so Paul, even more because of the accomplishment of the redemptive work, rejoiced in the ministry of reconciliation. Beautiful to him upon the mountains were the feet of those who bring good tidings, that publish peace.

The fifth and principal reason why the service of the New Covenant excels in honour, Paul adds, is this: that the Christ-glory is a living and self-communicating power, transforming both those who mediate it and those who receive it from glory to glory into the likeness of the Lord. Paul here again has in mind the difference between Moses and himself. Moses' own condition and appearance were only externally and temporarily affected by the vision on the mount. After a while his face became as before. And what he was unable to retain for himself he was unable to communicate unto others.

Over against this the apostle places the two facts, first that the servants of the New Covenant are internally and permanently transformed by beholding the image of the Lord, and second that they effect a similar transformation in others to whom through their ministry the knowledge of the glorified Saviour comes. In its first part this representation was doubtless connected with the apostle's personal experience. There had been a point in his life at which the perception of the glorified Lord had been for him attended with the most marvellous change it is possible to undergo. The glory that shone around him on the road to Damascus had in one moment, in the twinkling of an eye, swept away all his old beliefs and ideals, his sinful passion and pride, and made of him a new creature, to whom the past things were like the faint memory of some distant phase of existence. And what had happened there Paul had afterwards seen repeating itself thousands of times, less conspicuously, to be sure, but not on that account less truly, less miraculously. To express this aspect of his ministry he employs the formula, that it is a ministry of the Spirit, that is of the Holy Spirit, whereas that of Moses was one of the letter. The Spirit stands for the living, energizing, creative grace of God, the letter for the inability of the law as such to translate itself into action.

Now, in saying that the ministry of the New Covenant is a ministry of the glory of Christ and that it is a ministry of the Spirit, Paul is not really affirming two different things but one and the same fact. The glory and the Spirit to him are identical. As we have seen the glory means the equipment, with supernatural power and splendour, of the exalted Christ. And this equipment, described from the point of view of its energizing source, consists of the Holy Spirit. It was at the resurrection that the Spirit in this high, unique sense was received by him. There the Spirit transformed the Lord's human nature and made it glorious beyond conception. Besides this, the Spirit is with Christ in continuance as the indwelling principle, the element, as it were, in which the glorified life of the Saviour is lived. We need not wonder, then, that a little later the apostle gives almost paradoxical expression to this truth by declaring, 'The Lord is the Spirit,' and that we are transformed from 'the Lord, the Spirit'.

This language is not, of course, intended to efface the distinction between the second and the third Persons of the Trinity, but simply serves to bring out the practical inseparableness of the exalted Christ and the Holy Spirit in the work of salvation. So we begin to understand at least a little of the mystery, how the glory of Christ can communicate itself to and reproduce itself in the believer and transform him. As Spirit-glory it cannot fail to do this, for it is of the nature of the Spirit so to act. Hence also we read elsewhere that Christ 'became a quickening Spirit'. The main point to be observed, however, is how all this adds to the high conception held by Paul about the honour of his ministry as compared with that of Moses. The minister of the law, the letter, can never taste that sweetest joy of seeing the message he brings incarnate and reincarnate itself in the lives of others. The minister of the New Covenant does taste of this joy: he writes with the Spirit of the living God in tables that are hearts of flesh. This means more than what we sometimes speak of and feel as pleasure in the consciousness of power set free or good accomplished.

Paul undoubtedly knew this also, but to confine what he here describes to that would rob it of its most distinctive quality. Paul had the sensation of coming through his ministry into the closest touch with the forthputting of the saving energy of God himself. He was aware that to his preaching of the gospel there belonged an invisible background, that at every step his presentation of the truth was accompanied by a ministry from heaven conducted by the Christ of glory. His work was for him imbued with divine power, the life-blood of the supernatural pulsed through it. His service, at each point where it touched men, marked the line and opened channels for the introduction of divine creative forces into human souls. So vivid was this consciousness of involvement in the supernatural, that nothing short of a comparison of God's Word through him with the divine Word at the first creation could adequately express it to Paul's mind: 'God who said, Let light shine out of darkness, has shined into our hearts for the purpose of our imparting the light of the knowledge of his glory in the face of Jesus Christ.'

Nor was this close participation with God in a transforming spiritual process something glorious merely in itself. Paul also took into account its comprehensive effect. When the apostle says, 'We all are transformed', it is evident that the statement is not limited to the apostles or preachers of the gospel, but includes, so far at least as the passive experience is concerned, all believers. To the joyous consciousness of exerting extraordinary power there was added the delight of witnessing extraordinary results. There is a note of genuine Christian universalism in this. It was a reason for profound satisfaction to Paul that he need not stand in the midst of the congregation of God as another Moses, partaking of a light from God in which the others could not share, solitary in his splendour, but that the larger share of what he affirmed of himself had through him become the possession of the simplest believer, a transfiguration of spirit like his own by the beholding of the Lord. Refracted from numberless mirrors the light

multiplied and intensified itself for each on whom it fell.
Nevertheless even so a measure of incommunicable
distinction remained. Since the reproduction into the
likeness of Christ is dependent on and proportionate to
the vision of the Saviour, and since this vision from the
nature of the case is more constantly present to the
minister of the gospel than to the common believer, it
follows that in the former an altogether unique result
may be expected.

So it was undoubtedly with Paul. He had no need of
testing the principle in others; a more direct and convincing evidence lay in its effect upon himself. He was
aware of a renewal of the inner man, progressing from
day to day, and in which there was observable this
law of increase, that the more he did to make Christ
known, the deeper the lineaments of the character of
Christ were impressed upon his soul. Even the hardships
befalling his flesh in the service of the Lord were con-
tributory to this: 'We are always bearing about in the
body the dying of Jesus, that the life also of Jesus may
be manifested in our mortal flesh.' And: 'Our light
affliction, which is for the moment, works for us more
exceedingly an eternal weight of glory.' 'Therefore we
faint not, though our outward man decay, yet the inner
man is renewed day by day.' Thus the apostle's ministry,
while exercised upon others, became unto him a
continual ministry to his own soul, ever increasingly
assimilating him to the glory of Christ.

Such was Paul's conception of the ministry of the
New Covenant. It bears upon its face the marks of
the historical situation in which he was called upon to
present it. None the less it has abiding validity, for it is
drawn from the nature of the gospel itself, and the

gospel is the gospel of him who remains the same yesterday and today and forever. Even of the errors over against which Paul placed these glorious views it is in a certain sense true that they are not of one age but of all ages; they lead a life of pseudo-immortality among men. In the Judaistic controversy which shook the early church, forces and tendencies were at work deeply rooted in the sinful human heart. In modernized apparel they confront us still to the present day. There are still abroad forms of a Christless gospel. There prevails still a subtle form of legalism which would rob the Saviour of his crown of glory, earned by the cross, and would make of him a second Moses, offering us the stones of the law instead of the life-bread of the gospel. And, oh the pity and shame of it, the Jesus that is being preached but too often is a Christ after the flesh, a religious genius, the product of evolution, powerless to save!

Let us pray that it may be given to the church to repudiate and cast out this error with the resoluteness of Paul. There is need for her ministers of placing themselves ever afresh in the light of the great apostolic consciousness revealed in our text. They should learn once more to bear their message out of the fulness of conviction that it is an unchangeable message, reliable as the veracity of God himself. God grant that it may become on the lips of his servants more truly from age to age a gospel from which the name of Christ crowds out every other human name, good tidings of atonement and righteousness and supernatural renewal; to preacher and people alike, what it was to Paul and his converts, a mirror of vision and transfiguration after the image of the Lord.

VI: Heavenly-Mindedness

Hebrews, 11:9-10: *'By faith he became a sojourner in the land of promise, as in a land not his own, dwelling in tents with Isaac and Jacob, the heirs with him of the same promise; for he looked for the city which has the foundations, whose builder and maker is God.'*

The chapter from which our text is taken is pre-eminently the chapter on faith. It illustrates the nature, power and effects of this grace in a series of examples from sacred history. In the context the prophecy of Habakkuk is quoted: 'The righteous shall live by faith.' We remember that in the Epistles to the Romans and Galatians also the same prophecy appears with prominence. Abraham similarly figures there as the great example of faith. In consequence one might easily be led to think that the development of the idea of faith in these epistles and in our chapter moves along identical lines. This would be only partially correct. Although the two types of teaching are in perfect accord, and touch each other at certain points, yet the angle of vision is not the same.

In Romans and Galatians faith is in the main trust in the grace of God, the instrument of justification, the channel through which the vital influences flowing from Christ are received by the believer. Here in

Hebrews the conception is wider; faith is 'the proving of things not seen, the assurance of things hoped for'. It is the organ for apprehension of unseen and future realities, giving access to and contact with another world. It is the hand stretched out through the vast distances of space and time, whereby the Christian draws to himself the things far beyond, so that they become actual to him. The earlier epistles are not unfamiliar with this aspect of faith. Paul in 2 Corinthians declares that for the present the Christian walks through a land of faith and not of sight. And on the other hand this chapter is not unfamiliar with the justifying function of faith, for we are told of Noah, that he became heir of the righteousness which is according to faith.

Nevertheless, taking the two representations as a whole, the distinctness of the point of view in each should not be neglected. It can be best appreciated by observing that, while in these other writings Christ is the object of faith, the One towards whom the sinner's trust is directed, here the Saviour is described as himself exercising faith, in fact as the one perfect, ideal believer. The writer exhorts his readers: 'Let us run with patience the race that is set before us, looking unto Jesus the leader and perfecter of our faith.' Faith in that other sense of specific trust, through which a guilty sinner becomes just in the sight of God, our Lord could not exercise, because he was sinless. But the faith that is an assurance of things hoped for and a proving of things not seen had a large place in his experience. By very reason of the contrast between the higher world to which he belonged and this dark lower world of suffering and death to which he had surrendered himself it could not be otherwise than that faith, as a projection of his soul into the unseen and future, should have been the fundamental habit of the earthly life of his human nature, and should have developed in him a degree of intensity not attained elsewhere.

But, although, for the reason stated, in the unique case of Jesus the two types of faith did not go together, they by no means exclude each other in the mind of the Christian. For, after all, justifying faith is but a special application in one particular direction of the frame of mind here described. Among all the realities of the invisible world, mediated to us by the disclosures and promises of God, and to which our faith responds there is none that more strongly calls into action this faculty for grasping the unseen than the divine pronouncement through the gospel, that, though sinners, we are righteous in the judgement of God. That is not only the invisible, it seems the impossible; it is the paradox of all paradoxes; it requires a unique energy of believing; it is the supreme victory of faith over the apparent reality of things; it credits God with calling the things that are not as though they were; it penetrates more deeply into the deity of God than any other act of faith.

What we read in this chapter about the various activities and acts of faith in the lives of the Old Testament saints might perhaps at first create the impression that the word 'faith' is used in a looser sense, and that many things are attributed to it not strictly belonging there on the author's own definition. One might be inclined in more precise language to classify them with other Christian graces. There is certainly large variety of costume in the procession that is made to pass before our eyes. The understanding that the worlds were framed out of nothing, the ability to offer God an acceptable sacrifice, the experience of translation unto God, the preparing of the ark, the responsiveness to the call to leave one's country, the power to conceive seed when past age, the willingness to sacrifice an only son, Joseph's mention beforehand of the deliverance from Egypt, and his commandment concerning his bones, the hiding of the child Moses, the choice by Moses, when grown up, of the reproach of God's people in preference to the treasures of Egypt, all this and more is represented as belonging to the one rubric of faith. But let us not misunderstand the writer. When he affirms that by faith all these things were suffered and done, his idea is not that what is enumerated was in each case the direct expression of faith. What he means is that in the last analysis faith alone made possible every one of the acts described, that as an underlying frame of mind it enabled all these other graces to function, and to produce the rich fruitage here set forth. The obedience, the self-sacrifice, the patience, the fortitude, the exercise of all these in the profound Christian sense would have been impossible, if the saints had not had through faith their eye firmly fixed on the unseen and promised world.

Whether the call was to believe or to follow, to do or to bear, the obedience to it sprang not from any earth-fed sources but from the infinite reservoir of strength stored up in the mountain-land above. If Moses endured it was not due to the power of resistance in his human frame, but because the weakness in him was compensated by the vision of him who is invisible. If Abraham, who had gladly received the promises, offered up his only-begotten son, it was not because in heroic resignation he steeled himself to obedience, but because through faith he saw God as greater and stronger than the most inexorable physical law of nature: 'For he accounted that God is able to raise up even from the dead.' And so in all the other instances. Through faith the powers of the higher world were placed at the disposal of those whom this world threatened to over-whelm, and so the miracle resulted that from weakness they were made strong.

No mistake could be greater than to naturalize the contents of this chapter, and to conceive of the thing portrayed as some instinct of idealism, some sort of sixth sense for what lies above the common plane of life, as people speak of men of vision, who see farther than the mass. The entire description rests on the basis of supernaturalism; these are annals of grace, *magnalia Christi*. Even the most illustrious names in the history of worldly achievement are not, as such, entitled to a place among them. This is the goodly company of patriarchs, prophets and saints, who endured the reproach of Christ, of whom the world was not worthy, who form the line of succession through which the promises passed, who now compose the cloud of witnesses that encompass our mortal strife, men of whom God is not ashamed to be called their God, with whom the Saviour himself is associated as the leader and finisher of the same faith.

In our text, however, we meet faith in its more sim-ple and direct mode of operation. It appears as dealing with the unseen and future. From the life of the patri-archs the more militant, strenuous features are absent. In their lives it is allowed as in a region of seclusion and quietness to unfold before our eyes its simple beauty. Faith is here but another name for other-worldliness or heavenly-mindedness. Herein lies the reason why the writer dwells with such evident delight upon this particular part of the Old Testament narrative. The other figures he merely sketches, and with a rapid skilful stroke of the brush puts in the highlights of their lives where the glory of faith illumined them. But the figure of Abraham he paints with the lingering, caressing hand of love, so that something of the serenity and peaceful- ness of the original patriarchal story is reproduced in the picture: 'By faith he became a sojourner in the land of promise, as in a land not his own, dwelling in tents with Isaac and Jacob, the heirs with him of the same promise; for he looked for the city which has the foundations, whose builder and maker is God.' The charm spread over this part of the subject to the author's vision also appears in this, that, after having already dismissed it and passed on to the portrayal of Abraham's faith in another form, as connected with the seed of the promise, he involuntarily returns to cast one more loving glance at it: 'They died in faith, not having received the promises, but seen them and greeted them from afar, and having confessed that they were strangers and pilgrims on the earth. For they that say such things make it manifest that they are seeking after a country of their own. And if indeed they had been mindful of the country from which they went out, they would have had opportunity to return. But now they desire a better country, that is a heavenly; wherefore God is not ashamed to be called their God: for he hath prepared them a city.'

The other-worldliness of the patriarchs showed itself in this, that they confessed to be strangers and pilgrims on the earth. It found its visible expression in their dwelling in tents. Not strangers and pilgrims outside of

Canaan, but strangers and pilgrims in the earth. The
writer places all the emphasis on this, that they pursued
their tent-life in the very land of promise, which was
their own, as in a land not their own. Only in this way
is a clear connection between the staying in tents and
the looking forward to heaven obtained. For otherwise
the tents might have signified merely that they considered themselves not at home when away from the holy
land. If even in Canaan they carried within themselves
the consciousness of pilgrimage then it becomes strikingly evident that it was a question of fundamental,
comprehensive choice between earth and heaven. The
adherence to the tent-life in the sight and amidst the
scenes of the promised land fixes the aspiration of the
patriarchs as aiming at the highest conceivable heavenly
goal. It has in it somewhat of the scorn of the relative
and of compromise. He who knows that for him a
palace is in building does not dally with desires for
improvement on a lower scale. Contentment with the
lowest becomes in such a case profession of the highest,
a badge of spiritual aristocracy with its proud insistence
upon the ideal. Only the predestined inhabitants of the
eternal city know how to conduct themselves in a
simple tent as kings and princes of God.

As to its negative side, the feeling of strangeness on
earth, even in Canaan, the writer could base his representation on the statement of Abraham to the sons of
Heth: 'I am a stranger and a sojourner with you,' and on
the words of the aged Jacob to Pharaoh: 'The days of
the years of my pilgrimage are an hundred and thirty
years: few and evil have the days of the years of my life
been, and have not attained unto the days of the years of
the life of my fathers in the days of their pilgrimage.' As

to the positive side, the desire for a heavenly state, there is no such explicit testimony in the narrative of Genesis. None the less the author was fully justified in affirming this also. It is contained by implication in the other. The refusal to build an abiding habitation in a certain place must be due to the recognition that one's true, permanent abode is elsewhere. The not-feeling-at-home in one country has for its inevitable counterpart homesickness for another. The writer plainly ascribes this to the patriarchs, and in doing so also ascribes to them a degree of acquaintance with the idea of a heavenly life. His meaning is not that, unknown to themselves, they symbolized through their mode of living the principle of destination for heaven. On the contrary, we are expressly told that they confessed, that they made it manifest, that they looked for, that they desired. There existed with them an intelligent and outspoken apprehension of the celestial world.

Let us not say that such an interpretation of their minds is unhistorical, because they could not in that age have possessed a clear knowledge of the world to come. Rather, in reading this chapter on faith let us have faith, a large, generous faith in the uniqueness and spiritual distinction of the patriarchs as confessors, perhaps in advance of their time, of the heaven-centred life of the people of God. In other respects also Scripture represents the patriarchal period as lifted above the average level of the surrounding ages, even within the sphere of special revelation. Paul tells us that in the matter of grace and freedom from the law Abraham lived on a plane and in an atmosphere much higher than that of subsequent generations. Anachronisms these things are, if you will, but anachronisms of God, who does not let himself be bound by time, but, seeing the end from the beginning, reserves the right to divide the flood of history, and to place on conspicuous islands at successive points great luminaries of his truth and grace shining far out into the future. The patriarchs had their vision of the heavenly country, a vision in the light of which the excellence or desirableness of every earthly home and country paled. Acquaintance with a fairer Canaan had stolen from their hearts the love of the land that lay spread around like a garden of paradise. Of course, it does not necessarily follow from this that the author credits the patriarchs with a detailed, concrete knowledge of the heavenly world. In point of heavenly-mindedness he holds them up as models to be imitated. In point of information about the content of the celestial life he places the readers far above the reach of the Old Testament at its highest. To the saints of the New Covenant life and immortality and all the powers of the world to come have been opened up by Christ. The Christian state is as truly part and foretaste of the things above as a portal forms part of the house. If not wholly within, we certainly are come to Mount Zion, the city of the living God. And in this we are more than Abraham.

No such gospel broke in upon the solitude of these ancient shepherds, not even upon Jacob, when he saw the ladder reaching up into heaven with the angels of God ascending and descending upon it. But do you not see that precisely on account of this difference in knowledge the faculty of faith had addressed to it a stronger challenge than it has in us, who pilgrim with heaven's door wide open in our sight? For this reason it is so profitable to return again and again to this part of the Old Testament Scriptures, and learn what great faith could do with less privilege, how precisely because it had such limited resource of knowledge, it made a sublimer flight, soaring with supreme dominion up to the highest heights of God.

Let us try briefly to analyse what this other-worldliness of the patriarchs involved, and in what respects it will be well for us to cultivate it. The first feature to be noted is that it is not essentially negative but positive in character. The core lies not in what it relinquishes but in what it seeks. Escape from the world here below and avoidance of the evil in the world do not furnish its primary motive. That is true only of the abnormal, morbid type of other-worldliness, that connected with pessimism and monastic seclusion. From an unwarranted identification with these the true grace portrayed by Scripture has been exposed to much ill-considered criticism and fallen into disrepute. If heavenly-mindedness were an upward flight in the ignominious sense of the word, it would be the very opposite to the heroism of genuine faith, a seeking for a harbour of refuge, instead of a steering for the haven of home.

Do not misunderstand me. It is only right that in some measure the bitter experience of sin and evil should contribute to the Christian's desire for heaven. The attraction of heaven is in part the attraction of free-dom from sin. And not a little of the contempt poured upon it, while pretending to protest against cloistered withdrawal, springs in reality from a defective percep-tion of the seriousness of sin. Where the eye has not by divine grace been opened to the world's wickedness, it is easy to look with disdain on the Christian's world-shyness. But the Christian, who knows that the end of sin cannot come until the end of this world, looks at the question in a light of his own. He is fully warranted in considering ridicule of this kind part of the reproach of Christ and bearing it with joy.

Nor should we forget that an excess of interest in the present life, when shown in the name of religion, is apt in our day to be a symptom of doubt or unbelief in regard to the life to come. Still the principle remains in force, that the desirability of heaven should never possess exclusively or mainly negative significance. It is not something first brought into the religious mind through sin. The lineage and birthright of other-worldliness are of the oldest and noblest. By God himself this traveller's unrest was implanted in the soul. Ever since the goal set by the covenant of works came within his ken, man carries with him in all his converse with this world the sense of belonging to another. This is but to say that supernaturalism forms from the outset the basis of true religion in man.

Man belongs to two spheres. And Scripture not only teaches that these two spheres are distinct, it also teaches what estimate of relative importance ought to be placed upon them. Heaven is the primordial, earth the secondary creation. In heaven are the supreme realities; what surrounds us here below is a copy and shadow of the celestial things. Because the relation between the two spheres is positive, and not negative, not mutually repulsive, heavenly-mindedness can never give rise to neglect of the duties pertaining to the present life. It is the ordinance and will of God, that not apart from, but on the basis of, and in contact with, the earthly sphere man shall work out his heavenly destiny.

Still the lower may never supplant the higher in our affections. In the heart of man time calls for eternity, earth for heaven. He must, if normal, seek the things above, as the flower's face is attracted by the sun, and the water-courses are drawn to the ocean. Heavenly-mindedness, so far from blunting or killing the natural desires, produces in the believer a finer organization, with more delicate sensibilities, larger capacities, a stronger pulse of life. It does not spell impoverishment, but enrichment of nature. The spirit of the entire epistle shows this. The use of the words 'city' and 'country' is evidence of it. These are terms that stand for the accumulation, the efflorescence, the intensive enjoyment of values. Nor should we overlook the social note in the representation. A perfect communion in a perfect society is promised. In the city of the living God believers are joined to the general assembly and church of the first-born, and mingle with the spirits of just men made perfect. And all this faith recognizes. It does not first need the storms and stress that invade to quicken its desire for such things. Being the sum and substance of all the positive gifts of God to us in their highest form, heaven is of itself able to evoke in our hearts positive love, such absorbing love as can render us at times forgetful of the earthly strife. In such moments the transcendent beauty of the other shore and the irresistible current of our deepest life lift us above every regard of wind or wave. We know that through weather fair or foul our ship is bound straight for its eternal port.

Next to the positiveness of its object the high degree of actuality in the working of this grace should be considered. Through the faith of heavenly-mindedness the things above reveal themselves to the believer, are present with him, and communicate themselves to him. Though as yet a pilgrim, the Christian is never wholly separated from the land of promise. His tents are pitched in close view of the city of God. Heaven is present to the believer's experience in no less real a sense than Canaan with its fair hills and valleys lay close to the vision of Abraham. He walks in the light of the heavenly world and is made acquainted with the kindred spirits inhabiting it. And since the word 'actual' in its literal sense means 'that which works', the life above possesses for the believer the highest kind of actuality. He is given to taste the powers of the world to come, as Abraham breathed the air of Canaan, and was refreshed by the dews descending on its fields. The roots of the Christian's life are fed from those rich and perennial springs that lie deep in the recesses of converse with God, where prayers ascend and divine graces descend, so that after each season of tryst he issues, a new man, from the secrecy of his tent.

Because it had this effect for the patriarchs, faith had so intimately joined to it the exercise of hope. It is no less the assurance of things hoped for than the proving of things not seen. It annihilates the distance of time as much as of space. If faith deals with heaven as it exists, hope seizes upon it as it will be at the end. Hope attaches itself to promises; it sees and greets from afar. As the epistle describes it, it does not contemplate purely provisional and earthly developments, does not come to rest in the happenings of intermediate ages, but relates to the end. In one unbroken flight it soars to the goal of God's work in history, which is none other than the finished heaven. For heaven itself is subject to a process of preparation, so that its full content became accessible only to the patriarchs through a projection of their faith in time. The heaven for which they hoped was the heaven of redemption, enriched through the ages, become peopled with the successive generations of the saints of God, filled with the glory of Christ, the recreated paradise, towards which all the streams of grace springing up in time send their waters. The believer requires this new heaven, not simply the cosmical place that resulted from the first creation. Hence his heavenly-mindedness can never destroy interest in the unfolding of the ways of God throughout the history of the present world. Neither grows he impatient when the promise seems to tarry. For his hope also is in him a vitalizing power. It lives by the things that are not as though they were already, and makes the future supply strength for the present. Amidst all the vicissitudes of time the Christian knows that the foundations of the city of God are being quietly laid, that its walls are rising steadily, and that it will at last stand finished in all its golden glory, the crowning product of the work of God for his own.

But the faith of heavenly-mindedness in yet another, even profounder, sense surmounts time. In contrast with what is transitory it lays hold of the unchanging and eternal. The text expresses this by describing the city looked for as the city which has the foundations. The difference between the well-founded enduring edifice and the frail, collapsible tent has induced this turn of the figure. Already in the prophet Isaiah Jehovah declares: 'Behold, I lay in Zion for a foundation a stone, a precious cornerstone of sure foundation: he that believeth shall not make haste.' In this word the two ideas of sure foundation and faith are brought into close connection. Because the foundation is sure the believer can lay aside all disquietude and impatience in regard to the working out of the divine purpose. He need not make haste. It is of the essence of faith to crave assurance; hence it cannot come to rest until it have cast its anchor into the eternal. And heaven above all else partakes of the character of eternity. It is the realm of the unchangeable. In this lower world time with its law of attrition is king. Nothing can escape his inexorable rule. What is must cease to be, what appears must vanish, what is built must be broken down, even though the human heart should cherish it more than its own life. And this applies not merely to objects of natural affection; it involves also much that is of transitory purpose in the service and church of God. Even our religion in its earthly exercise is not exempt from the tragical aspect borne by all existence in time. The summons comes again and again: 'Get thee out of thy country, and from thy kindred, and from thy father's house,' and after a brief spell of comfort and delight we anew find ourselves in tents roaming through an inhospitable world. There is no help for these things. Like Abraham we must resolutely confess that we are strangers and pilgrims in a land of time, and that the best this land can offer us is but a caravanserai to tarry in for a day and a night.

Abraham would have undoubtedly rejoiced in the vision of the historical Jerusalem around which gather so many glories of God's redemptive work. But, suppose it had risen up before him in all its beauty, would that have been the soul-satisfying vision his faith desired? No, there is neither quietness nor repose for the believer's heart except on the bosom of eternity.

There and there alone is shelter from the relentless pursuit of change.

The inspired writer tells us that the two most momentous events in sacred history, the giving of the law on Sinai and the end of the world, signify the removal of things that are shaken, in order that such things as are not shakeable may remain. And the second shaking is so radical and comprehensive that it involves not only the earth but likewise the heavens: it will sweep the transitory out of the life of the people of God even in the higher regions, and will leave them, when the smoke and dust of the upheaval are blown away, in a clear atmosphere of eternal life. But in this sense also faith is not purely prospective: it enables to anticipate; it draws down the imperishable substance of eternity into its vessel of time and feeds on it. The believer knows that even now there is in him that which has been freed from the law of change, a treasure that moth and rust cannot corrupt, true riches enshrined in his heart as in a treasury of God. Have we ever been impressed in reading the narrative of Genesis by the peacefulness and serenity enveloping the figures of the patriarchs? There is something else here besides the idyllic charm of rural surroundings. What enviable freedom from the unrest, the impatience, the feverish excitement of the children of this world! Our modern Christian life so often lacks the poise and stability of the eternal. Religion has come so overmuch to occupy itself with the things of time that it catches the spirit of time. Its purposes turn fickle and unsteady; its methods become superficial and ephemeral; it alters its course so constantly; it borrows so readily from sources beneath itself, that it undermines its own prestige in matters pertaining to the eternal world. Where lies the remedy? It would be useless to seek it in withdrawal from the struggles of this present world. The true corrective lies in this, that we must learn again to carry a heaven-fed and heaven-centred spirit into our walk and work below. The grand teaching of the epistle that through Christ and the New Covenant the heavenly projects into the earthly, as the headlands of a continent project into the ocean, should be made fruitful for the whole tone and temper of our Christian service. Every task should be at the same time a means of grace from and an incentive to work for heaven. There has been One greater than Abraham, who lived his life in absolute harmony with this principle, in whom the fullest absorption in his earthly calling could not for a moment disturb the consciousness of being a child of heaven. Though, like the patriarchs, he had no permanent home, not even a tent, this was not in his case the result of a break with an earthly-minded past. It was natural to him. In his mind were perfectly united the two hemispheres of supernaturalism, that of the source of power behind, and that of the eternal goal of life beyond every work.

A religion that has ceased to set its face towards the celestial city is bound sooner or later to discard also all supernatural resources in its endeavour to transform this present world. The days are perhaps not far distant when we shall find ourselves confronted with a quasi-form of Christianity professing openly to place its dependence on and to work for the present life alone, a religion, to use the language of Hebrews, become profane and a fornicator like Esau, selling for a mess of earthly pottage its heavenly birthright.

There are two more aspects of the patriarchal faith of

heavenly-mindedness to be briefly considered. The first is its spirituality. Heavenly-mindedness is spiritual-mindedness. This pervades like an atmosphere the entire epistle. We have already seen that even in the promised land the patriarchs remained tent-dwellers. God had a wise purpose in thus postponing for them personally the fulfilment of the temporal promise. Although Canaan was a goodly land, it was yet, after all, material and not of that higher substance we call spiritual. While capable of carrying up the mind to supernal regions, it also exposed to the danger of becoming satisfied with the blessing in its provisional form.

That this danger was not imaginary the later history of Israel testifies. In order to guard against such a result in the case of the patriarchs God withheld from them the land and its riches and made of this denial a powerful spiritualizing discipline. By it they were led to reflect that, since the promise was theirs beyond all doubt, and yet they were not allowed to inherit it in its material form, that therefore it must in the last analysis relate to something far higher and different, something of which the visible and sensual is a mere image. Thus the conception of another sphere of being was introduced into their minds: henceforth they sought the better country. Not as if the things of sense were worthless in themselves, but because they knew of something transcendent that claimed their supreme affection. Their tastes and enjoyments had been raised to another plane. The refinement of grace had been imparted to them. For bodily hands there had been, as it were, substituted spiritual antennae, sensitive to intangible things. They had come to a mountain that could not be touched and yet could be felt.

In all the treasures and promises of religion the one valuable thing is this spiritual core. In the Word that God speaks we can taste all his goodness and grace. Hope itself is spiritualized, remaining no longer the hope of imagination but grasping in God the ideal root from which the whole future must spring and blossom in due time. The heavenly world does not appear desirable as simply a second improved edition of this life; that would be nothing else than earthly-mindedness projected into the future. The very opposite takes place: heaven spiritualizes in advance our present walk with God. Each time faith soars and alights behind the veil it brings back on its wings some of the subtle fragrance that there prevails.

This also is an important principle in need of stress at the present day. If there is danger of Christianity being temporalized, there is no less danger of its being materialized. How easily do we fall into the habit of handling the things of our holy faith after an external, quantitative, statistical fashion, so that they turn flesh under our touch and emit a savour of earth? If at any time or in any form this fault should threaten to befall us, let us revisit the tents of the patriarchs and rehearse the lesson that in religion the body without the soul is worthless and without power.

The other point to be observed is this: heaven is the normal goal of our redemption. We all know that religion is older than redemption. At the same time the experience of redemption is the summit of religion. The two have become so interwoven that the Christian cannot conceive of a future state from which the redemptive mould and colour would be absent. The deepest and dearest in us is so much the product of salvation, that the vision of God as such and the vision of God our Saviour melt into one. We could not separate them if we would. The simple reason is that precisely in redeeming us God has revealed to us the inmost essence of his deity. No one but a redeemed creature can truly know what it is for God to be God, and what it means to worship and possess him as God.

This is the fine gold of the Christian's experience, sweeter to him than honey and the honeycomb. The river that makes glad the city of God is the river of grace. The believer's mind and heart will only in heaven compass the full riches, the length and breadth and depth and height of the love of God. No one can drink so deeply of it here, but he will more deeply drink hereafter. Blessed be God, no stream of Lethe flows this side of his city to wash away from our minds the remembrance of redeeming grace! The life above will be a ceaseless coming to Jesus, the Mediator of a better covenant, and to the blood of sprinkling that speaketh better than Abel. The Lamb slain for our sins will be all the glory of Emmanuel's land.

Finally the highest thing that can be spoken about this city is that it is the city of our God, that he is in the midst of it. Traced to its ultimate root heavenly-mindedness is the thirst of the soul after God, the living God. The patriarchs looked not for some city in general, but for a city whose builder and maker was God. It is characteristic of faith that it not merely desires the perfect but desires the perfect as a work and gift of God. A heaven that was not illumined by the light of God, and not a place for closest embrace of him, would be less than heaven. God as builder and maker thereof has put the better part of himself into his work. Therefore those who enter the city are in God.

The thought is none other than that of the seer in the Apocalypse: 'I saw no temple therein: for the Lord God, the Almighty and the Lamb are the temple thereof. And that city has no need of the sun, neither of the moon to shine upon it, for the glory of God lightens it, and the throne of God and the Lamb are therein: and his servants shall do him service, and they shall see his face, and his name shall be on their foreheads.' And the faith is the faith of the psalmist, who spoke: 'Whom have I in heaven but thee? and there is none upon earth that I desire beside thee.' Here it is impossible for us to tell how truly and to what extent our relation to God is a relation of pure, disinterested love in which we seek him for his own sake. There, when all want and sin-frailty shall have slipped away from us, we shall be able to tell. It was because God discerned in the souls of the patriarchs, underneath all else, this personal love, this homesickness for himself, that he caused to be recorded about them the greatest thing that can be spoken of any man: that God is not ashamed to be called their God, and that he has prepared for them the city of their desire.

VII: Running the Race[1]

Hebrews 12:1-3: 'Wherefore seeing we also are compassed about with so great a cloud of witnesses, let us lay aside every weight, and the sin which doth so easily beset us, and let us run with patience the race that is set before us, Looking unto Jesus the author and finisher of our faith; who for the joy that was set before him endured the cross, despising the shame, and is set down at the right hand of the throne of God. For consider him that endured such contradiction of sinners against himself, lest ye be wearied and faint in your minds.'

These verses stand at the beginning of one of the five hortatory sections which are so character-istic of the Epistle to the Hebrews. There is perhaps no other book in the New Testament in which the two elements of theological exposition and practical application are so clearly distinguishable and yet so organically united as in this epistle. The writer never makes exhortation a substitute for doctrine. His practi-cal counsels are always based on a carefully managed presentation of the truth addressed to the intellect of his readers. It must have been in many respects an extremely critical situation in which he found them and from which he endeavoured to rescue them; but nevertheless he attacks it in his thoroughly objective, calm, reasonable and confident manner. He relies upon

[1] Preached in the Chapel of Princeton Theological Seminary, Princeton, New Jersey on 6 April 1902.

the inherent power of the truth to commend itself and work its way as applied by the Spirit of God. He appreciates the mighty weapon which a full command of the truth puts into the hand of the preacher. He knows that the Word of God is living and active and sharper than any two-edged sword, piercing till it divides the soul and the spirit both in their joints and in their marrow (i.e. till it reaches the very skeleton and what is within the skeleton of the innermost consciousness of man, and becomes the judge of the thoughts and intents of his heart). And you will observe that where he deplores the general backwardness of the Hebrew Christians, he has just as much in mind their failure to make progress in the doctrinal apprehension of Christianity as the lack of development in the more practical province of their religious life. His complaint is distinctively the teacher's complaint as you can best see from the fifth chapter. There he charges his readers with having become dull of hearing, declares them to be in need again of someone to teach them the rudiments of the first principles of the oracles of God, and characterizes them as babes without experience in the word of righteousness (*Heb.* 5:12, 13).

It is quite in keeping with all this that in the passage before us he also gives such a turn to his exhortation as to gather up in it the gist of the whole preceding chapter, in which the nature and possibility of a life of faith had been exemplified from the sacred history of the old covenant. The personal appeal he makes to his readers is contained in the words: 'Let us run with patience the race set before us.' The figure is a familiar one, especially in the epistles of Paul, and would easily suggest itself to a writer who came at all in contact with the pagan athletic life of the times. The figure was also strikingly apposite to the religious situation of that time. In these early days, Christianity bore a most strenuous character; internal and external causes combined to impose upon its adherents the straining of every nerve in order to maintain their faith. Still, there were probably special reasons why the representation of Christianity as a race to be run was extremely appropriate under the conditions of the readers to which the writer of the epistle addressed himself. The readers seem to have been lacking in the energy of faith. Instead of having their faces resolutely set forward towards the future, they were given to looking backward at the antiquated forms of a ceremonial religious system. And in the mistaken love of this system they overlooked the far greater privileges and treasures to which Christianity had given them access. Repristination [to restore to an original state or condition] may sometimes be necessary, but even at its best, even when it is repristination of that which is good and of permanent value, it is little conducive towards a healthy spiritual growth and development, least of all so when it aims at the revival of something that has served its purpose and is close to vanishing.

As well as lacking the energy of faith, these Hebrew Christians also seem to have been abnormally restive under the trials, afflictions and persecutions that had befallen them. In the midst of these difficulties, they had failed to develop that Christian fortitude and heroism which on the whole were so characteristic of the early church in the sub-apostolic period. For these two reasons, it was peculiarly appropriate that the author clothe his exhortation to them in the athletic figure of the running track, which contains the central thought of the passage. The way in which he introduces the athletic metaphor, and the motives which he advances for its enforcement, enable us to trace to some extent the situation which it was intended to meet. Let us for a few moments look at the figure and what its implications are.

1.   The writer exhorts his readers to the exercise of an energetic Christian faith by pointing them to the example of the Old Testament saints which he had depicted in the preceding chapter: 'Having therefore so great a cloud of witnesses lying around us, let us also lay aside every weight, and the sin which doth so easily beset us, and let us run with patience the race set before us.' We shall get somewhat closer to the author's meaning by observing the intimate connection in which these words stand with the two last verses of the eleventh chapter. The thought that the Old Testament saints are witnesses may have been suggested by what is said about them in the thirty-ninth verse: 'And all these, having had witness borne to them.' But the idea expressed is a different one since there they are the objects of the witness borne by God or men to the nobility of their character, while here they appear as witnesses themselves. The only doubtful point is whether they are called witnesses in the same sense that they speak to us through the historic testimony of their heroic faith recorded in Scripture; or whether we must bring the idea into closer connection with the figure of the race so as to conceive of them as actually witnessing, surveying us as spectators of the struggle in which we are engaged. Something may be said in favour of either view: the preceding chapter as a whole perhaps favours

the former interpretation, that they bear witness to us as
figures in history. But over against this, we must place
not merely the admirable manner in which the other
interpretation fits into the figure, but also the fact that
they are called 'a cloud of witnesses', 'encompassing' us
(an expression which naturally suggests the great crowd
of spectators seated or standing around the arena). It
does not necessarily follow, if we adopt this latter view,
that the writer means to represent the saints in heaven as
'conversant with our life here and fascinated by the
interest of it'. Evidently, the emphasis does not rest on
what we are for the departed saints, but on what they
ought to be for us. The writer intimates as much as
this by saying that we have this cloud of witnesses. The
whole conception is figurative and ideal, and the only
question that can be raised is whether the author wants
us to imagine the Old Testament heroes of faith as
speaking to us from out of their own historic situation
or as gathered figuratively and ideally around us. Looked
at closely, it will be seen that the latter interpretation to
a certain extent includes the other as the more comprehensive of the two. For if the Old Testament saints
appear as encompassing us, the effect which their ideal
presence should produce upon us must be largely due to
the fact that they themselves were at one time runners
in the same race. They influence us not merely through
the thought that they once passed through the experience we now have—all the memories of what they
endured and accomplished crowd in upon us when we
imagine them as watching us.

There is certainly an important lesson embodied in
this noble figure for us as well as for the first readers of
the epistle. I do not know whether we always make

enough of this retrospective communion of the saints, of this spiritual continuity with the church of the past. In natural relations, we are not slow to take pride in our descent from those who have left an honourable record behind them in the annals of history, and we feel the obligations which such a connection imposes upon us. Why should it be different in the religious sphere? In the exercise of faith as well as in that of the natural virtues, we ought to feel the force of the principle *noblesse oblige.* Sometimes we are altogether too much concerned with what the present world will say about us—whether it will regard us as progressive, enlightened and liberal; while too seldom considering what would be the historic judgement passed upon us by the church of the former ages if its great figures could gather around us and review the part we take in the making of the history of the present—whether they would be shamed or gladdened by our doings. So let us, sometimes at least, endeavour to view our condition and performance in this light, and ask ourselves whether we can without shame and self-reproach allow the soundness of our faith, the purity of our life and the consecration of our service to fall below the attainments of any earlier generation in the church of God. And on the other hand, though the world may look down upon us as reactionaries and antiquated people, if we can conscientiously say that we have remained faithful to the principles which God himself stamped with his historic approval in the past, let us derive comfort from the thought that we do not walk alone, but are compassed about on every side by an innumerable host of friends who will honour us as God has honoured them.

2.   The next important point of comparison when the author represents the Christian life as a race to be run lies in this: its whole character ought to be prospective; everything in it ought to be determined by the thought of the future. It is a race to which the inheritance of the final Kingdom of God forms the goal. Just as one who is on the track running for a prize makes the attainment of this end his supreme—his only—concern, so the true believer only obeys the fundamental law of his Christian calling when he concentrates his mind and energy upon the future. This is the reason why the author in the fortieth verse of the eleventh chapter emphasizes that the fathers did not receive the promise. For although this, on the one hand, implies that we have an advantage over them because we already have at least a partial possession of the promise in this life; yet, on the other hand, it is obviously the writer's intention to remind the readers of the resemblance which their life ought to bear in this respect to that of the Old Testament saints. They were not to be made perfect without us. We had first to join them in their looking forward to, in their reaching out after, the world to come before this world could actually appear. We and they form one great assembly of believers, animated by the same thought, inspired by the same vision of the ideal life, the ideal kingdom. From this point of view the survey of Old Testament history which the author made was peculiarly adapted to put the Hebrew Christians in the frame of mind required in those who are to run a spiritual race. The Old Testament was pre-eminently a prospective period, a period of anticipation, a period in which the believer was reminded at every step of something higher and better yet to appear. Enoch, Moses,

Abraham and all the prophets bore witness by their whole manner of life that they appreciated this, that the present was to them something provisional.

Now just as it would have been a grave defect in them if they had lost sight of this fact and had been reconciled to these Old Testament conditions as final and sufficient, it will have to be regarded as a serious spiritual fault in the New Testament believer if he ceases to give the future world that dominating influence over his entire life and thought which, as the goal of his Christian calling, it can properly claim. Whatever the difference in other respects, we are one with the whole church of God of every age, from the beginning of the history of redemption until now, in this fundamental trait—that we seek the absolute, the final, the perfect. Hence the race is represented as being in reality a race of faith in which the energetic exercise of faith corresponds to the running, and faith not so much in its general sense but specifically in its eschatological bearings—that faith which puts one in vital contact with and impels one irresistibly forward towards the unseen realities of the heavenly world. The same thought is expressed in a negative form by what the author adds concerning the laying aside of every weight and the sin which does so easily beset the Christian. Of course, this metaphor is again borrowed from the racetrack. As a runner would lay aside every encumbrance of dress as well as every other burden that might endanger his success in the race, so the believer who has his face set towards the future, heavenly life must divest himself of every concern with the present world which would retard his steady progress towards the higher kingdom.

Perhaps the author had specifically in mind the

entanglement of the Hebrew Christians in the ceremonial forms of the Old Testament religion and regarded these as a weight which dragged them down, making it impossible for them to rise to a truly spiritual apprehension and appreciation of the heavenly realities in which Christ ministers at the right hand of God. But whether this is so or not, at any rate the words allow a more general application in which they have significance for every believer. We may say that the things here called 'weights' embrace everything that might in any sense turn away the heart from the pursuit of heaven, even though these things might in the abstract be unobjectionable or even comely. It should be remarked, however, that properly speaking the innocent associations or engagements with our earthly life do not constitute the weight, for that would be equivalent to saying that we must adopt the principle of monasticism. The believer should not be indifferent to the natural environment in which the providence of God has placed him; but he should not have his portion in the present life in the same sense as the children of the world have it. He must gravitate towards the future life and must make every contact into which he comes with earthly concerns subordinated and subservient to this. Instead of weights these affairs must become wings speeding him onward and upward in his flight towards God. If he fails to do this, he becomes unfaithful to the claim which the spiritual world has upon him, a fornicator, as the author drastically expresses it, resembling Esau who for one mess of pottage sold his own birthright.

But while such weights must be laid aside because they hinder the believer in running well and involve a temptation to falling, the Christian's attitude towards sin should be even more resolute. Observe how the author singles this out from the general category of weights, distinguishing it as a separate category from the latter: 'Let us lay aside every weight and the sin which doth so easily beset us.' Sin requires special, radical treatment; it must, as he says immediately afterwards, be resisted unto blood. Here again the author may have had in mind that specific sin which the Hebrew Christians were in imminent danger of committing, if some of them had not committed it already: the sin of open unbelief in the gospel and the God of the gospels and a consequent relapse into Judaism or into something worse than Judaism—a state of rebellion against God as such. In several passages of the epistle the word 'sin' occurs with this specific connotation. Nevertheless, here also the words allow a more general exegesis. What the author says of sin is true generically of every form of sin: namely, that it must be laid aside if the believer is to run his race with alacrity and success. Sin interposes a barrier between us and the goal of our Christian striving. It does not merely prevent further progress, but it throws him who commits it back to a position less advanced than he had reached before. It obscures the vision of the heavenly state; it weakens the desire for its enjoyment; it breaks the energy of the will in pursuing it. This is especially clear if we place ourselves upon the standpoint from which the author is accustomed to view sin, as an impediment in our approach to God. God is the centre of attraction in the kingdom of glory; so that to lose touch with God inevitably means to stop in the midst of the race towards heaven.

Moreover, sin finds such ample opportunities for

barring our way of access to God and the higher world. For this reason the author characterizes it as the sin 'that doth so easily beset us', a statement not intended to refer to any particular form of sin (as we might be led to think from the analogy of our phrase 'a besetting sin') but applying to sin generically. It is for sin an easy thing to approach us; we always carry it with us; it runs, as it were, the race with us; it is at the same time the most dangerous and the most ubiquitous of our spiritual foes. So the characterization of sin as that which easily besets us is meant to suggest to the readers the most powerful motive for laying it aside, for breaking with it utterly, while they bend all their energies to the race of sancti-fication. This is an enemy with whom no compromise should be made. Every sin which we allow to stay with us may at any moment cause us to fall. What is demanded therefore is a positive and aggressive attitude towards sin. We must not merely resist it, but lay it aside—in dependence upon the grace of God, cut ourselves loose from it. Sanctification ought to be to every child of God not a desultory matter, but an intell-igent systematic pursuit.

3.   The next point upon which the passage throws emphasis is that the Christian race must be run with patience. Patience in this connection means more than perseverance or persistence; it describes the endurance of what is hard and painful. In the figure, the striving after the prize exposes the runner to hardship which, in order to succeed, must be met with such a spirit of fortitude that not only does it fail to impede him, but positively assists him in reaching the goal. In the same way, in the Christian pursuit of the kingdom of God,

suffering and trials are the inevitable concomitants; and far from hindering him in his progress, they must become the means of helping him onward through the development in him of patience. We may say that the cultivation of this virtue forms an integral part of the running of the race itself. The examples given in the eleventh chapter show that heroic endurance appeared to the writer as one of the aspects of faith; therefore it must be in his view something which speeds the believer onward towards the goal. The conceptions of faith as a spiritual vision of the eternal world, of faith as the source of Christian fortitude, and of faith as the principle of Christian obedience are closely associated in the epistle.

The manner in which patience becomes subservient to the attainment of the prize can be variously conceived of. In the case of Jesus, of whom the author speaks in the immediately following statement, there was a direct meritorious connection. What he endured in the race of his earthly life became the legal ground on which God based the bestowal upon him of all the glory and blessedness of his exalted state. The joy he received was the natural reward for the cross endured and the shame despised. It is not possible, of course, and the author does not mean to transfer this connection in the same sense to the case of the believer. No amount of patience displayed by us in our earthly trials and afflictions can give us the least semblance of a claim upon the glory that awaits us at the end. And yet the author clearly claims that there is if not a meritorious, yet a reasonable, logical nexus between the one and the other. As a broad supposition this view underlies everything said in the preceding chapter about the heroic conduct in the suffering of the Old Testament saints. The principle on which these were crowned was a principle of free grace, but on that account it was not arbitrarily applied.

The reason can be seen if we remember that in the first place these trials are endured for the sake of and in obedience to God; and in the second place that the patience with which they are endured is the direct result of the believer's vital connection with the heavenly world in which the prize awaits him.

To express the first thought the author says that the race we run is set before us by God. Everything that meets us in it is an object of God's appointment. In obedience to him we ought to endure it without murmuring, especially if, as is frequently the case (as was probably the case with the Hebrews) it is the outcome of our identification with the cause of God. What is more natural than that God should in his grace reward with the heavenly life those who thus suffer for him, so that patience and glory appear in relation to one another as the race does to the crown? God cannot but honour this loyalty to himself evinced in suffering; of such patient runners he is not ashamed to be called their God and he has prepared for them a city.

In the second place, the Christian virtue of patience is something that can spring only from true, vital connection with the spiritual, heavenly world. It is something entirely different from stoical apathy or resignation. If the Christian patiently endures, it is because he sees the invisible; because there is a counter-power, a counter-principle at work in his life which more than offsets, by the joy it creates, the pain of tribulation. This is nothing else but the power of the spiritual, heavenly world itself to which through faith he has access. Although in one sense the inheritance of this world lies yet in the future, yet in another sense it has already begun to be realized in principle and become ours in actual possession. The two spheres of the earthly and the heavenly life do not lie one above the other without touching at any point; heaven with its gifts and powers and joys descends into our earthly experience like the headlands of a great and marvellous continent project-ing into the ocean.

Now it is the secret enjoyment of a real communion with the celestial sphere that is the source from which all Christian patience is fed, and without which it could not exist for a moment itself. In point of fact, patience—negative as the conception may superficially appear to us—is in its Christian sense a most positive thing; at least it is the manifestation of a most positive thing, the manifestation of the supernatural energy that works in faith itself. The heavenly world is to the believer what the earth was to the giant in ancient mythology; so long as he remains in contact with it, an unintermittent stream of new spiritual power flows into his frame. Is it strange that patience thus engendered should become, under God's appointment, the great prerequisite and in a certain sense the measure of reward at the end of the race? In the example of Christ which the author holds up before his readers, we can most clearly observe the manner of working of the principle in question because he was the Leader and Perfecter of faith, the ideal believer, and therefore the ideal pattern of patience. What else enabled him to endure the cross and despise the shame, but that in faith undimmed he had his eye constantly fixed upon the joy that was set before him and in uninterrupted intercourse with the world of heaven received daily strength sufficient for the running of his race? The thought is the same as that expressed in the beautiful catena of Paul in Romans 5 with which I will conclude my remarks: 'We rejoice in tribulation, knowing that tribulation worketh patience and patience probation, and probation hope, and hope maketh not ashamed, because (even in this present life already) the love of God (as the principle and earnest of eternal blessedness) is shed abroad in our hearts through the Holy Spirit given unto us' (*Rom.* 5:3-5).

VIII: The Christian's Hope[1]

1 Peter 1:3-5: 'Blessed be the God and Father of our Lord Jesus Christ, which according to his abundant mercy hath begotten us again unto a lively hope by the resurrection of Jesus Christ from the dead, to an inheritance incorruptible, and undefiled, and that fadeth not away, reserved in heaven for you, Who are kept by the power of God through faith unto salvation ready to be revealed in the last time.'

We are all undoubtedly familiar with the characterization of Peter as the apostle of hope. The well-known distinction runs: Paul the apostle of faith; John the apostle of love; Peter the apostle of hope. Of course, generalizing definitions like this are apt to be somewhat misleading. They would be wrong if they were to give us the impression that in Paul hope was not particularly prominent or for John faith was not especially important. A single glance at the writings of these two apostles would suffice to convince us of the contrary. These three characteristics are necessary ingredients of all Christian life. The only question can be—which of the three virtues is the most characteristic in each; or, to put the same thing in a different

[1]   Preached at Princeton Theological Seminary, Princeton, New Jersey on Conference Sunday, 13 November 1904.

way, in connection with which does the individuality of each apostle find clearest expression?

These great Christian virtues are not something arbitrary. They correspond closely to the fundamental dispositions and activities in the natural constitution of man. What a man is temperamentally by nature he will, as a rule, be temperamentally in the state of grace. Evidently Peter's was a temperament of hope. We can observe this in all that is recorded of him in the Gospels and Acts. And so in his regenerate, Christian life he retains this peculiarity. That side of redemption which has to do with hope most deeply impressed and most strongly appealed to him. Therefore he was used by the Spirit as the apostle to interpret for us the nature and influence of Christian hope.

The whole of Peter's first epistle bears witness to the prominence of this factor in the writer's mind. It is, of course, highly significant that it emerges here at the very beginning before anything else is mentioned and that it is immediately introduced in such a way as to make us feel that the essence of what Christians are consists in this—that they have a hope. They are born again for that. When they were made new creatures, it was that they might have a new hope. In the thirteenth verse of this chapter, he exhorts the readers as follows: 'Wherefore girding up the loins of your mind, be sober and set your hope perfectly on the grace that is to be brought unto you at the revelation of Jesus Christ.' In the third chapter, the fifteenth verse, he enjoins the readers to be always ready to give an answer to every man who asks them for the reason for the hope that is in them. He even makes hope the keynote not only of the religious life of his readers, but of religious life in general, especially of the religious life of the old covenant. Of the holy women of old, whom he holds up as examples to the Christian women of his own time, he has nothing greater to say than this, that 'they hoped in God' (*1 Pet.* 3:5).

And what is even more characteristic is the close connection which the apostle establishes between faith and hope. In the seventeenth verse of this chapter he exhorts the readers to pass the time of their sojourning in fear: fear in view of the holiness of God who as Father without respect of persons judgeth according to each man's work. But fear is not the whole of the Christian consciousness. There is another side to it and that is hope. The God who is judge is also the one who has given Christ as a Saviour. The Christians are believers, through Christ, in a God who raised him from the dead and gave him glory for the express purpose that their faith might also hope in God. For thus, it seems, we must render the close of the twenty-first verse rather than 'that your faith and hope might be in God'. In thus closely connecting faith and hope, our epistle bears a certain similarity to the Epistle to the Hebrews, with which it also possesses some other interesting points of contact. In Hebrews, you will remember, faith is in one place defined as 'the substance of things hoped for' (*Heb.* 11:1).

Let us consider this idea of the Christian hope and the significance the apostle ascribes to it for the practice of religion.

1.   We notice first that the hope of which the text speaks is not a general sort of hopefulness—the expectation of future blessedness in an indefinite sense. It is true

the Christian is a man of hope in that his outlook upon the future, whether near or far, is bright and cheerful. But what Peter means is something different from this, something far more specific. The hope he refers to is the hope of the future Kingdom of God, the final state of blessedness, the hope of heaven, as we would call it. This is stated in so many words; for the apostle, after having first said that we were begotten again unto a living hope, goes on to substitute for the conception of hope that of the inheritance reserved in heaven for us. And he adds still further that while this is reserved for us, we are also guarded for it as for a salvation ready to be revealed in the last time. The Christian is a man, according to Peter, who lives with his heavenly destiny ever in full view. His outlook is not bounded by the present life and the present world. He sees that which is and that which is to come in their true proportions and in their proper perspective. The centre of gravity of his consciousness lies not in the present but in the future. Hope, not possession, is that which gives tone and colour to his life. His is the frame of mind of the heir who knows himself entitled to large treasures upon which he will enter at a definite point of time; treasures which will enable him to become a man and develop his powers to their full capacity, and every one of whose thoughts therefore projects itself into the period when he shall have become of age and enjoy the fruition of his hope.

It is characteristic of youth to live in the future because youth knows instinctively that the true realities, the great possibilities of life, lie before it; that what it now is is merely provisional and preparatory; that growing is for being. Yet this is even more emphatically true of that youthful stage of Christian life which believers spend here on earth. For after all, that which young people expect in the future is indefinite and uncertain. They know that what they have is not yet the true life, but what the true life, when and if it comes, will bring they cannot tell. Here hope is negative. But the Christian's hope is positive. His youth is like that of the heir who knows precisely what awaits him. No, more than this, the Christian has the assurance which no heir in temporal things can ever have. He knows with absolute certainty that the inheritance will not merely be kept for him, but that he will be kept for it. Here, then, there is something that possesses all the requirements necessary to make hope a safe and normal life-principle. The Christian can hope perfectly. He is the only one who can hope perfectly for that which is to be brought to him. For him not to have his face set forward and upward would be an anomaly, sickliness, decadence. To have it set upward and forward is life and health and strength. The air of the world to come is the vital atmosphere which he delights to breathe and outside of which he feels depressed and languid.

Undoubtedly the early Christians, as we observe them in the New Testament and even later, had more of this youthful spirit of the faith than you and I and Christians of the present day can boast of. Christianity in a certain sense has grown old in us. We do not, as much as we ought to, have our hearts in eternity. What is the reason? It is easy to say that the Christians of the apostolic age expected the speedy return of Christ which would soon make an end of the present world, and that for this reason they had a great advantage over us. To some extent this may be true, although to a far larger extent I believe that a precisely opposite connection between these two facts might be affirmed. I venture to say that the apostolic church was so interested in the return of the Lord and the time of his coming because spiritually it was predisposed for making this a question of supreme concern. In other words, because it was a church full of hope, it pondered with eager interest the problem of how and when its hope was to be realized.

There is a very easy way of testing this. To us, to every believer individually, death and through death the eternal world is just as near as the second advent could have appeared to the Christians of the time of Peter and Paul. Does the absolute certainty that we are so near to it have the same influence upon us as their belief had upon them? And if not, does not the difference plainly arise from this—that the forces of eternal life were so strong in them as to keep their hope ever fresh and green, whereas in our case they are frequently so weak as to make our hope little more than a profession, a name? Where are the few nowadays (we may ask it including ourselves) who carry with them the consciousness of belonging to another world, of being heirs to an unbounded future? Where are the few who are conscious to the same extent (I shall not say as Peter and Paul were) as the plain, average believer in those times was, so that for the whole New Testament wherever we open it, there blows upon us, as it were, a breeze fresh from the ocean of heaven? And what a pity that we succeed so little in creating and reproducing this atmosphere around us! What a dignity it lends to the Christian life to have such hope even theoretically. If you have ever moved for a time in circles where the

Christian faith has ceased to exist, where the belief in immortality has practically vanished, where people live consciously and professedly for this world only (and do not even attempt to break down the bars that shut them in), then you will have felt how sadly life was degraded, how pitifully brought down to the animal stage, even though it had all the advantages of worldly refinement and culture, simply because this element of hope had been taken out of it.

Modern paganism in this respect is not substantially better. In fact, it is worse than ancient paganism, being more self-conscious and confirmed. And of ancient paganism Paul already summed up the whole sad story in the double statement that it was without hope and without God in the world (*Eph.* 2:12), an exile from what is the noblest birthright of humanity. Now if this is so, how imperative becomes the duty of every true believer in the present age to cultivate the grace of hope; to make himself remember and to make others feel, not so much by direct affirmation but rather by the tone of life, that the future belongs to us and that we belong to the future; that we are children of the world to come and that even now we allow that world to mould and rule and transform us in our thoughts, desires and feelings. If we could only learn again what Peter calls 'to hope perfectly' (1:13), what a witness of the reality of the Christian religion, what a powerfully attractive influence might proceed from this one manifestation of our spiritual life! People without such hope would feel the difference between themselves and us, and their regret at not having it might in many instances offer the first inducement to regain an interest in Christianity and inquire about it.

2.   The necessary consequence of this life of the Christian in hope is that he learns to consider the present earthly life as a journey, a pilgrimage, something necessary for the sake of the end but which does not have any independent value or attraction in itself. This is a thought which pervades and colours the entire epistle. Peter in the very opening words addresses the readers as sojourners of the dispersion—two terms which strikingly express that they are away from home, a colony with regard to heaven, scattered in a strange world as truly as the scattered Jews were a diaspora to the holy land and Jerusalem. He tells them to gird up the loins of their minds as befits a traveller journeying through. And again he says: 'Pass the time of your sojourning in fear' (1:17). Once more: 'Beloved, I beseech you as sojourners and pilgrims to abstain from fleshly lusts which war against the soul' (2:11). Without a certain detachment from this world, other-worldliness is not possible. Hope cannot flourish where the heart is in the present life. Two things, however, ought to be remembered here in order not to misunderstand this teaching.

   (i) This detachment from the world is not and ought not to be an external matter, but an internal disposition. The question is not whether someone should deny himself all earthly, temporal possessions. He might do that and yet in his heart be far from a pilgrim, a sojourner. And on the other hand, he might not do this and yet inwardly obey the exhortation of the apostle because he had succeeded in disengaging his heart.

   (ii) Such an inward attitude towards the world cannot be assumed and maintained artificially by merely compelling ourselves not to love the present life. If this is to be a natural, healthy state of mind it must be the result of a greater, a supreme interest in the life to come. The negative must be the effect of the positive. The love of heaven must drive out the inordinate love of what is earthly.

Hence the author entirely directs his exhortation to the positive side. He does not urge the readers to make themselves strangers on earth or even to consider themselves so, but simply takes this for granted as a fact which none of them can be unaware of. All he does is to point out how their situation in the world bears out the truth of their not being of it. He tells them repeatedly that their sufferings are due to this. For you will observe, the suffering of which the epistle speaks so much was not suffering in general, but suffering of a specific kind—that brought upon believers by the enmity of the world; whence also it was prefigured by the suffering of Christ. And the world makes the Christian suffer because it instinctively recognizes that the latter belongs to a different, to an opposite order of things than itself. The malice of the world springs from reservations that the believer should refuse to identify himself with the world. If we are true believers, though we ourselves should sometimes forget, the world will not fail to remind us of the difference between it and us. And, on the other hand, if we at any time feel perfectly at home in the world, if our consciousness of its necessary antagonism to us is entirely in abeyance, then there is abundant reason for us to examine ourselves. And the probability is that we have been backward in cultivating our hope upon God and the world to come.

3.   We must note that this hope of the believer is

something into which he has come by being born again. Its origin is ascribed to God: 'Blessed be the God and Father of our Lord Jesus Christ, who according to his great mercy begat us again unto a living hope by the resurrection of Jesus Christ from the dead.' God had mercy upon us because he saw us leading a life without hope. And therefore by a new birth he radically changed our world for us so as to make it a world of hope. The peculiar way in which the apostle expresses this fact ought to be carefully noted. He might have said, 'God gave us a new hope,' or, 'God brought us into a new hope.' But what he says is, 'God begat us again unto a living hope.' Undoubtedly this representation is chosen in order to emphasize the comprehensiveness and persuasiveness of the hope which the Christian obtains. It means a change as great as the crisis of birth, a transition from not being to living, when the hope of the gospel breaks upon our vision. The change is not partial. It does not affect our life in merely one or the other of its aspects. It revolutionizes our whole life at every point. What this means is a total regeneration of our consciousness, a regeneration of our way of thinking, a reversal of our outlook upon things in their entirety.

The term 'to be begotten again' or 'to be born again' does not always have the same meaning in Scripture. Sometimes it stands for that fundamental act whereby God implants a new spiritual life in us deep beneath our consciousness and beneath all our experience in the centre of our nature. In that case regeneration is confined, as it were, to a single point and from this point the implanted life expands and unfolds itself. But there is also in the New Testament a wider conception of regeneration, according to which it describes the change in us as it presents itself to our own conscious experience and therefore the change not of a single point within us but the change as reflected in the entire compass of our consciousness. It is the coming in of the new life as a complex, rich world of new relations, new realities and new reactions. In this sense Paul says that when anybody is in Christ, he is a new creation (*2 Cor.* 5:17); not merely a new creature, but a new creation— behold the old things have passed away, all around him has become new. When a man becomes conscious of his being in Christ, there takes place such a transformation of his spiritual environment for him that it may be fitly compared to the great world-change that shall take place before our eyes when the new heavens and the new earth appear at the end of time. These two regenerations resemble each other in their pervasive, comprehensive character.

Now in this sense also, I take it, Peter affirms that believers have been begotten again unto a living hope. In all probability the representation, while applicable to all believers, was influenced to some extent by the apostle's memory of his own experience. There had been a moment in his previous life when all at once, in the twinkling of an eye as it were, he had been translated from a world of despair into a world of hope. It was when the fact of the resurrection of Christ flashed upon him. Under the two-fold bitterness of his denial of the Lord and of the tragedy of the cross, utter darkness had settled down upon his soul. Everything he expected from the future in connection with Jesus had been completely blotted out. Perhaps he had even been in danger of losing the old hope which as a pious Israelite he cherished before he knew the Lord. And then suddenly, the whole aspect of things had been changed. The risen Christ appeared to him and by his appearance wrought the resurrection of everything that had gone down with him into the grave. No, there was far more here for Peter than a mere resurrection of what he had hoped in before. It was the birth of something new that now, for the first time, disclosed itself to his perception. His hope was not given back to him in its old form. It was regenerated in the act of restoration. Previously it had been dim, undefined, subject to fluctuations; sometimes eager and enthusiastic, sometimes cast down and languishing; in many respects earthly, carnal and incompletely spiritualized. Apart from all of these defects, his previous hope had been a bare one, which could only sustain itself by projection into the future, but which lacked that vital support and nourishment in a present substantial reality without which no religious hope can permanently subsist.

Through the resurrection of Christ, all these faults were corrected; all these deficiencies supplied. For Peter looked upon the risen Christ as the beginning, the firstfruits of that new world of God in which the believer's hope is anchored. Jesus did not rise as he had been before, but transformed, glorified, eternalized, the possessor and author of a transcendent heavenly life at one and the same time, the revealer, the sample and the pledge of the future realization of the true kingdom of God. No prolonged course of training could have been more effective for purifying and spiritualizing the apostle's hope than this single, instantaneous experience; this bursting upon him of a new form of eternal life, concrete and yet all-comprehensive in its prophetic significance. Well might the apostle say that he himself had been begotten again unto a new hope through the resurrection of Christ from the dead. And, of course, what was true of him was even more emphatically true of the readers of his epistle, who, if they were believers from the Gentiles, before their conversion had lived entirely without hope and without God in the world.

4.   This substantial renewal which the consciousness of man undergoes when he is brought in contact with the resurrection-life of Christ is still more clearly expressed in the other statement of our text. For you will observe that the apostle describes the goal of this new begetting in two ways. First he says, 'unto a living hope', and then he says, 'unto an inheritance, incorruptible, undefiled and that fadeth not away'. What he means is evidently nothing else than that through the resurrection of Christ his hope has been made to terminate directly upon the heavenly inheritance in all its compass. It was a birth into a state of consciousness that knew itself infinitely rich in heavenly places in Christ. It was a birth in which all the thoughts and the aspirations have for their fixed background this sense of nobility, of being heir to untold treasures. What does it matter that the inheritance is not yet received, when our legal title to it and our ideal possession of it is assured! We have been born into it through the resurrection of Christ.

The three Greek adjectives translated 'incorruptible, undefiled, and that fadeth not away' describe the spiritual, heavenly character of the inheritance. They describe those aspects of it by which the hope of the believer can justly be called a new-born hope—distinct not only as a new fact, but distinct by its new qualities. They describe those qualities which make the inherit-

ance Peter expected after the resurrection different from
the one he expected before. These adjectives simply
unfold what is already given in the statement that the
inheritance is reserved (or rather preserved), kept secure
in heaven. Because by its very nature it belongs to the
heavenly, spiritual world, it is exempt from corruption.
The forces of decay that rule in this world of death cannot attack it. It is undefiled—the principle of moral evil,
the power of sin cannot invade it. It fadeth not away—
even the lapse of time which in a normal world destroys
the beauty and freshness of things cannot dim its glory,
for it is constituted under the laws of eternity and not
of time.

But it does not follow from this that because hope
exists under such laws and is so securely protected from
corruption, defilement and decay, that it is also debarred
from exerting its power in this world and acting upon us
while we form part of this lower order of things. For
the apostle, as you will observe, describes the hope to
which the Christian has been born again as a living
hope. This is only another way of saying that the inheritance unto which he has been born again is a living
inheritance; an inheritance that moves and sways, that
strengthens and inspires us not merely subjectively
through our knowledge of it, but objectively through
the spiritual power that proceeds from it. The word
'living' is used in two other passages in our epistle. It is
said of the Word of God that it 'liveth and abideth forever' (1:23). And Christ is called the 'living stone' (2:4),
with whom coming believers as living stones are built
up into a spiritual house.

From this we can infer what is meant by a living
hope. Just as living stones are different from ordinary

stones in that they do not wait passively until somebody comes and puts them into a building, but lend themselves in free spiritual activity for the purpose of edification; so a living hope is a hope which is not dead material in the mind of the believer, but an active force in his life—something that makes its influence felt and carries him along, that sustains and inspires him. The hope of the Christian can do this because it relates to something that is not purely future, but already exists in the present because it is a hope in an inheritance, the most real of all realities. The inheritance may be invisible, but this does not detract in the least from its power to become operative in our life. No, the very fact of its being invisible vouches for its efficacy, because this invisibility means that it forms part of the spiritual world and the spiritual world is infinitely more real and infinitely more powerful than the things which our eyes can see. Hence the Christian, while not having seen it, loves it and rejoices in it greatly with joy unspeakable and full of glory. He fashions himself according to it. He purifies his soul in harmony with the purity that intrinsically belongs to that world. He abstains from fleshly lusts because they war against the spiritual nature of the soul by which he is related to that spiritual realm which is the object of his hope. He is of sound mind, sober unto prayer. In all these things he conforms himself and responds to the claims which his heavenly destiny has upon him. He lives in the presence of the world to come and allows it to be the ruling factor in all he thinks and does.

5.   Finally, the living hope of which the apostle speaks has this for its peculiarity: that it possesses a personal

centre in Christ and God. All through the epistle this is strikingly brought out. That which controls and attracts the believer in this hope is not a confused mass of expectation, not a medley of fantastic dreams. There is a unifying idea in it; it is, in the last analysis, the certainty that there is a state in store for us which shall bring us face to face with God and Christ. The Christian is a sojourner here and must live in the future because he knows full well that under the present conditions he can never attain to that full possession of God and his Saviour for which in his best moments his heart and flesh cry out. The veil of sense lies between; the barrier of sin lies between. Even though he may lay hold of God as Moses did—seeing the invisible—there is something that lies beyond his reach, that eludes his grasp. And the believer knows, moreover, that as long as he cannot fully possess God, God cannot fully possess him nor be completely glorified in him. This sentiment lies at the basis of all genuine God-born Christian hope—the sentiment which enabled even the psalmist under the old covenant to transcend the darkness and mystery of death and then say, 'Thou wilt show me the path of life; in thy presence is fulness of joy; in thy right hand there are pleasures for evermore . . . As for me I shall behold thy face in righteousness; I shall be satisfied, when I awake, with thy likeness' (*Ps.* 16:11; 17:15).

IX: The Joy of
Resurrection Life[1]

1 Corinthians 15:14: *'And if Christ be not risen, then
is our preaching vain, and your faith is also vain.'*

⁂

Among the evils which threatened the life of the
church at Corinth (and to correct which was
Paul's chief end in writing this epistle) were
certain doubts and errors on the subject of the resurrection. Evidently Paul attributed very great importance to
these. You can infer this from the fact that in dealing
with the various abnormal conditions in the church, he
reserves the treatment of this particular evil for the close
of the epistle. He wanted the impression of what he had
to say on this point to be the final and most lasting
impression left upon the minds of the Corinthians. All
the other problems concerning such matters as divisions
and partisanship, the relapse into pagan modes of
living, marriages between believers and unbelievers—
important though they were in themselves—belonged
after all to the periphery, the outcome, not the root and
centre of Christianity.

But with the resurrection, it was a totally different
matter. Here the heart, the core, the very foundation
and substance of the Christian faith were at stake. Paul

[1] Preached at the Chapel of Princeton Theological Seminary, Princeton, New Jersey at Easter, 23 April 1905.

felt that if on this vital point a serious departure from the truth were allowed to develop unhindered, then sooner or later, by the inexorable law of organic disease, the whole body was doomed to destruction. This is the only way in which we can explain the intensely earnest, careful, thorough-going manner in which the apostle conducts the battle for this part of the Christian position. Paul was so profoundly impressed with the vital character of this truth that no other method of vindicating it could satisfy him than one by which it was placed in the centre of the Christian religion and all the light that streamed from its highest experiences and convictions focused upon it.

We may say Paul here exhibits the resurrection as that towards which everything in Christianity tends; the goal in which all thinking and striving and hoping of believers finds its perfect rest and triumphant solution. It seems to me we can set for ourselves no more appropriate or profitable task this Easter day than at the hand of the apostle to trace the inner nexus of our Christian faith with the resurrection of Christ. If the observance by the church of special seasons associated with the great epochs in the work of redemption is to be justified at all, it can be justified on no higher ground than that such seasons as Christmas and Easter and Pentecost invite us to rise for a moment from the poor frag-mentariness of our average consciousness of salvation to that clearer and more blessed vision whereby, as from a mountain top, we span the entire origin of our faith. Everything belongs to us of right because we are Christ's and Christ is God's; but we are consciously rich only in so far as we learn to place ourselves at least sometimes on those points of elevation from which we may survey the land of God's promises as a whole. Perhaps we do not sufficiently appreciate the extent to which the remembrance at stated seasons of these great facts of the incarnation, the atonement, the resurrection, the gift of the Spirit, has kept alive in the church the spirit of true evangelical piety. I am sure we shall not have meditated upon the words in vain if our meditation leads us to realize in some greater measure how entirely our holy religion stands or falls with the resurrection of Christ.

There are three trains of thought that I would like briefly to pursue with you. Let us ask in succession: what does the resurrection of Christ mean for our justification; what does it mean for our regeneration; what does it mean for our glorification?

1. *What Does the Resurrection of Christ Mean for Our Justification?*

For Paul, the resurrection stands in the centre of the gospel as a gospel of justification—of deliverance from the guilt of sin. To him, the one religious question which overshadows in importance all others is the question: 'How shall a sinful man become righteous in the sight of God?' Now if the resurrection of Christ had nothing to contribute towards the solution of this one stupendous problem, then (whatever significance in other connections might belong to it) it could scarcely be said to be of the heart of the gospel. It would have to recede into the shadow of the cross.

As a matter of fact, this frequently takes place in our minds when we think of the forgiveness of sins. That justification depends on the cross is one of the common-places of our evangelical belief; so much so that we hardly deem it necessary to ask whether the resurrection perhaps may not have an equally important bearing on this great concern of our souls with the righteousness of God. Now it appears from these words of our text that to Paul the resurrection is an absolutely necessary step in the work of atonement and justification. 'If Christ has not been raised,' he says to the Corinthians, 'your faith is vain.' That is to say, your faith is ineffective and worthless because 'Ye are yet in your sins.' It is justifying faith—faith in its connection with the forgiveness of sins—the efficacy of which is somehow bound up with the Saviour's resurrection. 'Ye are yet in your sins' means 'ye are yet under the condemnation of sin', subject to the wrath of God, exposed to eternal destruction. This appears still more clearly from what the apostle adds straight away: 'Then they also which are fallen asleep in Christ have perished.'

Nor is this the only place in the epistles of Paul where the justification of the believer and the resurrection of Christ are joined together. Elsewhere we read that our Christian faith, on which the imputation of righteousness depends, is in God as the one who raised Jesus from the dead (*Rom.* 10:9). Christ was delivered for our sins; he was raised for our justification (*Rom.* 4:25). Nobody can lay anything to the charge of God's elect; God justifies and none can condemn because it is Christ Jesus who died and was raised from the dead (*Rom.* 8:33, 34). To speak in one's heart despairingly, as if righteousness were still to be provided, would be equivalent to saying: Who shall ascend into heaven for the purpose of bringing Christ down to his life of suffering and humiliation, and who shall descend into the abyss for the purpose of bringing Christ up from the realm of death? The two things, therefore, on which righteousness depends are the descent of Christ from heaven to bear our sins and the resurrection. Hence, 'if thou shalt believe in thine heart that God raised Jesus from the dead, thou shalt be saved' (*Rom.* 10:9).

From all this, it is perfectly plain that we are not dealing here with an isolated form of representation, but with something which stood out in the apostle's teaching as a fundamental truth on which he dwelt repeatedly in the most various connections. We are therefore bound to put the question: 'What is it that the resurrection contributes to our becoming righteous in the sight of God?' I think we can put the answer in the most simple form by saying, 'The resurrection stands related to righteousness in the same way that death stands related to sin.' If we once clearly understand what death meant to the apostle, then it will immediately become plain what the resurrection of Christ meant to him. Death is a word that looms large in the Pauline epistles. By no one perhaps has the terribleness of death been so intensely realized as by the apostle. Death appears to him personified as a great enemy, a huge spectre, casting its dreadful shadow over human existence, something that it is impossible to become reconciled to, more horrible than any other shape or form to be encountered in the spiritual world. Now to what does death owe this unique terror in the mind of Paul? Is it simply the inevitable aesthetic recoil from its loathsomeness as a process of physical dissolution? Or shall we say that the apostle shrinks from death because of the strong, instinctive desire to live, as every living being shrinks from that which threatens to cut short its existence? Both of these feelings are to a greater or lesser degree present in the mind of every man. They were undoubtedly present in the mind of Paul and coloured to some extent his intense consciousness on the subject. But they do not explain this consciousness exhaustively. In the apostle's attitude towards death there is something more than this, something different from this; there is an element of moral revulsion. Paul abhors and hates death because it is the wages, the penalty of sin. Whatever else it might be, to him it appeared first of all as a minister of condemnation, the personified, incarnate sentence of God against sin. This is what death is when you strip it of all accidental features. Death is the exponent of sin. Its sentence and penalty is one with which the criminality of sin ineffaceably stamps the sinner. The sting of death is sin, and the power of sin is the law, and the law is nothing else than God himself personally confronting the transgressor and rendering judgement: 'The soul that sinneth it shall die.'

Now if this is the significance of death in general, it follows that the death of Christ in particular must be interpreted on the same principle. Christ was made sin on our behalf. When he assumed our guilt, it became inevitable that not merely some general form of suffering entailed by sin should fall on him, but also that the one great typical punishment of sin should be visited on him—he should die. Though his whole life in the flesh was sin-bearing from beginning to end, yet it was specifically in the cross and in the death that took place upon the cross that the condemnatory power of the law was concentrated on Christ. There it was made manifest that he had become sin for us, the curse incarnate. But if this is so, then the significance of the resurrection for the atoning work of Christ immediately springs into view. If the Saviour's death was the embodiment of the curse which rests upon the world, then so long as he remained under the power of death there could be no assurance that satisfaction had been rendered, the condemnation of the divine wrath removed. On the other hand, as soon as at any point the process of death is suspended and life permitted to emerge from death, this will be equivalent to a practical declaration on God's part that the curse has exhausted itself, the penalty been paid. Now Christ's bodily resurrection was the only way in which this could be impressively declared. As the curse laid upon him had assumed the visible form of separation between body and soul, it was necessary that in the same physical sphere, in the same palpable form, the divine absolution should be solemnly pronounced and placed on record. By raising Christ from death, God as the supreme Judge set his seal to the absolute perfection and completeness of his atoning work. The resurrection is a public announcement to the world that the penalty of death has been borne by Christ to its bitter end and that in consequence the dominion of guilt has been broken, the curse annihilated forevermore.

And all this was true of Christ not in his personal capacity so much but as our representative. We were concerned—you and I and all believers—in this momentous transaction. The principle of our justification was given here as an accomplished fact. It is just as impossible that any one for whom Christ rose from the dead should fail to receive the righteousness of God as it is that God should undo the resurrection of Christ itself. Consequently, knowing ourselves one with Christ, we find in the resurrection the strongest possible assurance

GRACE AND GLORY

of pardon and peace. When Christ rose on Easter morning he left behind him in the depths of the grave every one of our sins; there they remain buried from the sight of God so completely that even in the day of judgement they will not be able to rise up against us any more. And not only is this true of the resurrection as an accomplished fact, it is true in an even higher sense of the risen Lord himself. The very life of the exalted Christ is a witness to the blessed reality of the forgiveness of our sins. In the living Saviour, Paul would have us by faith grasp our justification. In the same real sense in which on earth Christ was identified with our sin, he is now in his resurrection-life identified with our state of pardon and acceptance. According to the profound words of the apostle, we have become the righteousness of God in him (*2 Cor.* 5:20) because he has become the righteousness of God for us.

2. *What Does the Resurrection of Christ Mean for Our Regeneration?*

The resurrection of Christ is of basal importance for the renewal of our life, for our regeneration and sanctification. We are all conscious that the creative, regenerating power which transforms our life, which expels sin and infuses holiness proceeds from the Spirit of Christ. And by this again Paul does not merely mean that in accordance with the Trinitarian constitution of the Godhead the Son sends the Spirit as his representative and agent to execute his task. The apostle clearly teaches that Christ as God-Man—as Mediator—in his exalted state has in a special, unique sense the disposal of the Spirit; inasmuch as the Spirit dwells in his own human nature and invests it with transcendent power and glory. Christ is Lord of the Spirit; no, in even stronger language we say with Paul, Christ is the Spirit (*1 Cor.* 15:45; *2 Cor.* 3:17). Now the point to be noticed here is that this unique and close relationship between the Spirit and Christ dates from the moment of the resurrection. By the resurrection of the dead he was effectually decreed to be the Son of God in power (*Rom.* 1:4). At the resurrection he became the last Adam who is a life-giving Spirit (*1 Cor.* 15:45). In still another form the same thought is expressed when Paul represents the glory of Christ as the source from which supernatural power is brought to bear upon the believer (*2 Cor.* 3:18). This glory of Christ again is none other than his resurrection-glory.

From various points of view therefore, we are taught by the apostle that the resurrection of Christ, besides being the divine acknowledgement of his perfect righteousness, is also the fountain-head of all the renewing and quickening influences that descend from him to us. To preach a risen Christ means to preach a gospel which claims to come with the demonstration of the Spirit and with power. It means to assume that this world is dead in trespasses and sins; that no word of persuasion, no force of example, no release from the body, in fact nothing short of a new creation can give it life. This is where the old apostolic gospel of Paul and the modern moralizing interpretations of Christianity part ways. Because the modern world has ceased to take sin seriously, it has lost its sense for the necessity of the supernatural in the work of salvation; and to such a state of mind the message of the resurrection of Christ no longer appeals.

At present it is believed by many who call themselves

Christians that all that is necessary to reach a state of
perfection is the self-evolution of the natural man.
Now so far as purely inward processes are concerned
this modern naturalistic spirit finds it easy to clothe itself
in the old Christian forms and to retain the old
Christian ways of speaking. But it will immediately rise
up in protest when confronted with an intrusion of the
supernatural in the external, physical sphere, such as the
resurrection of the body. Need we wonder then that
where Christians have begun to give ear to this
seductive spirit, the doctrine of the resurrection should
gradually have come to be regarded as a source of weakness rather than of strength? The conviction seems to be
gaining ground that all practical ends of religion will be
equally well served and a possible cause of offence
removed by exchanging this doctrine for a simple belief
in the immortality of the soul with reference both to
Christ and believers. We may learn from Paul that
scepticism on this concrete point is symptomatic of
infection with the poison of naturalism in the very heart
of the Christian faith. The most striking feature of Paul's
treatment of the resurrection here and elsewhere is that,
far from representing it as an isolated fact, he makes it
part of an organic work of renewal involving both the
soul and the body of man. The resurrection is supernatural for no other reason than that from beginning
to end—in regeneration, sanctification and in everything—the work of grace is supernatural in the most
absolute sense of the word. According to Paul, the same
exceeding greatness of divine power is displayed in the
production of spiritual life in the sinner's soul as when
God raised Christ from the dead and made him sit at
his right hand in heavenly places. The one is no more

difficult to believe and no more essential to hold than the other. The great question for us all is not whether we shall believe or disbelieve the resurrection as a single historic event, but whether we shall maintain or surrender the character of Christianity as a resurrection-religion—a religion able to bring life out of death, both here and hereafter. Can the choice be difficult for any of us?

3. *What Does the Resurrection of Christ Mean for Our Glorification?*

The resurrection of Christ is fundamental for our glorification. Ours is a religion whose centre of gravity lies beyond the grave in the world to come. The conviction that the gospel is primarily intended to prepare man for a future life and that consequently neither its true nature can be understood nor its full glory appreciated unless it be placed in the light of eternity—this conviction broadly underlies the apostle's reasoning both here and elsewhere. Christianity does many things for the present life, but if we wish to apprehend how much it can do, we must direct our gaze to the life beyond. What more eloquent expression of this feeling can be conceived than is found in immediate proximity to our text in the words: 'If [nearing the end] we are such who have only hope in Christ in this life, we are of all men most pitiable'? What else does this mean other than that the Christian's main thinking, feeling and striving revolve around the future state; and that, if this goal should prove to have no objective reality, the absoluteness with which the believer has staked everything in its attainment must make him appear in his delusion the most pitiable of all creatures? What a gulf then lies between this statement of the apostle and the sentiment we sometimes meet with—that Christianity had better disencumber itself of all idle speculation about an uncertain future state and concentrate its energies upon the improvement of the present world. Paul could not have entertained such a sentiment for a moment because the thirst for the world to come was of the very substance of the religion of his heart. He felt deeply that the believer's destiny and God's purposes with reference to him transcend all limits of what this earthly life can possibly bring or possibly contain. Christ's work for us extends even farther than the restoration of what sin has destroyed. If Christ placed us back there where Adam stood in his rectitude, without sins and without death, this would be unspeakable grace indeed, more than enough to make the gospel a blessed word. But grace exceeds sin far more abundantly than all this: besides wiping out the last vestige of sin and its consequences, it opens up for us that higher world to whose threshold even the first Adam had not yet apprehended. And this is not a mere matter of degrees in blessedness, it is a difference between two modes of life; as heaven is high above the earth, by so much the conditions of our future state will transcend those of the paradise of old.

It is for this reason that we know so little, and that even in the moments of greatest clearness of our spiritual vision we form such inadequate ideas of what awaits us hereafter. But, thanks be to God, in the resurrection of Christ for once the veil has been lifted. When Christ rose from the grave he rose as one whose human nature had been transformed into harmony with heavenly conditions. This was true not merely of his body, but of all the faculties and powers of his humanity hitherto exercised in humiliation and now set free and made fit for their perfect use in heavenly glory. In this respect the resurrection of Christ is prophetic of that of all believers. As we have borne the image of the earthy, we shall also bear the image of the heavenly man (*1 Cor.* 15:49). In the resurrection, therefore, we have the assurance that we ourselves also shall be made fit in our entire nature for our habitation in heaven. It is only by understanding this that we can understand the true significance of the resurrection of the body. Not that the restoration of our bodies is the great hope of the Christian, but that they shall be restored to us in such a state as to resemble the resurrection-body of Christ; that through them our spirits may dwell in perfect accord with their heavenly surroundings and may lead in its consummate form the life that knows no end.

In conclusion, let us observe that these three aspects of the resurrection of Christ are not merely each for its own part fundamental, but are also, when taken together, a comprehensive summary of the gospel which we are commissioned to preach. Peace of conscience, renewal of life, assurance of heaven: what more than this could we endeavour to bring to our fellow men? What less than this could we dare to offer them under the name of the gospel? As preachers of Christ and the resurrection, let us always remember to give due prominence to these three great things. Is there not a special satisfaction in being able to proclaim a gospel which so completely covers the needs of a sinful world? 'If Christ has not been raised—then is our preaching vain and vain the faith of all that hear us.' But now that Christ has been raised from the dead and brought righteousness and life and heaven to light, now we can be steadfast, unmovable, always abounding in the work of the Lord, forasmuch as we know that our labour is not in vain in the Lord.

X: Songs From the Soul [1]

Psalm 25:14: *'The secret of the LORD is with them that fear him; and he will shew them his covenant.'*

The Psalter is of all books of the Bible that book which gives expression to the experimental side of religion. In the law and the prophetic writings, it is God who speaks to his people; but in the Psalter we listen to the saints speaking to God. Hence the Psalter has been at all times that part of Scripture to which believers have most readily turned and upon which they have chiefly depended for the nourishment of the inner religious life of the heart. I say that part of Scripture and not merely that part of the Old Testament, for even taking the Old and the New Testament together the common experience of the people of God affirms that there is nothing in Holy Writ which in our most spiritual moments—when we feel ourselves nearest to God—so faithfully and naturally expresses what we think and feel in our hearts as these songs of the pious Israelites. Our Lord himself, who had a perfect religious experience and lived and walked with God in absolute adjustment of his thoughts and desires to the Father's mind and will, our Lord himself found his inner life portrayed in the Psalter and in some of the highest moments of his ministry borrowed from it the language

[1] Preached at the Chapel of Princeton Theological Seminary, Princeton, New Jersey on 15 October 1902.

in which his soul spoke to God, thus recognizing that a more perfect language for communion with God cannot be framed.

Undoubtedly it is in the Psalter that the specific work of inspiration which the Holy Ghost performs in inditing the Scriptures and the more general task which he carries out in sustaining, directing, stimulating and guiding the religious thoughts and aspirations of believers are most closely united. Inspiration for the disclosure of truth is not always accompanied by the subjective appropriation of the truth in a saintly experience (a Balaam and a Caiaphas were among the prophets); but nevertheless it remains the more natural and ordinary procedure of God that the instrument through which his truth is brought to man should be a mind in intimate touch with his own; a mind responsive to that personal revelation of God himself which lives and throbs in the truth. And consequently we see that the great prophets (like a Moses, an Isaiah or Jeremiah) appear at the same time as the outstanding examples of a wonderfully rich and tender religious intercourse with God. But in the Psalms we can more clearly than anywhere else observe the interaction of these two things: supernatural reception of truth and spiritual nearness to God. Possibly the fact that in David's case the prophetic disclosures of truth that he received were so vitally connected with his own life and destiny may have something to do with the presence of this feature in the Psalms, whereas the other prophets sometimes stood more or less apart from the development of things to which their words applied. And then the prophets, of course, in many instances spoke to and for the nation collectively, whereas in the Psalter it is the individual soul which comes face to face with God.

Hence the lessons and encouragements which we obtain from other parts of the Old Testament are frequently drawn indirectly by a process of inference, for which we are not always in the right frame of mind and the proper spiritual mood. But in the Psalms, whatever our mood, whether we are exultant or downcast, vigorous or weary, penitent or believing, we can always find our hearts mirrored there. It needs no process of reasoning to make their sentiments our own. Here the language of the Bible comes to meet the very thoughts of our hearts before these can even clothe themselves in language and we recognize that we could not have expressed them better than the Spirit has here expressed them for us. At first sight, this may easily seem strange to us when we remember that the psalmists lived under the conditions of a typical and preparatory dispensation; that on many points they saw through a glass darkly, whereas we, who live in the full light of the complete gospel, see face to face. But for the very reason that the Psalms reflect that experimental religion of the heart, which is unvarying at all times and under all circumstances, we need not greatly wonder at this. The influx of the divine light, whether more or less strong, must always produce the identical effect of joy, hope and peace in every soul to which it comes. The well at which we drink may flow more abundantly than that at which the psalmists drank, but the experience of thirst, of drinking and of satisfaction must still be the same as it was in the time of David.

Now regarding the Psalms from this point of view as an inspired record of what goes on in the heart of man—where the religious consciousness is under the influence of the Spirit of God, its thoughts are purified and directed into their normal channels—we must be struck at once, I think, by one characteristic of the spiritual experience here portrayed. This is the predominance of the element of personal communion with God. In a variety of ways this finds expression. Sometimes we observe it in actual exercise, as in those instances where the psalm is a formal prayer, or even more strikingly where it develops into something like a dialogue between God and the soul. Compare, for example, the touching episode which David records in Psalm 27: 'Thou saidst, Seek ye my face; my heart said unto thee: Thy face, LORD, will I seek.' At other times, it is not the actual exercise of this privilege, but the strong elemental desire for it which finds utterance. The examples of this will immediately suggest themselves to all of us. It is unnecessary to quote more than the opening verses of Psalm 42: 'As the hart panteth after the water brooks, so panteth my soul after thee, O God. My soul thirsteth for God, for the living God: when shall I come and appear before God?'

At still other times, it is neither the actual exercise nor the desire for it, but the remembrance of what has been enjoyed in the past or the reflection upon what may still be enjoyed in the future that moves the writer: 'These things I remember and pour out my soul within me, how I went with the throng and led them to the house of God, with the voice of joy and praise, a multitude keeping holyday' (*Ps.* 42:4). This is the case in the passage before us: 'The secret of the LORD is with them that fear him, and he will show them his covenant.' The 'secret' means the secret counsel, the *homilia* as one of the old translations has aptly rendered it. It is the intimate converse between friend and friend as known from human life where there is no reserve, but the thoughts and feelings of the heart are freely inter-changed. And the notion of the covenant here expresses the same idea: the covenant being conceived not as a formal contract for the specific purpose, but as a com-munion in which life touches life and intertwines with life so that the two become mutually assimilated. Evidently the psalmists recognize in this private inter-course with God the highest function of religion—the only thing that will completely satisfy the child of God. And this becomes all the more touching if we remem-ber how much there was in the old covenant, with its complex system of ceremonies, which necessitated a sort of indirect service of God; and remember further how even where a more direct approach unto God was permitted, this had to remain partial and to be exercised under restrictions because the fresh and living way into the Holy of Holies had not yet been opened up.

We may well believe that it was with something of this consciousness in mind that the saints followed hard after God and sought to penetrate in their inner spiritual life into that immediate presence, from which in the public service of God in the tabernacle or temple the restrictions of the old covenant excluded them. It may be frequently observed in sacred as well as in natural affairs that where a thing is partially possessed and still partially missed there is the keenest appreciation of its value and the most intense longing for its full attain-ment. It is certainly striking that these expressions of passionate desire to come into living fellowship with God are found in the Old Testament rather than in the New. Is it not possible that we, because we have the privilege of approaching God at all times without restrictions, are sometimes in danger of underestimating its value or even neglecting its exercise? Must not a David put us to shame when he cries in Psalm 63: 'O God, thou art my God, earnestly will I seek thee: my soul thirsteth for thee, my flesh longeth for thee, in a dry and weary land where no water is. Because thy loving-kindness is better than life—my lips shall praise thee'? If he longed like this for the less, how much more earnestly ought we to cultivate the greater?

Another point to be noticed in the same connection is this: how concrete and familiar, one might almost say how realistic, some of the figures are in which this personal intercourse with God is described in the Psalter. In this respect, the passage before us, expressive though it is, may be called sober and restrained compared with other statements drawn from the same source. Figures are borrowed from the intimacies of human life, even of animal life, which in point of picturesqueness and forcibleness go far beyond that of a covenant or a secret counsel here employed by the psalmist. An example of this is the figure of the common house in which the believer desires to dwell with Jehovah so that there may be something of that same closeness and intimacy of fellowship between God and him which binds the members of one household together. Of course, this attaches itself to the typical expression God had given to the thought of religious fellowship with himself in the structure of the tabernacle or the temple. But it remains interesting that this divine thought embodied in the sanctuary is most clearly apprehended and most eagerly responded to in the Psalms: 'A day in thy courts is better than a thousand: I had rather be a doorkeeper in the house of my God, than to dwell in the tents of wickedness' (*Ps.* 84:10); 'One thing have I asked of the LORD, that will I seek after, that I may dwell in the house of the LORD all the days of my life, to behold the beauty of the LORD and to inquire in his temple. For in the day of trouble he shall keep me secretly in his pavilion: in the covert of his tent shall he hide me' (*Ps.* 27:4, 5). Even this metaphor is surpassed in a number of other passages where the psalmist chooses figures based on physical, bodily contact in order to satisfy himself in describing his vivid experience of standing in real personal communion with God. The two modes of statement are joined together in Psalm 61 where David first says, 'I will dwell in thy tabernacle forever' and then adds by way of climax, 'I will take refuge in the covert of thy wings'; as elsewhere we read the petition, 'Hide me under the shadow of thy wings' (*Ps.* 17:8) and three times the avowal, 'Therefore, men put their trust under the shadow of thy wings' (*Ps.* 36:7).

Now it should be noticed that, notwithstanding the concrete, realistic character of such expressions, the sentiment expressed remains well within the bounds of conscious, intelligent fellowship with God. There is no lapse into false mysticism here; no desire to lose one's self in God. What the psalmist strives after is nothing more nor less than that mutual revelation of person to person, that grasping of God himself in the various forms of his approach unto us which is the culminating act of all religion. It is safe to say that both in the guarding of this idea from every kind of mystical excess and perversion, and in the thoroughness on the other hand of its application within the proper limits imposed

[175]

by the personality of God, the biblical religion stands unique among the religions of the world. You may find enough elsewhere of absorption into the deity, just as you may find plenty in other quarters of co-ordination between the gods and men as if the two had separated spheres of life. But you will find nowhere such a clear grasp upon the principle that from the very nature of religion man is designed to hold converse with God and to become practically acquainted with him. Nor is it merely a subjective aspiration of man which underlies this idea of religion. At the basis of it lies the conviction that there is in God himself the possibility, no, the desire for this. Notice how our passage expresses it. The secret intercourse of the Lord is with them that fear him and he will teach them his covenant.

It is a condescension of God not an aspiration of ourselves which renders real this crowning act of religion. The psalmists are convinced that God himself desires to enter upon close fellowship with man; that if he institutes a covenant for his servants it is because he is in his very nature a covenant God. In the saints upon the earth is all his delight. We have no right to say that there was any lack or deficiency in God to be supplemented by the creation of man in his image and for communion with him, for that would be inconsistent with his character as God. The Scriptures teach that he is all-sufficient unto himself and forever blessed in himself. Nevertheless having created man, it is natural in God to receive man as an inmate of his house and companion of his own blessed life. God himself takes pleasure in the immediate personal fellowship with us to which he invites us. There is that in him which corresponds to the highest in our religion. The prayer of his people comes like incense before him; the lifting up of their hands as an evening sacrifice. And it is because the psalmists realize this that their own desire to meet with God and speak with God attains that intensely passionate character to which reference has been made. The opinion is gaining vogue nowadays that a considerable portion of the Psalter was composed during the period of the later Judaism. It would be an interesting question to pursue whether this atmosphere of religious nearness to God in which the psalmists so naturally breathe was actually the prevailing atmosphere of that later period which was wont to complain that God had withdrawn from his people, that there was no voice of prophecy heard any longer, and which had almost settled down to serving God by indirection through punctilious obedience of his law. Certainly it is difficult to believe that two so entirely opposite spiritual attitudes should have belonged to one and the same age.

A last point to which I would briefly call your attention in connection with this subject is the high disinterestedness to which occasionally the psalmists rise in their longing for communion with God. Of course it is in no sense to the discredit of our religion if we seek contact with God from motives of self-interest and self-preservation. Our very position as dependent creatures and God's very character as the source of all blessings render it absolutely of the essence of all religious approach to him that it should be accompanied and coloured by the consciousness of our need. But from this it by no means follows that the desire to obtain something from God distinct from himself can rightly be the only or the supreme motive impelling us to seek his face. This is the attitude of the unregenerate man;

the form which true religious instinct takes under the influence of his selfish isolation from God. But when the Spirit of God moves the centre of our life, transferring it from self to God, there immediately awakes a longing to come in touch with God and possess him and enjoy him for his own sake. We can best illustrate this from the relation of a child to its parents. We do not blame the child because it often turns to its father or mother for the simple reason that it wants something which it can procure in no other way. But what would you think of a child which never sought its father's arms or climbed upon its mother's lap unless there were some external want to be supplied? The true child will spontaneously, instinctively turn to the presence and smile of its parents as a flower will seek the face of the sun. And in the same way the true child of God will have moments in which he turns to his Father in heaven unconscious of any other desire than the desire to be near unto God.

It is on this point that the Psalms most touchingly and most eloquently express the filial spirit as it surmounted the barriers of the Old Testament form of religion and made its way straight to the heart of God. 'Whom have I in heaven, but thee? And there is none upon the earth that I desire beside thee: though my flesh and my heart shall fail, God is the strength of my heart and my portion forever' (Ps. 73:25-26). This and nothing else underlies all the passages in which the psalmists speak of their love for the house of God or deplore their compelled absence from it. Their attachment to the house of God is at bottom an attachment to the person of God himself, just as the love which we cherish for our house would, when analysed, ultimately appear to be a love fed not so much from association with the material structure but from that intimate contact with the spirit of our family and friends of which the house is, as it were, the external embodiment.

And most touching of all, I think, is the form which this sentiment assumes in the mind of the Old Testament saints in view of the mysteries, so much greater to them than to us, of the state after death. Did you ever observe what is the thought that seems to have most acutely distressed and perplexed the writers of some of the Psalms when they tried in vain to pierce this veil of mystery enveloping to them the future world? It was the fear that in these strange regions there might be no remembrance of God, no knowledge of his goodness, no praise of his glory. We may be assured that when a religious want is projected into the world to come in this way, so that the fear of its not being satisfied proves stronger than the fear of death in itself, we may be sure that there it has been recognized as the supreme, the essential thing in religion.

Finally, what is the lesson we ought to draw from the prominence of this feature in the spiritual experience portrayed by the Psalter? Are we sure that we feel with the frequency and intensity which our greater privileges demand the desire to meet with God? Or are we satisfied with that indirect relation to him which our service of him in his kingdom and our daily study of his Word leads us to sustain? I need not tell you that there is a tendency at the present day to make the religious life seek the surface, the periphery; to detach it more or less from its centre which lies in the direct face-to-face communion of the soul with God. The devotional is not so much in evidence as it has been in other periods of the church's history. There are two causes for this:

(i) The first of these may not concern us very much. It is found in the modern reluctance to lay emphasis upon any religious practice which at all involves the idea of a clear, definite, personal knowledge and experience of God—in other words, in agnostic tendencies. Its watchword is: we can know little about God, but we can know what our religious duties are towards our fellow man. With this, as I have said, you and I may have little to do, although to some extent we may still feel its influence.

(ii) The second cause concerns us directly. It lies in the stupendous multiplication of the out-going activities which the present practical age makes it incumbent upon every minister of the gospel to pursue. With all these centrifugal forces playing upon us, no wonder if sometimes the one centripetal force which ought to drive us to the heart of God for the cultivation of our own devotional life is less felt in our experience. And yet it is absolutely essential for us that we should not only have our seasons of communion with God, but that all the time we should carry with us into our outward and public work in some degree a living sense of our nearness to God and of his nearness to us, because in this way alone can we make our service in the Lord's Kingdom truly fruitful and spiritual. If the savour of this is wanting in our work, if we do not bring to the world when we come to it the unction and peace acquired in prayer, we cannot hope to impart any permanent blessing or to achieve any lasting results.

Let us endeavour to cultivate diligently the devotional spirit of the psalmists. Or, better still, let us take for our example the spirit of Jesus himself, for whom notwithstanding the busy scenes of a most public career no distractions existed, to whom every call upon his strength became an occasion for meeting with God, a real contact with God, because the fountains of his strength lay hidden deep in the recesses of his inner life where he and the Father always beheld each other's face.

XI: The Essence of Christianity [1]

Matthew 16:24-25: *'Then said Jesus unto his disciples, If any man will come after me, let him deny himself, and take up his cross, and follow me. For whosoever will save his life shall lose it: and whosoever will lose his life for my sake shall find it.'*

As we are all aware, these words were spoken by our Lord at a most critical juncture in his ministry, at Caesarea Philippi, where he elicited from Peter the confession, 'Thou art the Christ, the Son of the living God' and for the first time explicitly announced the necessity of his approaching passion and death. Of course there was method in his putting these two things so closely together. Even at that late time and even in the case of his most faithful disciples, it would not have been safe for him to dwell on his Messiahship without straightaway adding the qualification that this Messiahship was not to issue into immediate glory, but into suffering and ignominious death.

How little the most advanced of these disciples were prepared to appreciate the true nature and aims of his Messianic work appears from the answer which Peter, who had just made that notable confession, gave to

[1] Preached at Princeton Theological Seminary, Princeton, New Jersey on 22 November 1903.

[182]

the startling announcement of Jesus: 'Be it far from thee, Lord; this shall never be unto thee!' At first thought these words of Peter might seem to be only the expression of affectionate concern, such as would ward off all suffering from the Saviour; and perhaps to the consciousness of Peter himself, they bore at first no other meaning.

Our Lord, however, had a deeper insight than Peter into the hidden motives by which this apparently innocent request had been inspired. In the first place he recognized in it a temptation of Satan addressed to him through Peter. Hence his answer: 'Get thee behind me, Satan!' It was a repetition of the effort made by the Tempter in the wilderness at the beginning of our Lord's ministry. At that time, when the life of self-denial and suffering was just opening up before Jesus, Satan had instantly discovered how his only hope lay in making Jesus fall out of this role of self-sacrifice and humiliation. Satan grasped better than some human theologians have done in what lay the inner principle, the true essence of our Lord's redeeming work. However evil his intentions, he was sound in his doctrinal views on the atonement. He did not need to be instructed about the necessity of Jesus passing through great trials and sufferings in connection with his Messianic task. In the world of superhuman spirits the issues of our Lord's ministry were understood at a time when they were still veiled in obscurity to most of his followers. As the demons were the first to recognize in him the Son of God and to address him as such, so here Satan, the Prince of the demons, shows himself fully alive to the consequences which would follow from the vicarious death of Jesus. And therefore he here, at this second critical point, renews the temptation using Peter as an instrument in order that even now he might make the Saviour swerve from his determined purpose to bear the cross and so destroy his work.

Jesus recognizes the Satanic temptation in Peter's words: they were not merely adapted, they were intended to make him sin; he calls Peter in this capacity a *skandalon*, an offence, a stumbling-block, thrown into his way by the Prince of Darkness. How sharp were the contrasts in Peter's life. A moment ago he had been honoured by the Saviour as the recipient of a special revelation: 'Blessed art thou, Simon Bar-Jonah, for flesh and blood hath not revealed it unto thee, but my Father who is in heaven.' And here Satan lays his hand upon him and uses him as a tool for the fearful purpose of tempting Christ. It ought to be a warning to us; a reminder that we should never deem ourselves safe, not even in our best and most spiritual moments, from the assaults of the enemy of our souls. There is no state of privilege, no degree of sanctification, that can render us absolutely secure to the allurements of sin. It is only the continuous supply of the grace of God in answer to our prayer and our faith that can shield us.

Peter, however, was not a mere passive instrument in the hands of Satan. There was a point of contact in his own heart for the suggestion of the Evil One. Our Lord's rebuke, while clearly pointing to a superhuman Tempter standing behind Peter, certainly involves a degree of blame for Peter himself. This appears from the statement: 'Thou mindest not the things of God but the things of men' in which the contrast between God and men would not be applicable to Satan. Peter's words were not inspired by a concern for the accomplishment

The Essence of Christianity

of the saving purpose of God, to which Jesus had so clearly referred when he said, I must go to Jerusalem and suffer, but by a concern for human comfort and safety. This is what our Lord calls 'minding not the things of God but of men'. Perhaps the general form of the statement (which speaks of men in the plural) may be taken to indicate that Peter's concern had not merely related to the Saviour's human comfort and freedom from suffering, but that he had also been thinking of his own safety and ease when he spoke those impertinent words: 'This shall never happen unto thee!' At any rate it will be observed that our Lord's answer is not in the main a reaffirmation of the necessity that he himself should suffer and die, but rather an emphatic assertion of the consequences which this will involve for the disciples and of the duty which it will impose upon them to follow him along the same pathway of suffering: 'If any man would come after me, let him deny himself and take up his cross and follow me. For whosoever would save his life shall lose it: and whosoever shall lose his life for my sake shall find it.'

Now let us look for a moment at the principle expressed in these words in the light of the connection described. If any man would come after me, would be my disciple, my follower, let him deny himself as resolutely as I deny myself; let him be ready, when the necessity arises and the call comes, to take up his cross, as I will take up my cross, to sacrifice his life, as I will surrender mine. Identification with me, the Lord means to say, will probably entail the loss of life. The primary reference is undoubtedly to the sharp conflict of persecution upon which the cause of Christ was to enter. To take up the cross is not to be understood in the first

place in the figurative sense we are accustomed to attach
to it as a metaphor for the endurance of trials in general.
Our Lord literally meant to say: 'If any man would be
my disciple, let him be ready to go on the scaffold with
me!' The immediately following words show this, for
there Jesus speaks without metaphor of the losing of life
and of the finding of life, i.e., of the losing of temporal
life here for his sake and of the finding of eternal life in
the day of judgement when he shall come in the glory
of his Father with his angels. Our Lord could condition
these two things upon one another, could represent the
surrender of life as a guarantee of salvation and the
opposite as entailing everlasting loss of the soul because
in the situation to which he was looking forward, the
sacrifice of life would mean a profession of him and the
refusal to sacrifice it would mean a denial of him.
By holding up before their eyes both this glorious and
this awful prospect, he seeks to nerve his disciples for
the career of martyrdom that was awaiting so many of
them. And who can estimate the influence which sayings like this in their clear, pointed, antithetical form
must have exerted upon the first generation of early,
persecuted, cross-bearing Christianity? The echo of
such words is heard in almost every martyr's confession.
They may well have been in Peter's mind when his own
cross loomed up before him together with those other
words of the Saviour: 'When thou shalt be old,
thou shalt stretch forth thy hands, and another shall
gird thee, and carry thee, whither thou wouldest not'
(*John* 21:18).

Now it might seem as if with the altogether changed
circumstances of the present world, now that Christianity is no longer a forlorn hope, a persecuted cause, but a

great historic power, the words of this passage have no further message for us. We are not called upon (at least it is not likely that the majority of us will be called upon) to take up the cross, to lay down our lives in this realistic sense. And yet I think it would be a mistake to dismiss these words as possessed of a purely historical interest and having no bearing on our own life as followers of Christ. It is easy to show that these uncompromising sayings of our Lord about the denial of self, the renunciation of life are but the sharpest expression with reference to concrete cases of something which everywhere underlies his teaching as an element of universal significance. No, it is not in exceptional cases; it is not in periods of persecution alone that the duty thus described devolves upon the Christian. Christianity, as such, in its very essence is a religion of self-denial, cross-bearing and life-surrender.

The same thoughts found here appear in other contexts which do not impose upon them any historical limitation. This very saying in regard to the taking up of the cross is found in Luke, where there is no direct reference to our Lord's own crucifixion and moreover with a very significant variation bringing out the universal scope of the idea: 'If any man would come after me, let him take up his cross daily' (*Luke* 9:23). Every day we are called upon to obey this injunction and not merely in times of extraordinary trial. Our Lord throughout means us to understand that the life of discipleship to which his followers bind themselves is a life of serious import, of tremendous cost, to which no one should rashly commit himself without calculating the consequences. In the same context of Luke already quoted, he says: 'Which of you desiring to build a tower, doth not first sit down and count the cost, whether he have wherewith to complete it' (*Luke* 14:28);'Or what king as he goeth to encounter another king in war, will not sit down first and take counsel whether he is able with ten thousand to meet him that cometh against him with twenty thousand?' (*Luke* 14:31).

Nor can we dismiss utterances of this kind with the easy remark that these are paradoxical, hyperbolical sayings which do not allow literal interpretation and enforcement; for, granting that they are figurative and intentionally paradoxical, this does not absolve us from the duty, but rather ought to stimulate us in searching for the principles involved. Our Lord has given an extreme, pointed form to his words, certainly not for the purpose that we should brush them aside, but that our interest should be aroused and our minds react upon them and study them. Now in endeavouring to do this, it will, I think, be conducive to clearness to proceed both negatively and positively: to state first the false views of self-renunciation which are not only not implied but distinctly excluded by our Lord's teaching on the subject; and then in the second place to unfold the true conception of this duty which his utterances do present to us.

1. *False Views of Self-Renunciation*

Beginning then with the negative side of the matter, it is clear that our Lord did not uphold this principle in any pessimistic, ascetic spirit because he considered the natural life of man as such an undesirable thing. Life with all its legitimate pleasures he considered a gift of God and spoke of it as an invaluable possession. This is best seen from the fact that he used the ordinary enjoyments of it as figures to describe the blessedness of the higher eternal life. His own mode of life corresponded to this for in the popular estimate he was distinguished from John the Baptist (who neither ate nor drank and practised a certain degree of abstention) as a gluttonous man and a winebibber. The general tone of his life, notwithstanding its deep serious character, was not one of gloom but of joy, even to the very last when the shadows of death were gathering around him. In regard to his disciples, he expressly vindicates their right to be joyful. They were children of the bride-chamber who could not fast, could not mourn as long as the bridegroom was with them. All this distinctly excludes both every kind of philosophical and every kind of religious asceticism which rests on a depreciating view of the natural life of man. Of the former you find an example in Buddhism, which teaches that man should kill the desire to live, that extinction of this fundamental desire is salvation. Monasticism in many of its forms gives an example of the other. The Church of Rome has taught men to look down upon ordinary life as something comparatively worthless, inferior in dignity to an artificially produced and artificially maintained state of renunciation. Both these theories are irreconcilable with the teaching of Jesus.

Secondly, our Lord nowhere countenances the idea that foregoing the natural enjoyments of life is in any sense meritorious conduct in the sight of God; that by denying ourselves one set of pleasures, we can earn a title to others, bartering present pain for future happiness. On this point also his teaching is perfectly plain, for he came into frequent collision with a class of people who held precisely this opinion. The Pharisees interpreted and observed the law from a meritoriously ascetic principle. They prided themselves on the profitableness of their fasting, of their punctilious abstention from all pleasure on the Sabbath, of their wearisome observance of all the rites of purification. Jesus squarely took issue with this standpoint, not merely because it is impossible to earn anything with God, but also because, if anything were to be earned, even then the self-mortification, the suffering of man as such could have no value in the sight of God. What God desires in the law is not to afflict man, but to benefit him—a principle most strikingly affirmed in the statement that the Sabbath was made for man, not man for the Sabbath.

2. *Correct Views of Self-Renunciation*

In coming to the positive side, we can also distinguish more than one line of thought in our Lord's teaching. The most prominent and most easily understood is the demand for self-denial which results from the supreme law of love for our neighbour. This law is so absolute and so comprehensive that it is impossible to do our full duty to our fellow man without in many points denying ourselves—denying ourselves even in the matter of legitimate, sinless desires. The disciple must not merely give and so sacrifice his personal use of earthly goods, he must also serve and so sacrifice his enjoyment of natural pleasures. He must humble himself for his brother's sake. Even an infringement of our personal rights by another cannot for a moment exempt us from the duty of meeting him and dealing with him in a loving, self-sacrificing spirit. Even if he should smite us on one cheek, we must turn the other; if he should take our coat, we must give our cloak also; if he should compel us to go one mile, we must go two. Of course it must be remembered in applying this principle that our Lord seeks the value of such conduct not in the exercise of self-repression and self-denial as such, as a negative thing, but in the positive good which through it we seek to confer upon our neighbour. Therefore it is not the blind impulse of self-surrender that is required, but the intelligent appreciation of what the welfare of others requires and how it can best be served.

In this spirit, our Lord practised the great self-denial of his entire earthly life; he brought this sacrifice because he understood its necessity and the beneficial results that would accrue from it for the glory of God and the salvation of mankind. In all minor matters as well the same principle should be applied. We may sacrifice ourselves for the physical, temporal comfort and welfare of our fellow man. But it would be wrong to do this if by doing so, by indulging his natural desires, we were to endanger his higher moral and spiritual life. It would be a useless procedure if the natural life in one were to be curtailed in order that the natural life in another might be fostered. Both in the one who practises the self-denial and in the one for whose sake it is incurred, the supreme end sought for should always be the true moral and spiritual welfare of the soul; and this thought ought to control and in certain cases to limit the Christian in his altruistic conduct. It may render it necessary for us to deny ourselves the exercise of self-denial in order that the higher good of our brother may be promoted.

Next to this stands a self-denial which the disciple is required to practise for the sake of God and the kingdom of God. God claims our supreme affection. He asks that we love him with all the mind, all the soul, all the heart, all the strength; that there shall be no division of allegiance; that nothing else shall be interposed between ourselves and him as the great end for whom we exist; that we shall worship no other gods beside him. Now in a perfectly normal state of things, in a world free from sin, there would be nothing in such an absolute claim which would have to interfere in the least with the unrestricted exercise of all the legitimate functions of our natural life. For in man's normal condition, everything—whether he eats or drinks or does anything else—is made subservient to the divine glory, so that the natural instead of encroaching upon the spiritual becomes itself spiritualized and receives a religious consecration, thus rendering all self-denial superfluous. But in such a state the Christian does not exist for the present. He lives in a world of disharmony and conflicting forces in which the true balance and proportion of things has been lost. And therefore the natural constantly tends to engross him in such a sense and to such an extent as to draw him away from God. Hence it is necessary that he should force it back within its proper limits wherever it interferes with his undivided devotion to the service of God.

Our Lord frequently speaks of self-denial for the sake of God in this sense. The Kingdom of God and God's righteousness are to be sought first. The Christian ought to wean himself from that pagan seeking after the things of this life which treats them as if they were the ultimate realities, which virtually puts them in the place of God. Martha was burdened with much serving while only one thing was supremely needful; and by attending to this one thing Mary had chosen the best thing. How hard it shall be for those who have riches to enter into the Kingdom of God. Circumstances arose in which Jesus demanded the giving away of all earthly goods, where he even warned against yielding to the claims of natural affection, where he refused permission to go and bury one's father and advised abstention from marriage because the interests of the Kingdom of God could not be properly served without these renunciations. But here again he kept clearly in view the positive end to which all self-denial must be directed. The negative self-repression must be accompanied by a positive self-surrender to God and the concerns of his kingdom. Without the cultivation of the latter, the former would not only be useless but harmful. Our Lord himself is the great example in this respect. He not only perfectly glorified God in his use of the natural world, but also kept his detachment from the world free from every taint of unnaturalness and austerity by the positive joy and satisfaction he found in always serving the Father.

Finally, our Lord preaches the duty of self-denial because self has become identified with sin. So far we have only dwelt upon the renunciation of the natural instincts under special circumstances where they come in conflict with the higher, the paramount interests of the love of God and our neighbour. But in the heart of every man there are evil cravings and lusts which must under all circumstances and at any cost be suppressed if the higher life of the soul is to prosper. Even in the disciple, even in the Christian who has already entered the kingdom, there are two natures, two principles, two selves wrestling for supremacy. It is in reference to the duty of denying this lower, sinful self that our Lord has spoken the sharpest, most uncompromising words: 'If thy right eye causeth thee to stumble, pluck it out and cast it from thee: for it is profitable for thee that one of thy members should perish, and not thy whole body be cast into hell. And if thy right hand causeth thee to stumble, cut if off and cast it from thee: for it is profitable for thee, that one of thy members should perish and not thy whole body go into hell' (*Matt.* 5:29-30). That is to say, where the natural self has been so taken into the service of sin as to bring the very soul into peril, there the disciple must by the severest discipline, in a painful process cut himself loose, tear himself away from it. Here self-denial becomes so imperative because it amounts to the direct denial of the right of sin to rule over us.

Now our Lord does not mean this in the merely outward sense that the refusal to indulge in the act of sin is sufficient. He nowhere lends his authority to the view that sin can be effectually conquered by attacking its external manifestations. He had too profound a conception of the internal source and the inveterate nature of sin than to have relied on such a remedy. No mortification of the flesh can uproot a single evil desire from the heart. The penances may kill the body, but they cannot kill the sin. No—what our Lord refers to is something internal; something that only the true child of God can practise—it is a penance of the soul. From the overt act of sin even an unbeliever, a man of the world, may by force of will restrain himself. But this deeper, spiritual self-denial whereby the regenerate consciousness asserts itself against the stirrings of the lower nature and reduces the desire itself to silence and subjection, this is something which the unbeliever cannot know because only the grace of God renders it possible. There can be no renunciation of the sinful self unless there is first set up in us a purer, higher self which will plead in us the cause of God.

Looked at from this point of view, the whole Christian life, the whole process of sanctification is one continuous exercise of self-denial. It is especially the apostle Paul who has grasped most profoundly this element in our Lord's teaching and most consistently developed it. It begins in conversion, which is crucifixion of the old man, and it extends from there through the entire life in the flesh. Daily there is something to deny; daily there is something to subdue. I buffet my flesh and keep it in subjection, lest I myself should become a castaway. And what we call cross-bearing in the wider sense—the enduring of hardship and adversity—what else is it but one of the principal forms in which the grace of God leads us to exercise this denial, this suppression of our sinful selves? When God lays upon us a trial, a cross, he always adjusts it to our individual state, that it may be helpful to us in purifying ourselves of remaining sin. But here also it is not the external bearing of the cross, it is the inward taking up of it which can alone yield the gracious result God designs it to have for us. Just as our Lord Jesus did not merely bear his cross, but entered into its spirit, approved of it and made it by his obedience and submission effective for atonement, so we must take upon ourselves (or receive, as another passage says) the chastisement of the Lord. We must search ourselves to discover the purpose God has in sending it to us and then deliberately set ourselves to give effect to it.

The old divines like Calvin used to devote a separate

chapter to this subject in their discussion of sanctification. In their days of trial and persecution there were special reasons for this. But I am sure that even in our day of peace and security there is still ample need for exercising this grace. The minister of the gospel has as a rule enough trials and crosses laid upon him to discipline his soul. Let us endeavour then to obey the Lord in this. And let us not think that this is too hard a view to take of the Christian life. Denial of self, a course of action as if self did not exist, certainly does not seem a pleasant procedure. But remember that it is not the true, it is only the sinful self that we are called upon to abrogate. The law laid down by our Lord, 'Whosoever shall lose his life for my sake shall find it' applies not merely to martyrdom with its reward in the day of judgement. It applies to every cross that we daily bear. Even now, if we are his true followers, the Son of Man comes to us in the glory of his Father and with his holy angels to impart unto us and strengthen in us that higher, heavenly life which needs no repression, no denial and with which trials of the present are not worthy to be compared.

XII: The Eternal Christ[1]

Hebrews 13:8: *'Jesus Christ the same yesterday,*
and today, and for ever.'

T hese words of the epistle attach themselves in
the most direct manner to what immediately
precedes. Although there is no connecting
particle, there can be little or no doubt that the author
wishes to urge a reason for the exhortation he had just
addressed to the readers: 'Remember them that had
the rule over you, which spake unto you the word of
God; and considering the issue of their life, imitate their
faith.' The exhortation is not meant in this sense—that
the Hebrews ought to imitate their former rulers by
adhering to the same faith—for the reason that the
Christian doctrine is the same and unalterable for all
times. In that case 'Jesus Christ' would stand here for the
content of the Christian religion in the sense of the
doctrine about Christ. It is certainly far more natural to
take the phrase Jesus Christ in the usual personal sense
which it elsewhere has in the epistle and to find here
accordingly the affirmation of the unchangeableness of
the personal life and character of the Saviour.

The question then is what bearing this personal
unchangeableness of Jesus Christ has on the duty of the
readers to imitate the faith of their former rulers by

---

[1]   Preached at Princeton Theological Seminary, Princeton,
New Jersey on 11 January 1903.

considering the issue of their life. Because this is not immediately apparent, some have thought it necessary to go back to the fifth and sixth verse for making the connection where the author quotes from the Old Testament: 'For himself has said, I will in no wise fail thee, neither will I in any wise forsake thee. So that with good courage we say, the Lord is my helper; I will not fear: What shall man do unto me?' To which this verse would then add the reason: we can rely upon the Lord not failing us nor forsaking us; we can consider him our helper; we need not fear because Jesus Christ is the same yesterday and today, and for ever.

But this also is less plausible. When we look clearly at the immediately preceding words, we perceive that the connection, while not at first apparent, is nevertheless of the closest and most convincing character. The author had been speaking not merely in general of the life and faith of their former rulers and pastors, but particularly of the issue of their life. The issue of their life does not mean the effect of that life either for themselves in the future state or for others in the present world; it refers to the manner in which their life has come to an end, the manner in which at the time of death they had exhibited and triumphantly maintained their faith. In all probability, the end of life referred to had been the end of martyrdom. The rulers who had spoken unto them the word of God had sealed their faith and crowned their profession of Jesus Christ with the testimony of their blood. Now the author looks upon this triumph of martyrdom not so much as a single exhibition of faith but as the ideal culmination of the entire career of faith. The words used in the original prove that by the issue of life he does not mean the end of physical life, but the climax of spiritual life. It is not the *telos tes zoes* but the *ekbasis tes anastrophes* that he speaks of. This is the reason why a consideration of this climax of the life of their rulers in martyrdom can be held up by him before the readers as a model upon which to fashion their own faith. What the author means to say, I take it, is nothing else but this: Behold in them, whose martyrdom you have witnessed, what the highest point is to which faith can attain; therefore keep your faith to this—shape your walk in such a manner that in your own case also, when the necessity arises, it will not be a hard and strange thing to lay down your lives for the sake of Christ, but a natural thing, the issue of your whole previous Christian conversation because it has been at every point inspired by the thought of self-denial and suffering and voluntary renunciation.

There is in general a heroic strain in this conception of faith as the author writes it out, especially in the eleventh chapter of the epistle. There, martyrdom also appears as the supreme exhibition of the spirit of faith. The whole catalogue of the great exemplars of faith issues into the description of those who were tortured and would not accept their deliverance and had trials of mockings and scourgings and of bonds and imprisonment and were stoned and sawn asunder and thus had witness borne to them through their faith. The twelfth chapter also agrees with this theme, where the writer exhorts the Hebrew Christians to follow in the footsteps of this great cloud of witnesses, reminds them that they have not yet resisted unto blood and urges upon them as the fundamental grace of which they stood in need, the exercise of patience in the midst of suffering.

Now the motive for the cultivation of such heroic

GRACE AND GLORY

faith is to produce a faith that had thoroughly familiar-
ized itself with the idea of hardship and could face the
crisis of martyrdom as the natural issue of its own course
without shrinking. It is as a help for the cultivation of
such faith that the author tells his readers: 'Jesus Christ is
the same yesterday and today, and for ever.' This means,
first of all, the same grace that sustained those who
preached unto you the Word of God so that not only
resignedly but joyfully and triumphantly they laid down
their lives—the same grace stands at your disposal. If, as
some modern writers of name think, the epistle was
written to a company of Christians in the city of Rome,
there might be a reference in this to the martyrdom of
Paul and possibly of Peter (at least if the statement 'who
spake unto you the word of God' is not understood of
the first preaching of the gospel). In that case, the
reminder would come with peculiar force and richness
of association since it would mean in substance: remember that the Christ in whose strength the great apostolic
leaders fought their battle of faith and gained their
crown is still the same Christ today, who can nerve you
also to an equally glorious and triumphant fortitude in
your conflict with the world.

But be that as it may, even though those who had
had the rule over them were less illustrious leaders of
the church than Peter and Paul; at any rate the appeal to
the unchangeableness of Christ has great force in this
connection. And to us it gives an insight into the spiritual condition of the Hebrew Christians to which the
letter addresses itself. Evidently after the first transport
of enthusiasm in the earliest days of the Christian
profession of these believers, there had followed a
period of reaction in which their zeal had begun to

decrease, their courage had begun to wane, their hope had become drained, and in which they had lost the strength of faith to maintain themselves on the same high plane they had lived on at the beginning. All through the epistle we can feel that this was the situation which filled the writer with solicitude because he discerned in it not merely the symptoms of a deplorable retrogression in Christian attainment, but even more because he perceived in it the forebodings of apostasy. It was true then as it is now that, strictly speaking, there can be no standing still in the spiritual life; for precisely because it is life—a growing, developing thing— progress is of its very essence. The suspension of progress means that there is something wrong, that a decline has set in which, if not arrested, must lead to a fatal issue. Such a thing as a stationary Christian in reality does not exist. It is only the outside appearance of the Christian life that may seem stationary—within the forces and processes are always working either in one direction or in the other.

How appropriate, then, it was for the author to unroll before them in their state of languor and depression not merely the annals of Old Testament history in which faith shines in its full glory; not just to hold up before them the example of their former leaders or their own noble past, but above all to point them to Jesus Christ, the same yesterday and today and for ever, through faith in whom their Christian life might be lifted above all danger of fluctuation. By laying hold of the unchanging Christ they could bring back into their wavering souls the same all-conquering strength and courage which had been theirs before. And perhaps there was one specific element in their spiritual discouragement which made such a reference to the unchangeableness of Christ even more pertinent than has been indicated. In all probability, they felt keenly the loss of those leaders who had formerly stood between them and the world as living examples of the Christian ideal and had communicated to them something of their own faith so as to draw them upward to the same height of courage and joy in believing. But now these fathers in Christ were gone and they were thrown back upon their own spiritual resources. Distrust of themselves had taken hold of them and for the moment they did not know whither to turn for that guidance and inspiration on which they had become so dependent. For this reason also the writer reminds them that although men may come and go; while the human supports on which the Christian's faith has sometimes to lean are from the nature of the case transitory; nevertheless Jesus Christ goes with his church through all the changes and vicissitudes of time, the same yesterday, today and for ever. He is always accessible, under every condition reliable and therefore the one proper object of faith, the only safe source of confidence because in him alone is that eternal certainty which faith needs to rest upon if it is to be faith at all.

This is a truth which we ourselves may well lay to heart, especially at the present time in the history of the church. It is easy in our days to come to feel as if the common people of God were more than ever left without great leaders such as former generations have known, exceptional men of God, who by their extraordinary power of faith and by the mighty utterances of their word rallied around them the army of believers, inspired them with ever new courage and thus prevented the enemy from gaining advantage over them. But if it does not please God to raise up such men in his church for the present or if it pleases him in his wisdom to take them from us, we should not allow ourselves to be tempted by this to unbelief and despondency. We should remember the truth of which the author here reminds his readers—that Jesus Christ is the same yesterday and today and forever; that even when the plain people of God seem most destitute of leadership, the greatest leader is always there, that not for a moment does he leave the helm or abandon either a single believer or the church as a whole to the waves of the world. Perhaps this will explain to us why the writer has placed the two propositions together without a connecting particle. First: 'Remember them that had the rule over you . . . and imitate their faith.' And then: 'Jesus Christ is the same yesterday and today, and forever.' The proper frame of mind is at the same time to honour and appreciate all the gifts and graces which God has bestowed upon eminent men for the service of the church, to honour them especially by imitating them, and yet to go behind all this and cast the anchor of our faith for the future of God's kingdom in the world in Jesus Christ himself: remember the men of the past, but trust in him alone who has the power of an endless life and dwells in an everlasting present.

This, then, seems to be the primary meaning of the words as determined from the connection. But I would not want you to forget that these words have behind them the whole peculiar teaching of the epistle in regard to the person and work of Christ. And it is only because the author assumes his readers have assimilated the gist of this teaching that he expects his appeal to come with convincing force to them. They would understand that Jesus Christ must indeed be the same yesterday and today and forever because they remembered who Jesus Christ was and in what terms he had been described to them in almost every sentence of the epistle. He was the Son of God, the effulgence of the Father's glory, the very image of his substance. To him the author had applied the words of Psalm 102: 'Thou, Lord, in the beginning hast laid the foundation of the earth, and the heavens are the work of thy hands: they shall perish; but thou remainest. And they all shall wax old as doth a garment, and as a mantle shalt thou roll them up. But thou art the same and thy years shall not fail' (26, 27). To him, therefore, belongs the attribute of unchangeableness that is inherent in the conception of divinity itself. Indeed the very form of the words—the same, yesterday and today and forever— reminds us most vividly of the sublime description which the New Testament Apocalypse gives of God himself as the one that is and that was and that is to come, who fills with his being all the possible categories of time because he is eternal; and also it reminds us of that other no less sublime description which we find in the same book of both God and Christ himself as the Alpha and Omega, the first and the last, the beginning and the end. Christ belongs throughout the epistle to the heavenly world in which everything bears the character of the unchangeable, the abiding. In this respect, the teaching of the epistle stands nearest to our Lord's own teaching concerning himself in the fourth Gospel where the emphasis is also continually thrown on this— that Jesus is from above and not from beneath, and that consequently he is free from all the relativities, imperfections and vicissitudes that necessarily belong to everything earthly. Christ is the truth, the reality of God incarnate, and therefore we can sustain to him the same religious relationship, address to him the same religious trust that we sustain and address to God himself.

Now this is not a mere speculation of the epistle, just as little as it is a mere speculation in the Johannine teaching of our Lord. For we must observe that the whole beautiful representation which the author gives of the saving work of Christ as both Revealer and as High-Priest is the direct outcome of this conception of Christ as a divine, eternal person. If you take this away, you take away the foundation of everything that is taught concerning Christ as the Saviour, not merely because it would be impossible for us to approach him in a religious spirit were he divested of these attributes, but even more so because it would be impossible for him to approach us, encompass us, enlighten us, atone for us and bring us back to God if he was not rooted with his personal life in the soil of divinity and eternity. There is nothing in the New Testament which teaches so emphatically the absolute indispensableness of the divine nature of Christ for the work of redemption as the Epistle to the Hebrews. He is the climax of all prophecy because he is the Son who does not speak the truth for a small portion or in a limited manner as it came to the fathers through the prophets, but who speaks it as the echo of the voice of God himself and therefore speaks it to all ages so that we may say not only of himself but also of his speech—it is the same yesterday and today and for ever. It is the same in authority, the same in freshness, the same in vital power as when it first resounded from the background of eternity.

And the same is similarly literally true of his priestly work. In that also we recognize the impress of what he is. The whole epistle is full of this thought. It is not necessary to state more than the main lines along which its profound and splendid exposition of Christ's priest-hood moves. The central theme from which the author starts and to which he returns is: he is a priest forever after the order of Melchizedek. And what this means is shown us in the type. When Melchizedek appears in Scripture as a priest who derives nothing from ancestors or predecessors in office, but everything from his own royal personality, it is only because he has been by inspi-ration made in this respect like the Son of God, so that he might prefigure the Son of God. Christ draws the qualification for his priesthood from his divine nature as well as from his human nature because it can be said of him that he is without beginning of days and end of life; therefore he remains a priest forever. He has an unchangeable priesthood because the power of an end-less life is in him. He transcends and abrogates by his ministry the Levitical priesthood because in his, the undying person, he has forever assumed all its functions and prerogatives in an infinitely higher sense. Through the eternal Spirit, he offered himself without blemish to God and therefore he has perfected forever by one sacrifice all those who are sanctified.

Finally, his eternity and priesthood are seen most closely united in this—that according to our epistle for the main part the discharge of his priestly functions takes place in heaven, where he ministers in his glorified state. The two are so inseparable that the author simply says: 'If he were on earth, he would not be a priest at all.' But being in heaven, he is the one priest, and his priestly state partakes of the unchangeability which is the supreme law of that world. He is a priest upon his throne (to use an Old Testament phrase) and his throne, as we have seen, is everlasting since it stands at the right hand of the throne of God himself. Even when the priestly work in the specific sense of the application of his redemption shall have ceased, when it will no longer be necessary for him to make intercession or plead his merit for us because all sin and all consequences of sin shall have been removed—even then he will remain the everlasting High Priest of humanity offering up to God the united adoration and praise of the redeemed race of which he is the Head.

It is necessary to keep this in mind because we sometimes emphasize the other side too much. Undoubtedly his earthly experience as a weak, limited, suffering man was necessary to qualify him for his office. Without it he could not have the experimental knowledge of our temptations and the sympathy, the assurance of which is so precious and consoling to us in our times of trial and affliction. But let us not forget that it lay far from the author's thought to make this sympathy work for us merely in a subjective way, just as we say that the sympathy of a person helps us though he can do nothing more for us than express to us a fellow-feeling with our infirmities. No—the sympathy of Christ works for us with all the endless resources that his divine nature and his glorious humanity put at its disposal. It is the sympathy of one who is the same yesterday and today and for ever; of one who remembers, as only absolutely perfect human nature can remember, what he himself passed through while on earth, when he offered prayers and supplication with strong crying and tears. It is the sympathy of one with whom to feel for us and to act upon us is one and the same thing. It is the sympathy of one who has access at every moment to every part of any distressing or perplexing situation in which any believer may find himself as well as to every recess of our heart, to the most secret fears and the most silent griefs which we can share with nobody else. And then it is the sympathy of one who can never grow weary of our complaints because in him there is an inexhaustible store of pity which is adequate for the consolation of ages of believers, which flows as freely now for you and me as it flowed in the day of the Hebrew Christians, for the simple reason that Jesus Christ is the same yesterday and today and for ever, unchangeable in this as in everything else. It is only by thus uniting the divine and the human, the temporal and the eternal aspect of Christ's activity for us that we can draw from them that rich profit and consolation which the reading of this wonderful epistle is intended to supply to us.

XIII: The Spiritual Resurrection of Believers[1]

Ephesians 2:4-5: *'But God, who is rich in mercy,
for his great love wherewith he loved us, even when we
were dead in sins, hath quickened us together with
Christ (by grace ye are saved).'*

I n the thirty-seventh chapter of his prophecy, Ezekiel
describes for us how the hand of the Lord was upon
him, and how he was led out in the Spirit and set
down in the middle of a valley full of bones. There
lay parts of human skeletons spread over the ground in
such great numbers that the prophet had to walk around
them in order to view them all. Then came the voice
of the Lord with the question: 'Son of man, can these
bones live?' Ezekiel answered: 'Lord God, you know,' as
if to say, 'For men this is impossible; if it is to come to
pass, you, the Lord God, must do it.' And in confirma-
tion of this answer, he received the task of prophesying
to those dry bones: 'You dry bones! hear the word of
the LORD. Thus says the Lord God: "Behold, I shall
cause breath to enter you, and you shall become alive."'

---

[1]   (A translation of *De Geestelijke Opstanding der
Geloovongen. Leerrede Over Ephese 2:4-5*, Grand Rapids:
J.C. Melis, Drukker, n.d.).

The prophet did as he was commanded and, as if the bones had understood his words, there was noise and commotion among them. At first it seemed impossible to detect any kind of order in the agitated mass, but before long they drew near to each other, bone to bone. What had just been scattered about in pieces now became articulated human skeletons. Look! The dry bones were clothed with flesh, and the prophet saw how delicate tendons intertwined among these bones and a pale skin was laid upon them so that the hideous skeletons changed into well-formed bodies.

Still, with that the prophecy was not yet fulfilled because there was no spirit in those bodies. Therefore, the command of the Lord again came to Ezekiel: 'Prophesy to the spirit, prophesy, son of man! Say to the spirit, "Oh spirit! come from the four winds, and breathe into these dead that they may become alive."' Hardly had this taken place than a mighty rustling was heard among those pale dead, the breath of life flowed over their lips, warm blood coloured their cold cheeks red, dull eyes began to sparkle with the light of life, they stretched out their arms, and rose up on their feet a well-prepared people that God had fashioned for himself out of dry bones through his mighty power.

All this was a symbolic prophecy of the national recreation of God's covenant people, who mourned in exile. Those bones were the entire house of Israel. The Lord would open their graves, raise them up, and bring them back to their land. And it is a strikingly similar image, of the resurrection of the spiritual Israel out of the graves of its sin and impurity, which we wish to explore, according to the word of the apostle in Ephesians 2:4-5: 'But God, who is rich in mercy, through his great love with which he loved us, even when we were dead through transgressions, has made us alive together with Christ, (by grace you have been saved).' It is, as was just observed, 'the spiritual resurrection of believers' which demands our attention. We will endeavour to consider it under the following points: (1) What it flows from; (2) What it presupposes; (3) How it is accomplished; (4) What it obliges us to.

1. *What Does the Spiritual Resurrection of Believers Flow From?*

According to our text, it is God's mercy and love out of which salvation is born. These two are the springs out of which it wells up, and therefore its entire character must correspond to this source. What springs from the bowels of God's mercy and love must in its entire course overflow with love and mercy. What comes from God, without our being able to prepare for or take away from it in any way, cannot in its duration be dependent on us but is, like God himself, unchangeable and eternally faithful; 'I the Lord do not change, therefore, O children of Jacob, you are not consumed.'

It is to a *rich* mercy and a *great* love that Paul points the Ephesians, as the source of their resurrection. And that is so as the latter is the foundation for the former. God was rich in mercy through his great love. Not until we rightly understand this will there be opened to us something of the riches that brought these glorious words of thanksgiving to the lips of the apostle.

What then is the situation? Imagine for a moment that the text read: 'God, who is rich in mercy, has made us alive together with Christ,' and that the words, 'through his great love with which he loved us' were omitted. What a different outlook on the matter would immediately result! It would then say: God saw us in the misery of our sins and was moved in mercy to save us in Christ. Thus the foundation of our salvation would be nothing but a natural feeling of pity in God because of the wretchedness of his creatures.

To be sure, that alone would already be inexpressibly much. When the holy God has dealings with sinful creatures such that he is moved to pity and mercy towards them, that is such a miracle of divine grace that it constrains us to kneel in adoration before him who accomplishes it.

But the great love leaves the rich mercy far behind and is at once distinguished from it. That can be easily grasped. Suppose yourself to be mortally ill without nursing care and someone comes who, out of pure mercy and moved by your pitiable state, cares for you. What do you think, would the hand of that person make your bed as gently as the hand that a loving father or mother or spouse would extend to you? Well then, the situation in our text is no different. It makes a great difference whether a redeemed person must say: God saw me in my misery and therefore he said to me, 'live', or whether, along with that, he may voice the glorious thought: God has loved me with an everlasting love, *therefore* he has drawn me with cords of loving kindness.

This great difference, which we immediately sense, may be given a satisfactory explanation. In order to grasp the proper relationship in which mercy and love appear here, we will look briefly at the respects in which they are different.

(i) Love has a more noble origin, provided it is born

of the one who loves. Mercy is different. There the reason why one shows mercy comes from outside, prompted by the wretched situation of the object. Where there is no misery, there is no place for mercy, and as soon as the distress has subsided your compassion for the sufferer ends. Dependent on external circumstances and temporary in origin and duration, mercy cannot be compared with love. What if we had to think that it were only our sins which had moved God to save us? Oh no! It was love, which was not aroused by us but was grounded from eternity in the depth of divine being, whose length, breadth, depth and height cannot be measured by our finite comprehension but by the infinite comprehension of God. It never ends, even as it never had a beginning.

Moreover, a distinction has to be made between divine and human love. The latter loves because it beholds and admires something beautiful and lovable in its object. Not so with God. He loved his own before the mountains came to be, before the earth and the world were brought forth. It was not at all that he knew, by virtue of his eternal foreknowledge, that they would be lovable. Oh no! All that they would be in this respect, he himself had decided to make them. He saw them dead in their sins and crimes, without form or glory, covered with their own blood. This is the great mystery that no man can solve—how God could love sinners, without there being anything in them worthy of his love. Mysterious, eternal love of God, you are beyond comprehension!

(ii) Love has a nobler nature. It is the firstborn of all God's virtues. 'He who does not love, does not know

God, for God is love,' testifies the apostle John. God's being consists of love, and therefore when it is said that he loved those who were his in Christ Jesus, that means that his whole being expressed itself in that love and carried over to its objects. It was not a part of his affection that he bestowed upon these who were loved from eternity, but the fulness of his own blessed being. He did not purpose for them a gift located outside of himself, but his love was so great and rich that it was satisfied with nothing less than giving itself: God gave himself in Christ Jesus, his only begotten Son, who is the reflection of his glory and the express image of his substance. Precisely because in this deed God gave himself for sinners, the Scriptures call this the greatest revelation of God's love, which includes all others. 'Greater love has no man than this, that he lay down his life for his friends,' testifies the Saviour. And the apostle asks: 'He who did not spare his own Son, but gave him up for us all, how will he not also with him give us all things?'

(iii) The distinction is seen in the object to which both reach out. Mercy is a common emotion, inherent in our nature, but love is something personal, the affection of a person for a person. Precisely this constitutes the richness of the faith of God's children, that every one of them can say with Paul: 'He loved *me*, and gave himself for *me*.' It is a discriminating love, which, although it encompasses the whole church, still has a personal relation to each one and knows every one of its own by name. The Scriptures compare it to the love of a man for his wife, a bridegroom for his bride. It follows its objects their whole life through with a care that protects, leads and blesses. It sets apart a Paul from the womb for his worldwide task, but the tears of even the least among God's children are numbered in its bottle, and none of them is forgotten by God. Its greatness condescends to the smallest, who through such exertions is made great. The blood of his own is precious in God's sight. So unique and personal is this relationship between him and those he loves that he himself declares: the one who touches them, touches the apple of my eye. In all their oppression he is oppressed, through his love and through his grace he delivers them; he takes them up and carries them, now as in days of old.

From these observations the meaning of our text becomes clear. Before all else, the apostle intends to say that love precedes mercy in order. In the second place, because that love was so great, mercy became so rich. *Through* his great love, literally, *for the sake of it*, God was so rich, so wonderfully merciful. That love desired to express itself and did so in a wealth of mercies. In spite of their unsightly form and their impurity, this love still declares: 'They are my people, children, whose lineage will not prove false. Thus he has become a Saviour for them.' For God, too, has a love that desires to work. Where he creates children for the glory of his great name and pours out on those children his tender mercies, there is a love that is impelled, a love that must disclose more and more of itself. Therefore it is absurd to think that he could let them go and consider them sufficiently blessed, before he had communicated to them all the riches found in his divine fulness, before he had raised them as high as they could go and endowed their being with that perfection of which it was capable.

For although he works all things according to his will, what is divine in that will is that the highest object of his glorious good pleasure is at the same time the greatest good of his children.

2. *What Does this Spiritual Resurrection Presuppose?*

This mercy, enriched and made tender by God's love, had an ample area in which to display itself. It found its objects, according to our text, 'dead in transgressions', that is to say, in the most wretched condition that one could imagine. And, what is most remarkable of all, this condition, however miserable in itself, was not such that, seen from a human point of view, it appeared capable of evoking mercy. Only when we clearly comprehend this will we in some measure have plumbed the deep meaning of Paul's words. To that end, we must consider what this spiritual resurrection presupposes, in other words, what the expression 'dead in transgressions' means.

On the surface it seems easy to say what 'death' is. 'It is the opposite of "life"', one will immediately answer. But here lies the difficulty. The greatest wise men in this world have never been able to explain what life is and how it originates, and therefore have had difficulty in clarifying the opposite.

Scripture, however, gives us an unambiguous answer to the question of what 'death' is, and it does so by showing repeatedly in the clearest light what it would have us to understand by 'life'. In the first place, according to Scripture, life is an attribute of God. He alone has true life in and of himself. In the second place, Scripture teaches that all creaturely life is derived from God and is nourished only in fellowship with him. So, at the beginning of all things, after the first creation, darkness covered the abyss and the earth was desolate and empty, a dead, formless mass. But as soon as the Spirit of God brooded, hovering over the waters, there was light and movement, the mass began to seethe and ferment, life originated in it by its contact with God. Again, when the Lord God had formed man out of the dust of the earth, he lay there like a dead man, lifeless and cold, until God blew into his nostrils the breath of life; thus man became a living being. From this it is plain enough that Scripture makes all life dependent on fellowship with God. Conversely, then, death can be defined as *being cut off from the source of life*. When we speak of temporal, spiritual and eternal death, repeatedly this thought lies at the foundation. In temporal death it is the body that is cut off from the source of its life, that is, the soul, and it slowly dissolves; there is no longer a living, animating principle that keeps it together; it returns to dust, from which it was taken. It is no different with the soul. In spiritual death it is cut off from the fountainhead of its life, the living God, and, accordingly, it dies, is completely torn from its context, loses its unity, perishes. Eternal death is the total separation of both body and soul, when these will one day be reunited, from the fellowship of God. In the outermost darkness, where no ray of divine light any longer penetrates, this alienation from God reaches its zenith and its most dreadful revelation.

From this it is immediately clear to us why Paul announces to the Ephesians that they were dead '*in* their transgressions'. Sin is nothing other than renouncing, abandoning God's fellowship, turning away from him and choosing one's own way. If, then, there is life only in this fellowship, for those who abandon it death must enter immediately. 'The mind of the flesh is death.' And so it came to pass. As soon as Adam ate, that is to say, as soon as he severed the thread of conformity to God's law and the blessed fellowship with his Creator, in that same moment he died the death.

We must, however, go a step further and examine not only the cause of death but also its manifestations. Here again what we see happening in every temporal death can provide us with a starting point. The first thing that strikes us in a dead person is that he lies there stiff and motionless. That same body that was formerly animated and suffused by the soul and in its most delicate fibres and nerves willingly lent itself as a tool to the soul, is now rigid and immobile, cold as a piece of marble. Not only has the activity of the soul upon the body ceased, but the body itself has lost the ability to obey that influence. It no longer receives impulses from the soul and shows no indication of being susceptible to them. A power is certainly still at work in such a body, but no other power than that which works in all matter, the natural power that leads to dissolution.

We also find all these characteristics in spiritual death. Here the same thing happens to the soul that we just saw taking place with the body. As soon as God takes away his Holy Spirit and withdraws his fellowship, the soul becomes insensible and hardened, spiritual numbness overpowers it. Where life is present, you will notice how it courses through all parts of the body: it beats in the heart, throbs in the pulse, hovers in the breath, gleams in the eye, and makes itself known by numberless marks. All this is missing in a dead person. Likewise, in a spiritually dead person one searches in vain for the heart throb of faith, the pulse beat of prayer, the breath of love, the look of sympathy for any expression of a hidden, inward life. The person dead in transgressions is a person, just as a dead body is a body, and yet, when you yourself possess spiritual life, you will feel the distance between yourself and that person, in the same way as living persons naturally recoil from the dead. You miss the image of God in their features, just as the image of the soul is missing in the face of the deceased. And just as death often leaves its stamp on the pallid countenance in misshapen and distorted lines, so the spiritual death of sin puts its horrible marks upon the destroyed soul.

But not only is the spiritually dead person incapable of moving and developing any power of himself, receptivity to impressions from the outside is also lacking. All life has these two sides: it makes impressions and receives impressions, and in doing so develops and grows. Both of these are lacking in the sinner in his natural state. He does not seek God, and when God comes to seek him, he does not answer, gives no signs of life, and remains insensible. When the Word of God, from which all spiritual life draws its sustenance, is brought into contact with him, his eye does not see it, his ear does not hear it, his heart does not give assent to it, it goes by him like an idle sound. 'The natural man does not comprehend the things of the Spirit of God, for they are foolishness to him, and he cannot understand them, because they are spiritually discerned.'

But there is more than this. In a dead body the powers by nature inherent in all matter are at work, they decompose and dissolve it. They were already present earlier, but were countered and made harmless by

GRACE AND GLORY

another, higher power. The life-power of the soul did not allow it to perish. However, as soon as that life-power receded, those natural forces were given free play, immediately began their work, and did not rest until the body was turned to dust. It is no different with a sinful man. The love of the world and selfishness work within him. As long as love and God's fellowship lived in him, they controlled all lower forces and led them in the right direction so that they could not harm him. But look! As soon as the person was cut off from God, and the life-power from God no longer exercised control in his soul, in that same moment the love of the world and selfishness began their horrible work, ruined the soul, and brought it unavoidably into destruction. It is impossible that a man who is 'dead in transgressions' should remain what he was. One would expect with just as much right that a dead body should remain as it was. So, if anything is clear, it is that sin makes man more and more abominable, and finally must be so displayed that all turn away with abhorrence and loathing. Although this may be less evident in some than in others, the principle of death is present in all and that principle, if it continues its work, can lead to nothing but open enmity against the Almighty.

Only when viewed in this light is full justice done to the expression of the apostle 'even when we were dead in transgressions'. *Even then still* he has made us alive. That can only be explained by God's great love. Were our spiritual death nothing more than a pitiable illness, the situation would be easily understandable. Were it no more than cold indifference, even then it would be thinkable. But now that it has developed into direct, straightforward enmity towards God, there is no alternative to solving this mystery of God's divine mercy than to assume that an eternal, mysterious love was at work behind it, was its foundation, and was expressed in it.

Imagine for a moment that you seek the good of someone with whom you do not have a relationship, that you do everything in your power to advance his welfare; you sacrifice yourself for him. But look! Instead of thankfully acknowledging that, he remains indifferent, begins to hate you, and ends up by cursing you. What do you think? Would the miserable condition of such a person be likely to evoke your mercy?

But now, imagine for a moment that all the circumstances just mentioned are the same, except that this time the scoundrel is not a stranger but your own son. Could you stop loving him because he hates you? Could you cease praying for him because he curses you? Could you restrain the urgings of your fatherly mercy because he has seared his conscience? I think not! You will say: 'He is still my son, whom I have carried in my arms.' The more such a rogue causes you shame and heartbreak, all the more will you watch, moved by deep pity for him, how he wilfully throws himself into ruin.

Where now is the distinction? Why can you not show mercy to a stranger who behaves like this but can towards your own child, although he may be ten times more vile than the stranger? The answer is simple: in the first case, no love drove you to pity; in the second, a great love had to be expressed in rich mercy.

Our case is no different. In themselves sinners are not objects of mercy but vessels of wrath. Sin is enmity and enmity as such does not fall within the scope of pity. But from eternity God had loved those sinners, those enemies, those spiritually dead, with a fatherly love.

This love was the foundation of everything and was before everything. It is useless to ask after its origin. It came from the inscrutable being of God and embraced the objects of its free choice even before they had existence. It determined to make them in such a way as to reflect that love. And look what happened! Those children fell, sank into sin and death. Instead of sons they became devils. Love was answered with hate. Nevertheless—and here lies the precious core of our text—all this was not able to extinguish that love, because it is impossible to tear the son from the heart of the father. On the contrary, it now came to light clearly that it was *love* and not just kindness. Where the latter would have stopped it went further and emerged triumphant. It did not love the righteous and virtuous, but the godless. In this 'God demonstrates his love toward us, in that, while we were still sinners, Christ died for us.' This is the deepest reason why Paul knows to ascribe to no other cause than a great, divine love the fact that those who lay in the midst of sin and death and were enemies of God were nevertheless endowed with the greatest benefits that could befall them, namely that God, according to his rich mercy, made them alive together with Christ, the Lord.

3. *How is the Spiritual Resurrection of Believers Accomplished?*

If we have clearly understood all this, then it is also immediately evident that only a divine creation, a new birth is capable of changing the sinner; for he is dead. This is no metaphor, but a reality. A dead person is no more insensitive and motionless in the natural domain than a sinner is in the spiritual sense. Where death has entered, all human help and advice ceases. Go to a dead person and see whether in a natural way you can call him back to life; use all available means. In fact, if necessary, bring back warmth to the departed one, restore breathing, cause blood to flow through the veins—all that will do you no good; the attempts of all the doctors combined are not enough to restore life to one single dead person.

But suppose that Christ the Lord comes, and by a word of power recreates the departed principle of life in that dead person. Then you can use these same means and the outcome will be that the dead will live again, and before long he will show by signs of life that his soul has returned.

In the spiritual sphere it is just the same. Here the dead person is the sinner. Here at the same time is the means God has given us to use: the Word of God—a brightly shining light, a life-nourishing power. But it is impossible for the spiritually dead person to open his eyes to see that light and to open his mouth in order to ingest that nourishment, unless a higher power has caused him to awake from the slumber of unrighteousness.

But if in the inmost being of such a person God the Holy Spirit causes his irresistible call to be heard: 'Wake up, O sleeper, rise from the dead, and Christ will shine on you,' then the blind eyes are immediately opened, the deaf ears unstopped, and the hardened heart begins, with a lively interest, to seek after God and his fellowship. When the dry bones hear the Word of the Lord, and the Spirit blows among them there is noise and movement, they approach each other, bone to its bone; they receive sinews and flesh, a skin to cover them and a spirit within them, and a human form appears.

Such a creative deed, therefore, is necessary. A question, however, arises: Is this possible? Can God justly bestow this benefit on a sinner, dead in transgressions, by creating a new life in him?

The answer to this must be a decisive 'no', God cannot do such a thing. It is true that his love is great and his mercy rich, but his justice is inviolable. It requires that the sinner be punished and that only the one who fulfils the demand of the law be rewarded. Justice draws its rigorous line without making distinctions between persons; on the left it assigns eternal death to the transgressor of the law and on the right eternal life to the keeper of the law.

If a person dead in transgressions is to be raised up, two conditions must be met. First, he must be relieved of the burden of his guilt which rests on him because of his sins. He must bear the threatened punishment and empty to its dregs the cup of God's holy displeasure. As long as this does not happen, despite God's great love and rich mercy, there can be no talk of God showing favour to the sinner.

But suppose that the punishment has been borne, the cup emptied—even that by itself is not enough. Second, the justice of the law must be fulfilled, that is to say, it must be perfectly obeyed and observed. Only to the one who does this can God restore life and impart his Holy Spirit.

To understand this clearly, let us imagine a criminal who must bear the punishment of imprisonment designated by the law. When he is released after serving his sentence, the law has been satisfied. But is the criminal's honour restored, have his civil rights been regained, can he count on all the privileges granted to someone who keeps the law without punishment? Of course not. Although the law cannot further require penal satisfaction from him, for the most part and all too often he finds himself without civil rights and honour, disgraced and an outcast in the midst of society.

Exactly the same justice applies in the kingdom of God. Assume that the sinner is able himself to bear the punishment of his transgression, by bearing it completely so that nothing remains to be borne. This is not the case, but assume it for a moment. What then would follow? Would this be the end of the matter for the sinner? God's wrath would be removed, but his favour would not be regained. The person would still be without citizenship and rights in God's kingdom, he would still remain a beggar who has no claim to anything. The unyielding law, with its 'Do this and you shall live' would still stand—with its accusation that it has not been fulfilled and its strict prohibition against giving life to the sinner.

You can immediately see where the great difficulty lies here. The law must be satisfied, because apart from keeping it there is no life. As far as we know, God does not grant eternal life to either angels or men on any other condition than perfect keeping of the law. But man cannot keep the law, he is dead in transgressions, spiritually impotent. If he is ever again to attain to keeping the law, it must be preceded by a creative act of God, by an infusion of life from God, whereby he is again put in a position to live according to the commandments of God.

Thus, two things are firmly established:

(i) God cannot make man alive from his spiritual

death in sin, unless he has first fulfilled the law.

(ii) As long as God has not made man alive, he cannot fulfil the law.

This crying contradiction demonstrates how hopeless the situation with man was. There was no solution in sight and it seemed there was nothing left for God to do but to abandon man to his miserable fate. And, indeed, if help would have had to come from man's side, it would not have appeared, not even in an eternity!

But through his great love God knew how to find a solution. He solved the riddle in a way that caused the angels to stare in wonder and the congregation on earth, in turn, to venture in joyful rapture before the heavenly authorities and powers. When the eye of God's love could find no resting place in all of sinful humanity, then it rested upon Christ Jesus, his only begotten Son, and saw in him the possibility of unravelling the sad riddle.

The Lord could not make us alive. We had forfeited the right to be made alive. There was no one who was worthy to be made alive—unless the Son of God became man, and by becoming such, restored the possibility that man be made alive and be saved. To make us alive *with Christ*—that was the answer that God's great love gave to the question raised by his mercy; otherwise there was no means by which sinners could be rescued from eternal destruction.

The two conditions just discussed were present in Christ. He was able to wipe out the debt, and he did. At the same time, because he was not dead in transgressions, by his perfect keeping of the law he acquired the right to eternal life. *Him* God could raise up by his sublime power and bring back in immortality. And with that the great work was accomplished in principle. Certainly there was only one point of departure found for the spiritual resurrection, but that point lay in the Mediator Christ Jesus. With Christ it is therefore possible for God to raise us up also. He took upon himself the curse and the demands of the law, we reap the fruits together with him. In his resurrection from the dead ours is given in fact and guaranteed by right. That new life, which he received as the reward for his obedience, passes over from him by the working of his Spirit to all that belong to him, so that they, awakened from the sleep of sin, let Christ shine on them, say 'Amen' with a living faith to all God's words of life, hunger and thirst after the righteousness of life, and end by praising God's rich mercy which, because of his great love, even when they were dead in their transgressions, made them alive with Christ the Lord.

4. *What Does the Spiritual Resurrection of Believers Oblige Us To Do?*

Finally, we must come to the recognition that nothing but God's love has accomplished this. In his final words the apostle draws the conclusion of our text and it is very simple: 'By grace you have been saved.'

The origin of this spiritual resurrection was an eternal, mysterious love, welling up from God's being. The objects to which it was applied were the spiritually dead, in whom not even the slightest spark of life glowed in the ashes. Its point of departure could not even be found in man; God had to make us alive with Christ, since he could not make us alive in ourselves.

Where then is boasting? It is excluded! All who with Paul's eye survey the plan of redemption from its ultimate origins in God's eternal choice to its final unfolding in a glorified soul, will not be able to do anything other than testify with Paul: 'Free grace has saved me; for me Christ Jesus has become wisdom from God, righteousness, sanctification and complete redemption.'

This spiritual resurrection compels such humble acknowledgement. God does not grant us his work of grace so that we should glory in it as our own. Therefore he so arranged it that it would manifestly be his work from beginning to end, a divine work, and he desires to be glorified in it.

Here lies the deepest purpose that God had in raising us *with* Christ. It was not merely impossible for it to be otherwise, but also magnificent and worthy of God that it took place in this manner. Just because it happened this way every possibility is cut off for the believer to nurture in his heart the unholy thought that there was still something of his own work involved.

That your guilt is atoned for in Christ is easy to see. This fact is so clear that no one who is truly Christian dares or is able to deny it. The danger, then, of self-righteousness creeping in does not lie here. It is, however, to be sought on that other side. How easy, how natural, how seemingly innocent, how tempting it is for you to suppose that, after your guilt is atoned for in Christ, you then have life of yourself; that, where your Surety has accomplished the first half by bearing your affliction, you can achieve the second half in your own power by earning eternal life for yourself.

This, in fact, is what Rome teaches us, and with such teaching it wrests the crown from God's work of grace. But God knew what sort of creatures we were, and that is why he has barred the way to this terrible error for everyone who truly fears him, by not making us alive in ourselves but by making us alive in Christ. First Christ, then, by his Spirit, we out of and with him.

As long as a believer fastens his eyes of faith on Christ Jesus, as long as he holds fast to the Mediator, he can do nothing else but testify with Paul: 'By grace I have been saved,' and, 'It was God's gift.' By that faith life flows from Christ to the believer. He not only knows that but feels it. 'Outside of Jesus there is no life,' his soul says to him. Or it repeats after Paul: 'I live, yet no longer I, but Christ lives in me, and the life which I now live in the flesh I live by faith in the Son of God, who loved me and gave himself for me.'

The unavoidable conclusion is that this life was in Christ before it came to us, that, consequently, it was not earned by us but acquired by him. He possessed it, long before we had performed any works; it was not manifested in us until we, by faith, came into contact with him, the living Christ. Thus our faith becomes an unimpeachable witness which, with every drink we take from the cup of God's redemption, cries out: 'By grace you have been saved!' So it becomes an ever-flowing stream, whose incessantly rushing waters do not cease mentioning: 'Not of yourselves, it is God's gift!'

Everyone who understands this language bows in humility in order to repeat it from the depths of his soul and thus respond to the glorious purpose of God, who created him as his creature in Christ Jesus, for good works, so that he might show in the ages to come the riches of his grace, through his kindness toward them in Christ Jesus.

And what does this language say to you? Does it appear to you as the narrow-minded expression of a dead and deadening doctrine, or as the most intimate core of the precious truth, that man is saved by pure grace, without consideration of anything in him? Seen in this light, does not the truth about which Paul boasted have another complexion than that to which we are interminably pointed, namely that it makes the door of salvation so narrow that only a few are able to enter, that it limits the free gospel and robs his preaching of power?

Where, then, has the apostle ended with his teaching? In an anxious concern as to how far he dared to go with the gospel of Christ? Oh no! The opposite was the case: he ended in glorious praise of the matchless, unsearchable love of God, whose kingdom is in all and over all, and with that glorious message he went from Antioch to Rome, and, wherever he went, his gospel was not in words but in power.

And with that we shall have to end. God's purpose with us in presenting this teaching in his Word has never been that we should sit down and attempt, by brooding, to find out whether we, too, are numbered among those who from eternity are loved in Christ Jesus. That is a hopeless task! It is like arithmetic without numbers. God has not put any data at our disposal by which we can determine the outcome as either 'yes' or 'no'. Such an approach would be an atrocious abuse, a turning of what is meant for God's glory into our destruction.

It is only in Christ Jesus that you can obtain certainty about the matter. Here, also, you must begin with him and end in him. If you are loved, it has been in him, as a member of his body. Therefore look to him! Only when he turns you away will you have the right to say that God has not loved you with an everlasting love, but not until then.

The most absurd conclusion that can ever be drawn from this truth is that it gives you the right to sit still. The opposite is true. In its deepest grounding this truth comes down to the fact that you are completely powerless, that you are wholly dependent upon God, that in yourself you are irretrievably lost. To what must such an awesome thought now lead you? To continue sleeping calmly upon the dregs of idleness? Or, with holy trembling, to call upon that God from whom alone your help can come?

You will want to agree to the latter. If you rightly feel your own helplessness and impotence, you will cry out to the mighty One of Jacob for mercy and will not cease until it is granted. For a sinking and perishing sinner who feels that he is slipping away it is impossible to keep still. He will cry out until the waters of destruction close over him. But that cannot happen. No one who cries out for mercy is turned away. 'The one who comes to me I will in no wise cast out,' the Saviour says. Oh, try that and you will discover that his Word is truth!

And for you who perceive that life-giving power of Christ in your own soul, this truth must be a new stimulus to humility and meekness. Your life came from Christ, it continues to be hid with Christ in God. You must draw all your lifeblood from him, so that the excellence of the power may be from God and not from you. Do not look for it anywhere else but from him. Let Christ dwell in your hearts by faith, so that you may be rooted and grounded in love. The more that happens the less you will become and will sink away deeper in your insignificance. God, on the other hand, will become greater and more glorious, and the more the language of your life will become that beautiful word of the apostle, in which prayer and thanksgiving fuse together: 'Now to him who is powerful to do more than abundantly, above all that we ask or think, according to the power that works in us, to him, I say, be the glory in the church, through Christ Jesus, in all generations, forever and ever.' AMEN.

XIV: The Gracious Provision [1]

1 Corinthians 5:7: *'Purge out therefore the old leaven, that ye may be a new lump, as ye are unleavened. For even Christ our passover is sacrificed for us.'*

The Old Testament feasts had, among other important features, this one peculiarity that they brought to the remembrance of Israel the great underlying facts and principles of their covenant-relation to Jehovah. They invited the pious Israelite at stated seasons to collect his thoughts and fix them upon those things which were fundamental in his religious life. Thus the feast of tabernacles reminded them of their dwelling in tents in the wilderness, and of the wonderful guidance and deliverance through which they had been enabled to overcome the perils of their journey and enter upon the possession of the promised land. In a similar manner, the feast of weeks, by requiring them to bring the first loaves of bread prepared from the new harvest to the sanctuary of Jehovah, reminded them that all the fruits of the land, all the blessings of their life, were on the one hand the free gift of God, on the other hand designed to be consecrated to God.

But it was especially in connection with the Passover

[1] Preached at Princeton Theological Seminary, Princeton, New Jersey on 1 October 1902.

that this peculiarity in the purpose which the feasts were intended to serve became most apparent. The Passover was pre-eminently a historical feast. It pointed back to the deliverance of the people from Egypt, a deliverance through sacrifice, a deliverance from the slaying angel, a deliverance in which manifestly the grace of God alone had made a distinction between them and their persecutors. Each time this feast was celebrated in the families of Israel, it proclaimed anew that redemption through blood, and by grace and sovereign choice was the great fact which lay at the basis of their historic existence; the source from which everything that Israel was and had or could ever hope to be and have ultimately flowed. And how significant it was that to this great feast there was immediately joined the feast of unleavened bread which marked the beginning of the harvest, and therefore gave a religious consecration to the tillage of the soil, on which the prosperity of Israel so largely depended.

All the gifts of God, which under the blessing of heaven were poured into the people's lap, were thus each year by a conjunction of these two feasts represented afresh as the fruit of a blood-bought redemption and the whole covenant-life was placed on the basis of the saving grace of God. Of course in a dispensation like that of the old covenant (in which there was a large and complex system of religious duties and ceremonies through which the mind of the believer might so easily be distracted and led to lose sight of the central facts and the central truths), there was more than ordinary need for such outstanding observances which compelled the church to centre her mind on the one great provision of God and the one great need of her own life, the realization of which was absolutely necessary, if she was to fulfil her calling in the world.

Now it occurred to me that on a day in which we have sat at the Lord's table to commemorate his death, it might be good for us to observe how the Lord (knowing our weakness, our forgetfulness, our tendency to look away from that which is most vital and essential in our religion, and to let ourselves be absorbed and distracted by a multitude of surface-duties and surface-experiences) has made gracious provision in the institution of the Supper for recalling us again to a sense of what is the centre and core of our relation to him, in order that we might not lose our contact with the heart of the gospel in which lie the issues of all true Christian life and activity. What the feasts were to Israel the sacraments are to us and the Lord's Supper especially ought to be to us. Our Passover also has been sacrificed and each time that we repeat its observance, the Lord himself invites us to call our thoughts home to the contemplation of that one thing on which our very life as believers depends, his atoning death.

But not only does the sacrament point us to the most fundamental fact of our religion, it is like the Passover also in this other respect—that it places before our minds in a condensed form the whole compass of what we have and are in Christ, the entire range of the salvation he has purchased for us, in its length and breadth and depth and height. Precisely because what it commemorates is so fundamental, it cannot help being comprehensive, for in the root of our redemption lies everything that this redemption can possibly embrace.

We may well, therefore, adore the wisdom of our Lord who has given us this ordinance. First of all, for the reason that it comes to meet our human weakness, that it brings his own person and grace within the reach of our senses, so that symbolically our eyes can see, our hands can handle, our mouth can taste the Word of life. Secondly it leads us, as I have already said, to seize upon the centre of the gospel. And thirdly, because it has served through the ages, wherever the ordinance has been observed in obedience to our Lord's command, as a perpetual proclamation of the great, comprehensive principle of salvation through Christ. It was certainly more than an appeal inspired by personal sentiment when he implored them in the night of his betrayal: 'Do this in remembrance of me.' He knew how often would arise in the subsequent history of the church the opportunity for his followers to forget if not his person, at least the true purport of his work and of that final act in which it was about to reach its climax. Many times when the spirit of the gospel was obscured, the table of the Lord has continued to be an eloquent witness on its behalf—sometimes perhaps the sole witness proclaiming to men the truth of salvation (and who shall say how many souls may have been saved through its ministry?). And similarly the apostle's words—'As often as ye eat of this bread and drink of this cup, ye proclaim the Lord's death until he come'—obtain a new significance to us when we regard the sacrament in this light as an epitome of the gospel of redemption.

Nor can we say that at the present time there is no need for such a witness of the sacrament because the ministry of the Word always and everywhere proclaims the central truth of the gospel with sufficient clearness and emphasis. It is true that there ought to be no need of this, for the church of the Reformation is pre-eminently a church of the Word, just as the Catholic Church is pre-eminently a church of the sacrament (for the very reason that in it, the ministry of the Word is kept in the background). But I am sure that there are churches in which a great many other things can be heard, yet where one could listen in vain for the plain preaching of the cross as the God-appointed means for the salvation of sinners. A man may attend a church where neither the preacher's word nor the preacher's prayer, but only the hymns that are sung, embody the elements of the gospel of grace and breathe the spirit of true evangelical piety; where the tradition of the past must fulfil the functions which the ministry of the present fails to perform, and where in consequence a powerful contrast is felt between the voice of the singing and that of the pulpit. And so it is possible to have a kind of preaching and an atmosphere of church-life and a type of ministry which enter as discordant elements into the true observance of the Lord's Supper simply because they are not keyed to the high spiritual and evangelical note that is struck in this sacrament of the Saviour's dying love.

Now I do not mean to affirm that in all such cases there need be the preaching of false doctrine which involves an open and direct denial of the evangelical truth. It is quite possible that both to the intention and the actual performance of the preacher any departure from the historical faith of the church may be entirely foreign. And yet there may be such a failure in the intelligent presentation of the gospel with the proper emphasis upon that which is primary and fundamental as to bring about a result almost equally deplorable as where the principles of the gospel are openly contra-

GRACE AND GLORY

dicted or denied. There can be a betrayal of the gospel
of grace by silence. There can be disloyalty to Christ by
omission as well as by positive offence against the
message that he has entrusted to our keeping. It is
possible, Sabbath after Sabbath and year after year, to
preach things of which none can say that they are
untrue and none can deny that in their proper place and
time they may be important, and yet to forego telling
people plainly and to forego giving them the distinct
impression that they need forgiveness and salvation from
sin through the cross of Christ.

I sometimes feel as if what we need most is a sense of
proportion in our presentation of the truth; a new sense
of where the centre of gravity in the gospel lies; a return
to the ideal of Paul who determined not to know
anything among the Corinthians save Jesus Christ and
him crucified. This does not mean that every sermon
which we preach must necessarily be what is technically
called an evangelistic sermon. There may be frequent
occasions when to do that would be out of place and
when a discourse on some ethical or apologetic or social
topic is distinctly called for. But whatever topic you
preach on and whatever text you choose, there ought
not to be in your whole repertoire a single sermon in
which from beginning to end you do not convey to
your hearers the impression that it is impossible for you
to impart to them what you want other than as a corre-
late and consequence of the eternal salvation of their
souls through the blood of Christ, because in your own
conviction that alone is the remedy which you can
honestly offer to a sinful world.

And in order to find out whether you are doing this,
whether your preaching meets this requirement or not,

a good test to apply is the frequent comparison of the purport of your sermon with the purport of the sacrament. The word and the sacrament as means of grace belong together: they are two sides of the same divinely instituted instrumentality. While addressing themselves to different organs of perception, they are intended to bear the identical message of the grace of God—to interpret and mutually enforce one another. If in the individual spiritual life of a Christian the Lord's Supper comes as something for which he is unprepared, something which requires a spiritual state of mind which he feels he cannot bring to it, something from which he shrinks because he realizes that it is so sadly unrelated to the usual tone and temper of his religious experience— then we would not hesitate to say that there is something wrong in the relation of that Christian to his God and his Saviour. And yet I think we will all be willing to confess that such has been frequently the case with ourselves. Is it not likely that a similar experience may be in store for us not as common believers but as preachers of the gospel? Let us therefore be careful to key our preaching to such a note that when we stand as ministrants behind the table of our Lord to distribute the bread of life, our congregation shall feel that what we are doing then is only the sum and culmination of what we have been doing every Sabbath from the pulpit.

It surely would be unnecessary, even if there were time for it, to do more than enumerate the great guiding principles which stand out prominently in the symbolism of the Lord's table and which ought to be constantly in the preacher's mind so that he may secure the result indicated. They are four in number:

(i) There is the plain, emphatic recognition of the fact of sin; not of any special, occasional form of sin, but of sin in its broad, general sense as an ingredient of all human life in this world. Though the people entrusted to your pastoral care may be all professing Christians, remember that you are to deal with them as sinners and that you ought to have no false delicacy about that because the Lord himself does not receive them on any other footing at his own table.

(ii) There is the positive and clear affirmation that the vicarious suffering and death of the Son of God, his body broken, his blood poured out and appropriated by faith are the only and all-sufficient means of obtaining the remission of sin, peace of conscience and the title to eternal life. It will be impossible for us to hold out any other hope to man so long as we have clearly before our minds the picture of the Saviour himself, who pointed his disciples to this and this alone as the great saving factor in his ministry.

(iii) There is the eloquent reminder that there can be no true participation in the merits which flow from Christ's atoning death except through such a faith as effects a personal union with him; a faith consisting not merely in the mental acceptance of his sacrifice as a historic fact, but a faith which mystically feeds upon him, the living sacrifice as he now exists in heaven. If we were to hold up Christ as a mere example to be followed by us in our own strength to the exclusion of the supernatural work of the Holy Spirit in the heart, would we not be silently corrected by our Lord's own voice speaking to us at his table: 'Except ye eat the flesh and drink the blood of the Son of man, ye have no life in yourselves'?

(iv) We have here impressed upon us the solemn obligation of everyone who receives Christ as his sacrifice and enters upon the communion of his sanctified life to abandon sin and walk in holiness. You will observe it is specifically this fourth principle which Paul has in mind when he says to the Corinthians—'For our Passover also has been sacrificed, Christ'—and derives from this the injunction:'Therefore let us keep the feast, not with the old leaven of malice and wickedness, but with the unleavened bread of sincerity and truth.'

So we see that the Lord's Supper spans the whole breadth of our Christian religion. Besides being what it must always primarily be, the means for strengthening our faith, it may also render to us the additional service of becoming to us an occasion for self-examination, a spiritual ideal by which we measure ourselves and ascertain in which respects, either as personal believers or as ministers of God, we may have failed perhaps to reach the normal standard prescribed for us by Christ himself.

XV: Christ's Deliberate Work[1]

Mark 10:45: *'For even the Son of man came not to be ministered unto, but to minister, and to give his life a ransom for many.'*

There are a number of reasons why great interest is attached to this saying. In the first place, the passages in which our Lord comments upon his own death as a saving transaction are rare in his teaching and their value is, of course, enhanced by this rareness. Although he did refer frequently and emphatically, especially towards the close of his life, to the subject of his death and emphasized that it was certain and necessary, yet an explanation of the purpose which it was to accomplish he did not add except just on two occasions—the one described here and the other the institution of the Supper.

In the second place, it is plain that a unique interest must attach to such a saying not merely because it throws light upon the mystery of the atonement, but particularly because the light comes from the inner mind of Jesus himself. We may feel sure that such a word as this will lead us straight into the heart of the matter and give us some conception of how the process

[1] Preached at Princeton Theological Seminary, Princeton, New Jersey on Conference Sunday, 12 October 1913.

presented itself from within to Jesus' own view. After all, he alone could fully understand with the understanding of experience what it meant to die for sinners. What first came to his mind in contemplating his saving death could not fail to be the centre and core of it, not some secondary aspect or bearing such as we might perhaps be disposed unduly to emphasize. The atonement becomes illumined with its own inner radiance. It is the consciousness of the cross itself that here speaks to us.

In the third place, this statement has value because it is peculiarly adapted to meet the doubts that have been raised against the historicity of the references to the atonement in the teaching of our Lord (often against this key passage). Suspicion has been cast upon the gospel account because after a long period of silence it makes our Lord all at once, during the closing days of his life, come forward with this new subject of his death and in such a mysterious way—positing the fact but not explaining why. Do you not see, we are asked, that that is just the result of carrying back the later doctrine of Paul and the others into the mind of Jesus himself; and do you not see that it brings him into conflict with his entire previous teaching in which no mention is made of his death as in any way essential to salvation, thus sacrificing the purity and simplicity of his true gospel to the speculations indulged in by the early church upon the tragedy of the crucifixion?

Now there is one element in the passage before us that has some bearing on the question here at issue. I refer to the purely incidental fashion after which the principle of the atonement is introduced by our Lord. As you will observe, it is not dwelt upon for its own sake as if the purpose were to communicate truth or give instruction regarding the cross. The cross is simply appealed to by way of illustrating quite a different subject: it serves to furnish an example of the self-sacrificing service which constitutes the law of life for the disciple in the Kingdom of God. It seems safe to draw from this the inference that the design of the passage cannot lie in any desire to import the apostolic doctrine of the atonement into the teaching of Jesus where it was originally lacking. For in that case a point would have been made of introducing it in a more positive and unmistakable fashion so as to place upon it the central stress of the statement. Someone who wanted the authority of Jesus for the doctrine of the atonement would have been sure to make him express it and vouch for it in a far more direct manner than is done here.

In the fourth place, this passage is equally decisive against the view which assumes that the idea of the cross was a late development in the mind of Jesus himself; that at first he contemplated a different method of salvation in which his death played no part and in which there was no provision for atonement, and that only towards the end, when his violent death became to him a certainty, did he modify his original belief in accordance with this and as an afterthought put the best possible construction upon his death by making it an atonement for sin. Against this view, too, the incidentalness of the statement would seem to be quite conclusive. The incidental nature of the reference shows that to our Lord's mind the conception was long since familiar, however strange it may have been to the mind of the disciples. Jesus had thoroughly accepted it as an established fact. He does not indulge in any reflection upon it, but simply takes it for granted and treats it as one of those things by an appeal to which other things can be confirmed and illustrated.

But even more conclusive on this point is the explicit avowal of the statement itself. For as you will notice our Lord affirms that he came to give his life as a ransom. The verb 'came' belongs not merely to the first thing named— the ministering—but belongs equally as much to the second thing named—the giving of the life by way of ransom: the Son of man *came* to minister and to give. I beg you to notice this form of the statement because many have tried to put upon it the weakening interpretation: Jesus came to serve and found, in the course of his life, that to serve to the full meant for him to die. But that merely makes the death the outcome of the service. What our Lord affirms is that it was the implication and the avowed end of the service from the outset. What he says carries the knowledge of his death and of the saving purpose of his death back into the initial act of his appearance upon earth: his coming was with this end and none other in view. He came to serve not merely to the possible limit of death, but to serve by the absolutely free and deliberate employment of death as the supreme instrument of his service. No one took his life from him. He gave it voluntarily. And he expected to give it from the very moment in which he received it. Hence the writer of the Epistle of the Hebrews represents him as entering the world with the words of the psalmist upon his lips: 'Lo, I am come to do thy will, O God' (*Heb.* 10:7, that is, it was God's will that he should suffer); and 'a body didst thou prepare for me' (*Heb.* 10:5, that is, God gave him a body in order that it might be possible for him to experience death as the true sacrifice for sin).

All this, therefore, excludes the view that our Lord only late in his career began to entertain the idea that his death might be a contribution to the success of his work. No—he carried the conviction that his work centred in his death with him in the silence of his inner life all the days of his pilgrimage. From the beginning he set his face deliberately towards this goal and unswervingly shaped his course with reference to its attainment. The gospel in the mind of Jesus did not need first to develop into a gospel of the cross. He took up the cross when he breathed the first breath of his earthly life. Thank God we are justified in reading the Gospels with this thought in mind. Jesus did not live the greater part of his life in a naive ignorance and uncon-sciousness of the web of destiny that was being woven around him. In his case, as in no other case, destiny and conscious purpose were identical. Not only that he died, but that he meant to die for us—this constitutes the preciousness of the gospel story for everyone who reads it with the eye of faith.

The passage speaks of our Lord's atoning death and yet is intended to place before the disciples an example to be followed by them in their own conduct of life. At first sight this might seem to involve an impossibility because the case of Jesus was so peculiar and unique as to be by its very nature and purpose inimitable. Of course it goes without saying that we cannot follow him and are not expected to follow him in this great act of sacrifice whereby he made his death a ransom for sin-ners. And even when we say it is not the death itself, but the mind of Jesus out of which the act proceeded—the spirit that animated him in his ministry of life and death—even then the example still remains something

so altogether by itself, so incomparable in its whole setting and in the attending circumstances that impart to it
its high meaning, that one might well feel disposed to
ask: how can a weak, sinful man, even though he is
regenerated by the grace and controlled by the Spirit of
God, ever attempt to reproduce this in his character or
conduct? For let us notice that it is not a human act but
a divine act—the act of a divine subject that is here set
before us as an ideal to model our mind upon. Just as in
Paul's statement in the second chapter of Philippians
where we read that Christ made himself of no reputa-
tion, emptied himself *(Phil.* 2:7); and in the other
statement of the same apostle in the second epistle to
the Corinthians to the effect that for our sake the Lord
became poor when he was rich (*2 Cor.* 8:9): just as in
these two instances, the reference in our passage is to a
self-denial, a self-sacrifice, a self-humiliation which
coincides with the entrance upon the incarnate state
and therefore, strictly speaking, precedes the incarnate
state and is predicated of the divine person who condescends to enter into that state. Our Lord says that he
came into the world to give his life as a ransom; not as a
man who had come, but as God who was in the act of
coming did he set us this example.

We must not overlook the contrast in which the state
of ministry and of death is placed with the state and
manner of life previously possessed by him through the
significant use of the name Son of man in the subject
of the statement: The Son of man came to minister and
to die. This name (Son of man) points back to the
glorious, heavenly figure that appeared in Daniel's
vision (*Dan.* 7:13-14); the one to whom the earth and
its fulness belonged; for whom the service of all nations

was destined as his rightful inheritance; this Son of man came to submit to and seek the very opposite—service, obedience, death. So the title Son of man brings before us as nothing else could do the unspeakable grace of our Lord, who being rich as God alone can be rich yet for our sakes became poor as only a dying creature can be poor that by his poverty we might be made rich.

And there is still another aspect in which the proportions of the example are equally overwhelming. When it is said that the Son of man came to minister, this form of statement makes the purpose of ministering cover his entire earthly life. Our Lord's incarnate life not merely had this purpose among others, it had this purpose exclusively. It consisted in this—was exhausted by this. There was never in human history such an absolute concentration of life upon the single specific task as our Lord here and elsewhere ascribes to himself. Everything else for him was swallowed up in the one great intent to accomplish this ministry. All the forces of his life flowed into this. Of course in this also there was something unique, something that can never be reproduced precisely in this form in the life of even the most consecrated servant of God. There was something absolutely unrepeatable in the manner in which our Lord made the sacrifice of his life redound to the service of others. He gave his life as a ransom in exchange for other lives. He died not merely for their benefit, but died in their place. This was a transaction which, strictly speaking, was possible to him alone. Others might minister unto death, or minister by their death, but no one else can minister through the payment of his death as a ransom in the literal, vicarious sense.

There enter, then, into the ministry of Jesus all these

elements of uniqueness by which it is and must ever
remain something apart and incapable of reproduction
by us. And yet after this is said, it ought to be equally
noted on the other hand that precisely in the incomparable manner of his service and the unapproachable
limit to which our Lord carried his service lies its force
as an example for our conduct. For these unique
features all point in one direction; they all have the
one effect of imparting to Jesus' life the character of
a service greater, more intense, more comprehensive
and more absolute than anything which can possibly
be conceived. Though the concrete circumstances are
unreproducible in our case, this not only does not
hinder them from being but is the very cause of their
becoming the most powerful incentives to us to make
our self-denying service of others as unlimited and
unqualified as it is possible within the range of our powers and opportunities to make it. We cannot, like the
Son of man, inaugurate our ministry by coming down
from a heavenly state of glory; but precisely because he
was willing to make this sacrifice in which we can never
equal him, what limit would we dare set upon the poor
little self-denial which the conditions of our earthly life
enable us to practise? We cannot concentrate our whole
existence upon the one purpose of saving sinners, but
precisely because our Lord condescended to shut up all
the riches of his infinite life within this narrow compass,
how can we ever dare to urge the excuse that the
Christian life, with its constant thoughts of others and
its consequent forgetfulness of self, is too narrowing and
stagnant a thing for us to submit to? We cannot put ourselves in the place of others as the bearers of their sin,
nor receive into ourselves the punishment of their

transgression with all the dreadful experiences which the atonement involved for our Lord; but precisely because he did not shrink from entering into these depths of shame and death and exposure to the wrath of God and to the hiding of his Father's face, how can we ever plead that any degree of humiliation, any extent of entering into the sorrow and shame and sin of man makes too great a demand upon our peace and purity to comply with it? And so the impossibility of our doing what Jesus did furnishes the most constraining argument for making the spirit in which he did it the supreme, governing principle of our Christian life and for recognizing that there simply are no limits which we can set upon its application.

What has been said will become clearer still if we look for a few moments into the supreme end of our Lord's service and the method pursued towards accomplishing this. His ministry had for its supreme end the procuring of freedom for those for whom he gave his life. It was a ministry with that specific thing in view. It was not to help them generally but to set them free. This is clearly given with the contrast between what he does and what the rulers of the Gentiles do (*Mark* 10:42). They lord it over them and exercise authority. That is to say: their striving is to make their subjects minister to them and increasingly reduce them to a state of bondage. Jesus' purpose is the opposite. He came to minister to men so as to place them in a state of freedom. But the same thing is also explicitly stated in the figure of the ransom-giving here employed by our Lord. A ransom is something which buys the freedom of a person. The many, therefore, for whom our Lord gives his life are in a state of bondage and his death procures their liberation. What then is this bondage? People have been over-quick to answer: it is the bondage of sin as a power reigning in the heart and life of man. While it is, of course, perfectly true that our Lord's work and also his death deliver us in this sense from the power of sin, I do not think that the answer exactly reproduces what Jesus had in mind on this occasion. We must try to refrain from inserting our general ideas into his words and endeavour to get at his own point of view. And the way to get at this is to ask: is there any other occasion on which he speaks of the giving of a ransom, and if so, the sense which he there connects with the figure will be entitled to the preference over all other interpretations in the present case.

Now our Lord does speak in terms of this same figure in the well-known passage where he urges upon the disciples the necessity of taking up the cross and following him (*Matt.* 16:24). He enforces this with the reminder that whosoever would save his life shall lose it and whosoever is willing to lose his life shall save it in the day of judgement. And then he adds: 'For what shall it profit a man if he gain the whole world and forfeit his life? For what shall a man give in exchange (ransom) for his life? For the Son of man shall come in the glory of his Father with the angels, and then shall he render every man according to his deeds' (*Matt.* 16:26-27). That is to say—in the hour of judgement when the Lord of the judgement shall declare a man's life forfeited, shall impose upon him the awful sentence of eternal death—in that hour, it will not avail a man having gained the whole world for himself if he were to bring this world with all its riches and offer it to God as a ransom for his lost soul. The offer would not be accepted for a whole world cannot satisfy God. His justice demands neither gold nor silver but the soul, the spirit, the life of man, because sin is a spiritual thing and it must be paid for in kind by the life of the sinner.

Here then it is perfectly plain what the ransom means, to whom it would be paid and what it would have to pay for (if such a thing were possible—a possibility which our Lord denies so far as all material riches are concerned). The ransom is nothing else but the price paid to God the Judge in the last day for the deliverance of a soul from eternal retribution. That this is actually the meaning of the passage becomes still clearer if we consider that in speaking these solemn words, our Lord plainly had in mind an Old Testament statement found in the Psalm 49, where the psalmist declares of the rich men who trust in their wealth that when God comes to judge, not one of them shall be able to redeem his brother by any means nor give God a ransom for him, and then assigns the reason for this impossibility— the redemption of their life is too precious, it must be let alone forever (*Ps.* 49:6-8). Here we have the same thought as formulated by our Lord in his own words: no material riches can serve as a ransom to satisfy the demands of God in the judgement. If now, in the word we are considering, our Lord speaks of a ransom paid for the life of many, it must be in the same sense and with the same situation in mind. He will pay in the judgement for sinners whose life is forfeited to God.

But how, we ask, can he here declare such a ransom-giving possible, whilst in the other connection he emphatically denied, as the psalmist had denied, that such an offer could ever be accepted or that enough could be offered to induce God to accept it? The answer

is found in this: that in the one case where the impossibility is affirmed, the reference is to a ransom consisting
of material things—silver, gold, the whole world—none
of which can pay for a life; whilst here, where the transaction is represented as actually to occur, the ransom
consists of a spiritual thing—the life itself and not
merely life in general but the precious inestimable life of
the Son of man who is the Son of God.

Therein lies all the difference. What the whole world
could not pay for, the life-giving of the Son of man will
pay for. For when it becomes a question of such a life
for that of sinners, God will consider the ransom sufficient and set the prisoner of his justice free. Just as our
Lord could refer to an Old Testament passage in the
Psalter for proof of the impossibility of a material
ransom, so he could have appealed (and possibly did
refer in his own mind) to a passage in the book of Job
for the possibility of the transaction in this other case. In
the thirty-third chapter of this book we read of the man
who lies under the judgement of the Almighty—how
he is chastened with pain and with strife in his bones,
his flesh consumed so that his soul draws nigh to the pit
and his life to the destroyer and all hope of his deliverance has been abandoned. But having shown him in
that extremity, the writer suddenly reverses the picture:
'If there be with him an angel, an interpreter, one
among a thousand, to show what is right for him, then
God is gracious unto him and says: deliver him from the
pit, I have found a ransom. His flesh shall be fresher
than a child, he returns to the days of his youth' (*Job*
33:23-25). That is to say: what gold and silver and the
world cannot purchase might be purchased if a mediator, an angel, one among a thousand were able to say to

God, 'I have found a ransom.' Such a mediator, such an angel, such a one among a thousand was our Lord Jesus Christ; and the ransom that he has paid and which he felt sure God would not disdain was none other than his own life.

Now in the light of this let us consider once more the extent to which our Lord went in his service; and I think we shall once more be prepared to say that it is beyond computation. We do not measure it by saying that he gave up his life; the mere doing of that might have been a small thing which others have done before and after him. No, what he did was to give that life as a ransom. That is to say he deliberately took his life and put it into the bondage of guilt and shame and death in which our lives were held by the divine justice. To become a ransom means to take the place of the other and accept all the consequences. And this Jesus did. I am afraid that as a rule we do not penetrate far enough into the mystery of the cross to realize this situation. What must it have meant to the Son of God whose blessed life had never been disturbed by the least cloud of trouble to enter into that tremendous strain of the divine justice, to feel the waves of guilt and wrath unleashing their fury upon him, so that he cried out in the bitterness of his anguish: 'My God, my God, why hast thou forsaken me?' All this and more than we can possibly realize lies in this single phrase—that he gave his life a ransom for many. But only in the same proportion that we realize something of all this shall we begin to measure what is meant by the other phrase, that he came to minister; and what is the unique force of the admonition that we should minister not like, but at an infinite distance minister as he ministered.

Let me in conclusion call your attention to other points implied in this statement. The first follows directly from what has just been said. It is this—that underneath the service rendered by Jesus to men lay a service rendered to God. He gave his life *for* men, but he gave it *to* God. The ransom which effected our freedom was paid to the divine justice, paid to satisfy God. And our Lord did not look upon this satisfaction of God as a hard necessity that could not be evaded if man was to be helped but in which he took no further interest. On the contrary, in this, as in all other matters with him, the service of God took precedence over the service, even over the salvation of men. He put his heart into the cross equally on account of what it meant for God than on account of what it meant for mankind. In dying, as in all else he did, he hallowed God's Name. That he was willing to make himself a ransom was a supreme act of love for God no less than for man. Let us not forget this. There is so much talk of service at the present day and it is so often deplorably noticeable that the idea people connect with this word is purely that of benevolence and helpfulness to man. If that is the meaning then the word is not fit to be the synonym of religion. The only true religious service is the one that puts foremost and guards foremost the supreme interest of God. That and nothing else is a true copy of the ministry of Jesus.

In the second place, because the service of Jesus was supremely a service of God, it had connected with it the promise of abounding fruitfulness. Notice the words: a ransom *for many*. These words are not of course meant to limit the atonement as if the meaning were not for all. This question, whether it is for all or *not for all,* lies altogether beside our Lord's intent. What he means to say is that the self-sacrifice of the one, because it was the sacrifice of the Son of man (of transcendent value inherently and brought to bear at the central point) would buy the freedom not of one but of many. It is the same thought which Paul expressed when he said that they who received the abundance of grace and the gift of righteousness reign in life through the one and that through one act of righteousness the free gift came unto all men to justification of life *(Rom.* 5:15-19). Because Jesus directed his service to this one central point where the source of all evil and misery lies—the guilt-relation of man to God—therefore in remedying this fundamental evil, he ministered unto mankind on the largest and most thoroughgoing and most comprehensive scale; the ransom of the one became the liberty of the countless many.

There is a lesson in this for us. We in our own way should also see to it that we do not foolishly squander our efforts at serving men in a thousand various directions when they will touch only the periphery of the evil of this world and can hardly expect to make a transitory ripple on the great sea of its sorrow. Rather let us concentrate our energies where alone they can permanently tell for the true betterment of things not for time merely but for eternity. Let us work for the salvation of souls from the judgement of God. If this is attained, then by the grace of God all the other regenerative, cleansing and uplifting effects are bound to follow in the wake of our service. The law from the one to the many as illustrated in the atonement of our Lord will repeat itself in our experience—we shall see of the travail of our souls and be satisfied.

XVI: Our Holy and Glorious God[1]

Isaiah 57:15: *'For thus saith the high and lofty One that inhabiteth eternity, whose name is Holy; I dwell in the high and holy place, with him also that is of a contrite and humble spirit, to revive the spirit of the humble, and to revive the heart of the contrite ones.'*

. . . is to follow of still more serious import for Israel. He begins to conceive of the world-power in the abstract, as a fixed principle in the history of redemption, whose significance is independent of its concrete embodiment in any single nation, be it Assyria or Babylon. This again influences his Messianic predictions in such a way as to give them the most universalistic scope they have ever attained in any prophet. Isaiah sees not only the mountain of Jehovah's house established in the top of the mountains and exalted above the hills and all nations flowing into it (2:2-3), but includes the material universe in the regeneration of the Messianic age. The whole realm of nature will be transformed and glorified; even the mute creation will, after its own manner, be full of the knowledge of Jehovah (11:9) and eager to celebrate the triumph of his kingdom.

[1] The first page of this manuscript is missing.
Preached at Princeton Theological Seminary, Princeton, New Jersey on 12 December 1896.

To this wide range of Isaiah's outlook the range of his prophetic lyre perfectly corresponds. There is no kind of music for which we listen in his prophecies in vain. With almost endless variety, he adapts his style to the ever-changing aspect of his discourse. 'All the powers and all the beauties of prophetic speech combine in him, and yet he is distinguished even less by any special excellence than by the symmetry and perfection of all his powers.'[2] Whether in the solemn monotone of the chant of judgement or in the rising swell of the song of triumph which greets the Messiah's birth; whether in the fearful words proclaiming vengeance or in the tender tones in which he consoles his mourning people—there is always the same unmistakable note of sovereign power which betrays the prophet and poet of the grace of God.

Is it permitted to inquire for the secret of this power? Undoubtedly it springs from the centre of Isaiah's personality and insofar belongs to a region of mystery where no human eye can penetrate. Individual character and endowment everywhere, but specially in the sphere of supernatural revelation, are products of the unsearchable working of the divine Spirit dividing to each of us as he wills and as the conditions of his

[2]   The thought of Jehovah's exaltation so absolute as to efface all relative distinctions in human greatness is quite familiar to the Old Testament. Having no rival and being no rival, it is his divine prerogative to take account of the weak and poor as much as of the strong and honourable. 'For Jehovah your God, He is God of gods and Lord of lords, the great God, the Mighty and the terrible, which regardeth not persons nor taketh reward. He doth execute the judgment of the fatherless and widow and loveth the stranger in giving him food and raiment' (*Deut.* 10:17-18).

plan require. But if we cannot hope to explain how the prophet's remarkable gifts and powers were imparted as a subjective equipment for his task, it is different perhaps in regard to the nature and range of the truth proclaimed. Here we are on objective ground. Although no prophecy ever came by the will of man (*2 Pet.* 1:21), yet the Holy Spirit has ordinarily adjusted the divine thoughts of revelation to one another and to some one central idea which was more congenial to the mind of his chosen organ. The prophet was not placed as a stranger in the midst of a mass of unassimilated material, but made at home in a world of truth where he would discover on all sides the correlates and implications of the supreme thought that filled his soul. In this sense then, it is entirely legitimate to ask what is the dominating thought in the mind of Isaiah and whether it may not furnish some explanation of the unrivalled breadth and depth of his teaching. What is there in the prophet's peculiar point of view that will account for the grandeur and richness of the scene he unrolls for us?

The answer to this question seems to be suggested by our text. Its opening words express the thought by which more than by any other both the contents and tone of Isaiah's prophecy have been determined, the fundamental thought of his life-work. It is the profound sense of the matchless glory of Jehovah as described in the sublime words: 'The high and lofty One that inhabiteth eternity, whose name is Holy.' Isaiah is the most theological of all the prophets; not of course in the scientific meaning of that term, but in the more simple and practical sense. His God is to him the one supreme reality from whom all other things derive their significance and to subserve whose end their history is shaped.

His mind is filled to overflowing with the thought of God. The whole secret of the wide extent of his vision lies in this elevation of his standpoint. But not only do we find here the explanation of what is unique in Isaiah's anthem upon the field of truth and history, the warm spiritual glow so uniformly present in all his preaching is kindled at the altar-fire of the purer and personal religion as this fire was kept forever burning in his soul by this vision of the divine glory.

Isaiah in this respect finds his great New Testament counterpart in the apostle Paul. Notwithstanding the immense difference necessarily created by the modified conditions of time and environment, these two favoured servants of God are remarkably alike in the distinctive features of their message. Isaiah is an Old Testament Paul and Paul a New Testament Isaiah. For both, there is the same deep impression of the infinite majesty and absolute sovereignty of Jehovah; the same intense realization of the awfulness of the divine justice and the inexorable nature of its claims; the unworthiness, the helplessness of sinful man; the same insistence upon the exclusive activity of God in the work of saving his people; the same prominence of the idea of faith as the only thing whereby man can appropriate the blessings of salvation; the same abounding truth in the marvellous condescension and overflowing grace of God; the same unlimited and unlimitable faith in the world-embracing character of the divine purpose. Paul seems to have felt something of the congeniality of Isaiah's mind to his own. He quotes from him often and with that fine spiritual insight which penetrates beyond the surface meaning of a passage into the innermost mind of the author and divines the subtle shade of his momentary thought and

feeling. 'Isaiah is very bold' (*Rom.* 10:20), he exclaims
with evident appreciation of a noble trait exemplified to
a high degree in his own character.

In boldness of conception there is perhaps no utterance even in the prophecies of Isaiah which equals the
words of our text. The thought trembles on the verge
of the paradoxical: Jehovah the high and lofty one,
inhabiting eternity, dwelling in the high and holy place,
declares his willingness to abide with the contrite and
humble. That Jehovah should dwell with individual man
at all is in itself a conception sufficiently startling on the
basis of the Old Testament. His presence among Israel in
the most holy place was the highest distinction
conferred upon the people of God, and even of this,
unrestricted enjoyment was not granted to the individual Israelite. It was to Israel as a whole that this
privilege primarily applied. Of the single believer, the
utmost that could be predicated was his appearing
before God in Zion and his dwelling in Jehovah's house.
But here the customary relation is boldly reversed;
instead of men dwelling with Jehovah, it is Jehovah
dwelling with man. And even this does not adequately
express the startling character of the conception. For we
must observe that Jehovah is here represented as coming
forth not from the partial seclusion of his dwelling-place
in Zion's temple, but from the unapproachable recesses
of his heavenly sanctuary to take up his abode with
man. The prophet throws upon the idea all the emphasis it can possibly receive from the united force of the
expressions in which it is his custom to describe the
transcendent heavenly glory of God. And the descent is
from the highest point of divinity to the lowest point of
humanity. It is not with man as such, but with those

among men of a humble and contrite spirit that Jehovah consents to dwell.

But we should fail to grasp the profound meaning and to realize the great preciousness of this word of God were we to regard it merely as a striking example of the effect that may be produced by a bold rhetorical contrast. The exaltation of Jehovah is far more than the measure of his condescension in bending down to man. It is not so much in spite of, but in virtue of God's infinite majesty that he delights to dwell with the humble spirit and the contrite heart. Observe, however, that the characteristics mentioned by the prophet describe man in reference to his self-consciousness. The small, the insignificant, the weak, the transitory are not contrasted here with the infinite and eternal, but the humble in spirit and the contrite in heart. Whatever may be the nicer distinction between spirit and heart in the scriptural usage, both terms are at one in this; that they denote those central seats of man's inner life in which the reality, mode and condition of his own existence reveal themselves to him.

Now the humble spirit and the contrite heart are nothing else than that specific attitude of self-consciousness which is sensitive and responsive to the loftiness, holiness, the eternal glory and divinity of God. And this is the reason why they are chosen as the conditions predisposing man for receiving the presence of God in his soul. Humility and contrition do not appear in this character as ethical dispositions having any meritorious value in themselves. It is not because through them man can in any way influence God, but simply because they enable God to impress himself upon man and to reflect in a created consciousness the infinite glory of his being that the humble spirit and the contrite heart receive this promise. We read here the very essence of Isaiah's conception of religion and find it to correspond perfectly to the prophet's idea of God. As sublime and transcendent as is the one, so profound and pervasive is the other. The figure of the in-dwelling of Jehovah in the human heart gains a richer meaning when interpreted in the light of this correspondence and will be seen to unite in itself both elements that enter into the religious intercourse between God and man, i.e. the mystical and the material. It does not stand for a description of the subconscious presence of God in the soul alone: far beyond the limited sphere of the feelings also, it gives to Jehovah as his dwelling-place the entire compass of man's conscious life with all its varied powers. The heavenly temple and its effulgence of the divine majesty reproduced in the spirit of man—this is the thought underlying the prophet's figure. A temple is not intended to contain God in the sense of a human habitation; it is intended to be filled with the glorious presence of God. The ideal temple in all its parts, in its ritual of sacrifice and service, with its music and incense, in its very construction is nothing but the receptacle and the reflector of the glory of him who inhabits it. The model of such a temple was shown to the prophet in that memorable vision which so deeply impressed itself upon his whole subsequent life and thought, the sublime reproduction of which opens with the words: 'I saw the Lord sitting upon a throne, high and lifted up, and his train filled the temple' (*Isa.* 6:1). And again: 'The house was filled with smoke' (verse 4). In this sense, the spirit and heart of man are to become the dwelling-place of Jehovah—the high and lofty one, enthroned in eternity, whose name is holy. The created mind a temple: that is to say, not merely in its innermost shrine a holy of holies where the immediate presence of Jehovah is felt, but from its centre to its farthest recesses resplendent with the light of God and re-echoing the voice of one crying, 'Holy, holy, holy is Jehovah of hosts'—such is Isaiah's conception of the perfect religion.

We find then in our text indirectly expressed if not explicitly formulated what must always be the governing principle of the highest worship of Jehovah. The relation here defined between Jehovah's exalted being and the humble spirits of his acceptable servants is typical of every God-centred attitude that may be properly called religious. Were we to seek an abstract name for this, we might say that it consists in the full adjustment of man's conscious life to the nature, the claims, the purposes of God; the joyful subordination of the creature to the Creator and his glorious kingdom. But it will be more profitable perhaps to look at it concretely and historically by analysing the elements of this frame of mind as we are able to observe it in Isaiah. In doing this we perceive that whereas the prophet lifts his soul directly to God and the specifically religious chord is struck, three distinct notes make themselves heard. The first is that of amazing and enraptured contemplation of the infinite perfection of Jehovah; the second is the note of intense realization of the finiteness and imperfection of man; the third is the note of blessed self-surrender wherein the prophet, at first almost overwhelmed by the sense of the divine majesty, regains his mental poise and recognizes as the only possible, the only satisfying purpose of created existence, the glory of God. From the blending of these three impressions in Isaiah's soul results what is peculiar in the prophet's religious consciousness.

We can clearly trace this effect of the self-revelation of Jehovah upon Isaiah everywhere in the cosmical, the moral and the redemptive sphere, and in each of these it appears to have been essentially the same. First of all observe the manner in which his religious nature responds to those attributes of Jehovah whereby he is exalted above the finite conditions of time and space and nature—those called in theological language the transcendental or metaphysical attributes of God, here represented by the words: 'The high and lofty One, that inhabiteth eternity'. This last phrase specially gives utterance with great simplicity and directness to the profoundest thought human reflection has ever been able to reach in this unfathomable subject. Eternity is the form of the divine existence, that in which Jehovah dwells, the atmosphere that surrounds him. Such a thought can find its full comprehension in him alone in whom it is reality. God himself is the only one able to compass its infinite content with the infinitude of his mind. But this impossibility of adequately thinking out the conception of the greatness of God, far from making it a useless element in Isaiah's experience is precisely that which imparts to it its religious significance and power to stir his soul to the deepest worship. On this point the prophet of the eighth century B.C. might have taught a lesson to the philosopher of our own day who denies the possibility of our knowing the infinite God. Isaiah would have answered him by saying that every futile attempt to comprehend the infinite being of Jehovah contributes by its very failure towards making our knowledge of it more real and practical. Though trembling at the vision, the prophet delights to fix his gaze upon this eternity which is Jehovah's dwelling place. He is the first and the last, beside whom there is no God, the Creator of all things, the King, Jehovah of Hosts. He sitteth upon the circle of the earth and the inhabitants are as grasshoppers before him, whole nations as a drop of a bucket, as the small dust on a balance. Lebanon is not sufficient to burn, nor the beasts thereof sufficient to prepare him a burnt offering.

The most striking element, however, of all the descriptions of the transcendent greatness of Jehovah lies in this—that they convey not abstractions of thought, but a sense of the living presence of a personal God. Isaiah does not shun the boldest anthropomorphic language to express this intensely personal character of his vision of the majesty of Jehovah. He speaks of his glorious eyes, his glorious voice, his glorious arm. And when the prophet thus scales Jehovah above every created being, it is not relative greatness he predicates of him. All comparisons in their inadequacy only impress us more strongly with the uniqueness of the divine nature and mode of existence. Isaiah knows of no gradations to fill up the distance between the Creator and the creature: it is an infinite distance which nothing can fill up, however exalted. The seraphim, though themselves belonging to a higher world, worship in Jehovah's temple and cover their faces and their feet with the same profound sense of their own insignificance as the earth-born prophet. Each time Isaiah proclaims the absolute greatness of God there follows without fail as an echo the confession of the absolute littleness of every creature. After painting that sublime judgement scene of the terror of Jehovah as the glory of his majesty shaking the earth, the first and only thought awakened in his soul is: 'Cease ye from man, whose breath is in his nostrils: for wherein is he able to be accounted of?' (*Isa.* 2:22); and 'the Egyptians are men, and not God; and their horses flesh, and not spirit' (31:3). The excited, sometimes sarcastic, language in which the prophet speaks of the worship of idols is inspired by this keen sense of the incommensurableness of God and what is not-God, even more than by the idea of Jehovah's spiritual nature. 'To whom then will ye liken me, that I should be equal to him? saith the Holy One' (40:25). 'I am Jehovah: that is my name: and my glory will I not give to another, neither my praise to graven images' (42:8). From the same source springs the prophet's belief in the absolute sovereignty of God over all created beings as expressed in his figure of the clay and the potsherd in the potter's hands (45:9). But enough has been said to show how this principle of the divine exaltation pervades and moulds the prophet's thought at every point.

We may well pause here for a moment to reflect upon the significance of this fact. Are there not many in our day who would stigmatize all that I have enumerated as the product of philosophy, which the sooner it is eliminated from the religious consciousness the better? We are invited to conceive of God under those aspects exclusively in which he is like ourselves; that is, possessed of the communicable or so-called ethical attributes. There and there alone we can know or understand and profit by it in a religious sense. Now if one thing is plain from the testimony of Isaiah it is this—that these so-called metaphysical abstractions lie at the very root of all religion, that there can be no living worship worthy of that name where these are ignored or neglected. Religion is love of God or a sense of dependence upon God but not entirely after the same manner as we cherish love for our fellow creatures or feel dependent on them in certain relations. Religion begins when we realize our dependence on the absolute, infinite being, the eternal, omnipresent, omnipotent, omniscient God. What men are urged to discard, therefore, is precisely that element which differentiates a religious experience from any other state of mind. Do not misunderstand me. I do not mean to say that the bare recognition of the greatness of God and the littleness of man is sufficient to produce true religion. For this the third element observed in Isaiah is indispensable—the element of joyous self-surrender to the greatness and sovereignty of God, whereby the creature feels uplifted and glorified. And this cannot enter until the coal of fire has touched the lips and the consciousness of sin forgiven has been imparted. When thus the soul inwardly delights in the infinite perfections of Jehovah, then and not until then is fear changed into reverence; or, as the prophet calls it, humility of spirit. But it is impossible to cultivate such worship (the highest flower of religion) where the perception of God's transcendent glory has been obscured. Religion may not be metaphysics, but there is a theology of the heart, the banishment of which means blight and starvation for all vital piety.

This will become still more obvious when we briefly consider how the exaltation of Jehovah affects Isaiah in the moral and redemptive sphere. In our text, contrition of heart corresponds to the divine holiness in the same manner as humility of spirit answers to Jehovah's inhabiting eternity. But the predicates of loftiness and highness belong to the former as much as to the latter. Indeed the peculiarity of Isaiah's teaching on the divine holiness consists precisely in this—that it unites the two elements of infinite majesty and moral excellence in a single harmonious conception. Jehovah's holiness appears to the prophet as the loftiness of ethical perfection, towering high above human sin and levelling it in judgement to the dust. This is the general conception of holiness in all prophecy and yet, here as elsewhere, simplicity and grandeur go hand in hand. The fundamental belief that God is glorious over every creature applied to the moral sphere is the source of this conception. While we are accustomed to speak of holiness in terms of intensity, the prophet speaks of it in terms of dimension. By it as much as by his eternity Jehovah is exalted above all finite being. Holiness in God has a peculiar divine glory distinguishing it from created holiness in angels or man. Even apart from the consciousness of sin, its revelation is so majestic as to fill the soul with awe. In Jehovah's holiness his divinity as it were concentrates itself. It involves not merely that his nature is stainless, empirically free from sin, but means that he is exalted above the possibility of sin—in him, as the absolutely good, evil cannot enter. (If owing to this the sinless seraphim hide themselves while proclaiming him holy, how should sinful man endure?)

Isaiah's whole doctrine of sin shows the influence of this conception. From first to last he emphasizes that aspect of sin in which it offends against the infinite majesty of Jehovah. This may be done by human pride and wealth as power infringing upon the divine right to unique greatness. Hence there is a day of Jehovah of Hosts upon all who are proud and haughty and upon all who are lifted up, to bring down the lofty works of man. Jehovah alone shall be exalted in that day. Jehovah will punish the fruit of the stout heart of the king of Assyria and the glory of his high looks because, although a mere tool in the hand of God, he usurped the praise of his achievements for himself. But the highest personification of sin in this sense is that king of Babylon who said in his heart: 'I will ascend into heaven, I will exalt my throne above the stars of God . . . I will ascend above the heights of the clouds; I will be like the Most High' (14:13-14). In this figure of the last representative of the world-power that came within his knowledge, the prophet has drawn the character of diabolical sin and we need not wonder that the name 'day star, son of the morning' here borne by the king of Babylon, was later (in the form 'Lucifer') transferred to Satan.

Isaiah could not have framed this bold conception of sin, however, had he not first been granted the vision of the King Jehovah of Hosts in the temple of his holiness. (All the sinister grandeur that invests the figure of Satan is here, as elsewhere, only the reflex of the majesty of him to whose throne he aspires. God's glory is so great that the bare attempt at usurping it renders the usurper half-sublime.) From still another point of view, the unique character of the divine holiness appears in Isaiah's preaching of judgement. Being not merely holy but majestic in holiness, Jehovah upholds and asserts his ethical glory for the punishment of sin. Isaiah has felt most keenly that God would not be God, would not respect his own divinity, did he not avenge evil. Because he is the absolutely good, because his name, the essence of his being, is holy; therefore in him holiness is attended with the sovereign right to vindicate its own supremacy. Nowhere else are we taught so clearly as in Isaiah that the vindicating justice of God is only the intensity of his holiness translated into action. We see the transformation under our own eyes when the prophet represents the Light of Israel as becoming a fire and his holy one a flame which burns and devours the thorns and briars of sin in one day (10:17).

Do we wonder, then, that our text requires contrition of heart as the only attribute in which man can venture to approach the moral majesty of God? The same threefold reaction observed above may again be witnessed here in the prophet. First his eye is dazzled by the view of an infinite perfection. Next he realizes the contrast that exists between this divine purity and the uncleanness of a sinful creature. Fear falls upon him, the fear of absolute moral dissolution, expressing itself in the words: 'Woe is me! for I am undone; because I am a man of unclean lips, and I dwell in the midst of a people of unclean lips' (*Isa.* 6:5). As this fear results from the consciousness of disharmony with an infinite holiness, there is no dread excited by any finite power in the universe worthy to be compared with it. When the sinful people tremble on account of human enemies, strangely forgetful of their exposure to Jehovah's judgement, the prophet is instructed by a special revelation not to fear their fear, nor to be in dread of it: 'Jehovah of Hosts, him shall ye sanctify, and let him be your fear, and let him be your dread' (8:13), words vividly reminding us of our Saviour's admonition to fear him alone who is able to destroy both soul and body in hell (*Matt.* 10:28).

But even this unique fear cannot be the final thought to which the vision of Jehovah's ethical glory moves Isaiah. True contrition involves more than the sense of guilt and pollution than fear and shame continued; it is the specifically religious response to these moral perceptions whereby the sinner abhors his unholiness not from any selfish motive but from the standpoint of God; from the profound conviction that it is a slight on his purity and infringes upon the supremacy of his glory. Spiritual penitence is God-centred and by this feature may be distinguished from the purely moral self-criticism and self-condemnation which does not presuppose a change of heart. The difference between these two is clearly described by Isaiah. It is mere terror of conscience that makes the sinner in Zion speak: 'Who among us can dwell with the devouring fire? Who among us shall dwell with everlasting burnings?' (33:14). 'Cause the Holy One of Israel to cease from among us!' (30:11). But genuine contrition acknowledges the propriety that sin, the sinner and everything defiled by sin should be swept away, and Jehovah of Hosts be exalted in judgement and God the Holy One be sanctified in righteousness. So powerful is this constraint of the moral majesty of God's law in the prophet's soul that he cannot conceive of any hope or future for Israel unless there arises one who by vicarious suffering shall satisfy the supreme interests of the divine holiness. And in harmony with this conviction, the idea of the Messianic king was deepened and enlarged in Isaiah's mind to that of the Suffering Servant, in whom perfect contrition is joined to perfect innocence, who humbles himself and opens not his mouth and makes his soul an offering for the sin of his people.

It would be interesting to trace the influence of the principle thus made supreme in the moral sphere throughout the whole range of Isaiah's doctrine of salvation. Objectively we should here find to predominate the glory of the divine grace and love and saving power, and subjectively faith sustaining the same relation to these attributes as humility and contrition to the greatness and moral majesty of Jehovah. (This is insofar suggested by our text as God's indwelling is said to unify the spirit and the heart, and as the bestowal of life is elsewhere associated by Isaiah with the eternal being and the creative omnipotence of God, being conceived as a strictly divine act. The experience of the effect of God's life-giving presence upon spirit and heart is an experience, therefore, in which man is made conscious of the unique glory of him who alone has life in himself.)

As time, however, forbids our following up this thought further, permit me to point out in conclusion one or two practical inferences that may be drawn from the facts we have been considering.

First let us observe in the whole history of Old Testament revelation there is not a second example as striking as this of the power of truth for the enrichment of religious life. The modern prejudice so widely spread that the intellect is an uninfluential if not injurious factor in the formation of spiritual experience is contradicted at well-nigh every point of the sacred record, but stands exposed in its utter folly when tested by the history of a spiritual giant like Isaiah. In his case, the influence of a pure and deep knowledge of God over all the other elements that enter into a harmonious religious development is plain beyond all possibility of

denial. What else but the great thought of God supernaturally introduced into the soul of this man produced
that untold wealth of spiritual power which even the
world, hostile as it is to divine truth, cannot help
honouring when it puts him with the most illustrious
examples of religious genius in all ages?

But we may go further than this and confidently
affirm that not only must truth from the nature of the
case be the prime mover in every religious activity of
the soul and in all progress of piety, but also that the
more fundamental and ultimate the truth apprehended,
the greater will prove the power stored up in it for
fructifying and quickening spiritual life. Many, while
admitting in a general way the importance of the truth
for the vesture of piety, yet seem to think that truth
cannot be made the truth, cannot be systematized to
any extent without straightaway losing this beneficent
quality and becoming a barren intellectual thing. If ever
we have been inclined to adopt this idea, let us learn
from the prophet how little it has to recommend itself.
With Isaiah the issue to view all things in the unity of
the divine plan and purpose was born from the very
love of God. Can we not conceive of a thirst for harmony in our knowledge of divine things so entirely the
expression of identification in thought and sympathy
with God as to be a worship in itself? And if we were to
seek for a single point of view that is likely to impart to
our study of God's Word this profoundly religious character, what higher or better could be found than this of
Isaiah? What could be more adapted to warm our hearts
than the constant thought of God's eternal excellence
and glory? It ought not to be difficult for us to assume
this standpoint. I deem it wholly within the limits of

historical sobriety to say that Isaiah represents among Old Testament writers most distinctly that aspect of revealed truth and religion with the embodiment of which in Christian thought and life we count it our privilege under the providence of God to be identified. This is not to say that other Old Testament writers could or did represent any view of Jehovah's relation to the world which was fundamentally different from his, but with Isaiah this principle bursts into the clear light of conscious recognition and acquires that intensity and fruitfulness which only the highest truths when consciously apprehended are capable of developing.

Let us not then hastily despise or think antiquated what comes to us associated by both history and the infallible Word of God, in holding to which we are in company with the most princely spirits of the old and new dispensation. I urge this upon you the more since you are to be ministers of God. If the character and tone of Isaiah's preaching are partly due to his representative position as a prophet of Jehovah, ought not the same to apply to your ministry? Is there any frame of mind more appropriate to the ambassador of God than that which is guided in its thinking and speaking and living by the supreme desire for the divine glory? Is there any consecration more entire, any inspiration more lasting, any comfort more unfailing than that derived from this principle? It would be difficult to find in the history of the church of God the record of a life more entirely consumed on the altar of service than that of Isaiah. But like everything else in this life, the cry 'Send me!' was a cry uttered under the constraint of the vision of Jehovah's glory. And only because this was so was there no recoiling when the disclosure followed that the prophet's ministry would be one of hardening and judgement. Isaiah knew that even when God does his strange work his purposes are accomplished and his honour vindicated; and that the ultimate significance of service in his kingdom is to be measured by this highest standard alone. And thus believing he spoke: 'I will wait for Jehovah that hideth his face from the house of Jacob, and I will look for him!' (8:17). It is not likely that any of us will be called to a ministry offering so little prospect of what the world calls success. But even if some of us were, if Isaiah's vision is ours, if like him we walk face to face with the glory of Jehovah, there need be no disappointment or discouragement. 'Hast thou not known? hast thou not heard? the everlasting God, Jehovah, the Creator of the ends of the earth, fainteth not, neither is weary; there is no searching of his understanding . . . they that wait upon Jehovah shall renew their strength, they shall run and not be weary; they shall walk, and not faint' (40:28, 31).